The Yale Ben Jonson

GENERAL EDITORS: ALVIN B. KERNAN AND RICHARD B. YOUNG

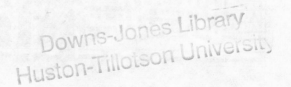

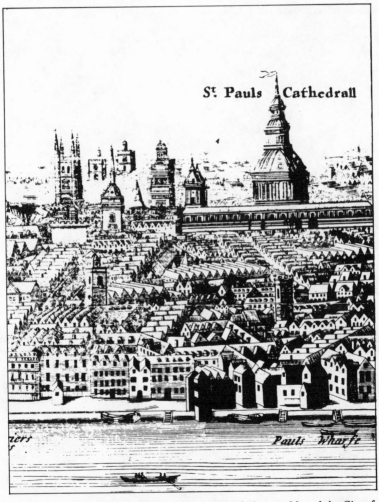

St. Pauls Cathedrall

Pauls Wharfe

Detail from the Yale reproduction of *A Large and Accurate Map of the City of London . . . by John Ogilby*, 1677. By permission of the Yale University Library.

Ben Jonson:

Every Man in His Humor

EDITED BY GABRIELE BERNHARD JACKSON

NEW HAVEN AND LONDON:

YALE UNIVERSITY PRESS, 1969

Published with assistance from the Kingsley Trust
Association Publication Fund established by the
Scroll and Key Society of Yale College.

Library of Congress catalog card number: 77–81419
Designed by Helen Frisk Buzyna,
set in Aldine Bembo type by Clowes,
and printed in the United States of America by
The Carl Purington Rollins Printing-Office of the
Yale University Press, New Haven, Conn.
Distributed in Great Britain, Europe, Asia, and
Africa by Yale University Press Ltd., London; in
Canada by McGill-Queen's University Press, Montreal;
and in Mexico by Centro Interamericano de Libros
Académicos, Mexico City.

Contents

Preface of the General Editors

The Yale edition of the plays of Ben Jonson is intended to meet two funda-
mental requirements: first, the need of the modern reader for a readily
intelligible text which will convey, as nearly as an edition can, the life and
movement which invests the plays on the stage; second, the need of the
critic and scholar for a readily available text which represents as accurately
as possible, though it does not reproduce, the plays as Jonson printed them.
These two requirements are not, we believe, incompatible, but the actual
adjustment of one to the other has been determined by the judgment of the
individual editors. In details of editorial practice, therefore, the individual
volumes of the edition may vary, but in basic editorial principle they are
consistent.

The texts are based primarily on the two folio volumes of Jonson's
Works, the first published in 1616, the second in 1640. The 1616 volume
was seen through the press by Jonson himself, and therefore represents to a
degree unusual for dramatic texts of the period what the dramatist intended
us to have. The 1640 volume presents more difficult textual problems;
though Jonson himself began preparing individual plays for it as early as
1631, these were carelessly printed—a fact of which he was painfully aware
—and the folio, under the editorship of the eccentric Sir Kenelm Digby,
was not completed until after Jonson's death. The quarto editions have also
been consulted, and where a quarto reading has been preferred by an editor
the necessary information appears in the notes.

In editing Jonson for the modern reader, one of the central problems is that of annotation, a problem that is complicated rather than solved by providing a catalogue of Jonson's immense classical learning or of his contemporary lore. We have believed that annotation is most helpful not when it identifies or defines details but when it clarifies the context of the detail. Consequently, citation of sources, allusions, and analogues, whether classical or colloquial, has been controlled by and restricted to what is relevant in the judgment of the editors to a meaningful understanding of the dramatic and poetic values of the passage in question and of the play as a whole. For the same reason, all editorial apparatus—introductions, notes, and glosses— frequently and deliberately deal with critical and interpretative matters in order to reanimate the topical details and give substance to the imaginative world each play creates.

To provide a readable text it has been necessary to revise some of the printing conventions of the seventeenth-century editions. In order to identify himself with the classical tradition of comedy, Jonson used as a model for his *Works* the first printed editions of Plautus, Terence, and Aristophanes, heading each scene with a list of all characters appearing in it, without marking individual entrances and exits. The present edition follows the more familiar practice of listing only those characters on stage at the beginning of a scene and indicates all entrances and exits. Stage directions, kept to an absolute minimum, have also been added where understanding of the dialogue depends on an implied but not explicit action, or on an unspecified location. With the exception of the first speech ascription in each scene, which is usually omitted by Jonson, all such additions and all material not in the original text have been enclosed in square brackets.

Where Jonson printed all verse in the metrical unit of the line, whether or not it represents the speech of one or more than one character, this edition divides the parts of such lines according to the speaker, and indicates the metrical unit by echeloning the parts of the line.

The original punctuation has been followed where its rhetorical effect has a dramatic value, but modern pointing has been used wherever necessary to clarify syntactical obscurities and to eliminate obvious errors or mere eccentricity. Spelling has been modernized except where orthographical change affects either meaning or meter. For example, where Jonson prints *'d* to indicate an unstressed ending of a past participle, this edition prints *-ed*, and where Jonson printed *-ed* to indicate stress this edition prints *-èd*. Jonson's frequent elisions, e.g. *th'* or *i'*, are retained, and all unusual accents are marked.

In the original text the entrance of a new character usually, though not invariably, initiates a new scene, so that there are many more scenes than a fully modernized text would allow. This edition retains Jonson's act and scene divisions in the belief that in most cases they represent the linking effect, the *liaison des scènes*, characteristic of the developing neoclassic drama; in all cases they represent Jonson's own conception of dramatic form; and the fact of form is part of the meaning of his plays.

Retaining the original act and scene divisions means that the act and scene numbers of the Yale Ben Jonson correspond to those of the standard edition of Jonson, edited by C. H. Herford and Percy Simpson (11 vols. Oxford, 1925–52). This enables the reader to consult with ease the notes of Herford and Simpson, who list all classical sources and analogues, and to refer without difficulty to the original text.

Introduction

When Ben Jonson placed *Every Man in His Humor* at the head of his collected works and alluded to it in his dedication as his first-fruits, both position and allusion were symbolically appropriate, as he was no doubt fully aware. He had earlier dramatic writing to his credit, including at least one full-length comedy; but unlike what had come before, this springtime production held all the flavors of the mature harvest. All Jonson's characteristic concerns, values, turns of mind and phrase, dramatic techniques, structural designs— all are here, ready to be selected, developed, recombined. The very copiousness is, from the point of view of dramatic consistency, this play's disability: it offers too much simultaneously, sometimes contradictorily. It exceeds itself, and so displays its author better than almost any single later play. It is quintessential Jonson.

Jonsonian comedy is the comedy of non-interaction. In the characteristic Jonsonian plot, a group of personages in a state of chronic introspection is brought together by a central action which loosely unites them, or rather, brings them into proximity. Each character, though responsive in his own way to outside stimuli, acts essentially alone; he moves along the line of force directed by his nature, and comes into collision, when time or a manipulator decrees, with another character moving along an intersecting line. It follows that Jonsonian plot is not plot in the ordinary sense. It does not develop outward from a coherent center, but moves inward from widely separated points to an accidental, as opposed to essential, meeting point—accidental in terms of action, though at its best essential in significance. For this reason, the plot of a Jonson comedy is peculiarly hard to recall; we remember individual characters and confrontations, as though the story were a means to achieve certain juxtapositions. These moments of intersection constitute characteristic Jonsonian comedy; the design is not organic but geometric.

A Jonsonian comic plot is a group of subplots collected in one place. How deeply this comedy of non-interaction differs from comedy of interaction is evident if we think of Shakespeare's comic plots: where subplot and main plot meet, they merge into one another, each clarifying the other: the moment of meeting is the moment of resolution—consider the confrontation of Portia and Shylock, the Duke and Malvolio, Oliver and Orlando, or Theseus joined in celebration with the midsummer-night's lovers and the workmen. The motto for Shakespeare's comedy could well be taken from this last play: "All the story of the night told over, / And all their minds transfigured so together, / . . . / . . . grows to something of great constancy." In Jonson there is no *together*; each mind is transfigured separately. If these separate transfigurations are simultaneous, their crisscrossing only exhibits more strikingly the need to avoid gullibility. They teach, perhaps, the source of transfiguration and the means of escaping it, but the condition itself contains nothing valuable. No mutual element of great constancy can be deduced from the interweaving of confusions. On the contrary, the moment when Jonson's subplots coincide is a moment of chaos; instead of merging, they rebound from one another; insteady of clarifying, they confound. The chaos is funny to the observer, who, aware of all the motivations which compose it, laughs at the disparities he, but not the characters, can perceive—for the audience, too, is detached. This comedy of non-interaction is what Theseus expressly rejects; when his master of ceremonies predicts that he will enjoy the workmen's botched play only if he "can find sport in their

2

intents," he rebukes him: "Our sport shall be to take what they mistake." In Jonson the sport of those who play audience is all in the performers' intents; as Wellbred says when he has aroused Dame Kitely's jealousy, "This may make sport anon."

Furthermore, the coming together of plots in Shakespeare is a moment of resolution and merging because the plots are already organically connected by the relationships between their central figures. Oliver and Orlando are brothers; the Duke and the midsummer lovers are court and courtiers, and besides the Duke's group includes Hermia's father; Olivia and Malvolio are two halves of a household; Portia defends her husband's best friend. When the plots make contact we experience relief and release, for what has been artificially fragmented is reassembled. It is what we have been waiting for. In Jonson, on the other hand, although families do exist, they occupy the same subsection of plot to begin with, so that the meeting of two or more plot lines has no reason to bring a sense of fitting union. The separate subplots are not interconnected by previous personal relationships. Corvino and Corbaccio happen to be fellow citizens, and the Would-bes happen to be visiting their city; Drugger and Dapper and Sir Epicure Mammon happen to encounter Face at different times; Cokes (or Wasp) happens to choose John Littlewit to draw up a marriage license. Of course, in these great plays the characters are brought together by a far more subtle relationship than that of family ties: they have similar complexions of soul. The "something of great constancy" which transfigures their minds is a capacity for similar evil (or folly —which Jonson always sees as weak evil). But since the evil is invariably such as to cut them off from other men, what metaphorically unites them actually divides them.

Now I do not think that Jonson was yet aware, when he wrote *Every Man in His Humor*, that his great comic genius lay in documenting and exploring this division; nor could he possibly foresee that the triumphs of that genius would be reserved for a time when he would find dramatic correlatives for his ultimately metaphysical belief that, while pursuit of an absolute good leads to unity and a constructive ordering of society, pursuit of evil leads to fragmentation and absolute isolation. But in *Every Man In* he is already attempting to introduce such a dramatic correlative in the debate about poetry; he sees, though perhaps but hazily, the direction in which he will have to move. The debate about poetry frames the play, whether one begins with the dedication to Camden, with the Prologue, or with Knowell's opening speech. Its settlement at the end by Clement, whose word is in every sense law, immediately precedes the proper ordering of society metaphorically ("I will do more reverence to him [a true poet], when I see him, than I will to the Mayor") and in fact (in the arrangements for rewards and punishments). General unification follows: Clement exhorts each participant to put off his divisive humor, to enjoy the symbolically unifying banquet; and he insists on a final procession properly emblematic of unity: "every one, a fellow!" (The occasion, of course, is a wedding.) So the identification of a metaphysically valid ideal, poetry, is forced into linkage with constructive organization of society—forced, because the society has no more than the most tangential concern with poetry and seems unlikely either to be constructive or to remain, under pressure, organized. Clement has to push and shove to make them "put off all discontent": "You, Mr. Downright, your anger; you, Master Knowell, your cares; Master Kitely and his wife"—this is hard work. The picture of a society in the process of being constructively organized is always the weakest part of Jonson, and in his most satisfying plays he cuts it down to a minimum. In his least satisfying, *Catiline* and *Cynthia's Revels*, he makes it, alas, the major part of the proceedings. In these two plays and in *Poetaster* he tried again to use poetry as the ideal which could unite society, in all three works making eloquence a centrally important part of the plot, whereas in *Every Man In* it is very lightly dealt with in the action, though given disproportionate symbolic

4

weight to bear. The relationship between the value of a society and the position of poetry within it was a theme dear to Jonson, but perhaps too indirectly dramatic to make a really great play, since poetry itself is still only a symbol for the moral and spiritual qualities it embodies.

That Jonson had not yet clearly perceived the drift of his own creativity is plain in his attempt to superimpose an organic unification on the arbitrary unification demanded by Justice Clement. The marriage between Edward and Bridget literally makes the "worthwhile" characters one big family. Even Cob and Tib are worked in as household retainers, with their allotted place in the buttery. Clement, who might be considered an exception, has his special role above and outside of the action, sanctioning and repairing family ties and providing the family mansion and the family dinner. Only Matthew and Bobadill remain literally unrelated on either side of the family; their position is evidently intended to correspond to their moral state, for they are specifically excluded from humanitarian concern as unsalvageable ("these two have so little of man in 'em, they are not part of my care"). Since they do not share in the communion of humanity they get no organic dinner, either. But while this gesture toward a discriminating interactive comedy provides an agreeable and symbolically correct ending to the played-out action, it is utterly mechanical. The marriage, a most unconvincing piece of work patched up by Wellbred ("Hold, hold, be temperate," the fortunate bridegroom begs him), is as much of a contrivance as Clement's final procession. Clement dedicates "this night . . . to friendship, love, and laughter" as though he were articulating the elements of the action, three motivations joined to bring about the final success. But major laughter in *Every Man In*, when connected with these two emotions at all, is based—as laughter typically is in Jonson—on perversions or negations of love (Kitely's for his wife, Knowell's for his son, Matthew's courtship of Bridget) and friendship (Kitely's suspicions of Cash, Brainworm's deception of Knowell, Edward's baiting of Stephen, and Wellbred's of Bobadill and Matthew). Clement is asking for the simultaneous celebration of effects opposed at the very root. All Brainworm's laughter-making talents have been dedicated, as talents in Jonson always are, to the pleasant task of self-aggrandizement, which separates father from son, brother from sister, husband from wife (with the false message delivered to Kitely), master from servant (Formal from Clement as much as Brainworm from Knowell), for as long as the laughter is able to continue.

To be sure, there is not much separation needed; as in the great comedies, all that is wanted is judicious intensification of a spiritual state that already exists. And Clement's conjunction of friendship, love, and laughter is only unconvincing, not, as it might be, offensive, for Brainworm is not yet Mosca or Face, the non-understanding between Knowell and Edward is not yet the deadly opposition of Corbaccio to Bonario, Kitely's treatment of his Dame is not Corvino's treatment of Celia, Brainworm's deception of Knowell is not Mosca's betrayal of Volpone, and to counterfeit a London Justice's warrant is not to pervert the Venetian courts. But as folly is a weak evil, so *Every Man In* is an incipient *Volpone* or *Alchemist*. The situations are basic to Jonsonian humanity: bonds of relationship are always denied by separation of spirit.

Clement, thus circumscribed by human nature itself, can only create, as family relationships do, a tenuous physical pairing. The characters Jonson would like, in *Every Man In*, to present as "fellows" are incapable of fellowship. Can there be anywhere in literature a more tedious pair of friends than Edward and Wellbred? Their sterile interchange of witticisms is outgone only by the silence of the stony young lovers, who exchange not a single remark either before or after marriage. The place for emotional activity is in soliloquy; there old Knowell can protest his paternal affection, but confronted with his newly-married son he does not address a word to him, until the opportunity to mock Edward's poetic inclination unseals his lips. His one disagreeable sentence is the sum total of communication between them. Kitely, even more lavish of passion in soliloquy, dredges up four direct remarks to his wife (one is "How now? What?"), of which the last seems promising: "Kiss me, sweetheart"; but his final pronouncement, "When air rains horns, all may be sure of some," does not augur well for the harmony of his union. Indeed, the Quarto text, continuing to the very end Kitely's suspicious questions—intermixed with his assurances that he is cured of jealousy—makes explicit the rocky future of his marriage.

The natural conclusion of Jonsonian comedy is complete fragmentation, coupled with (since this is comedy and not tragedy) an arbitrary reconstitution of some kind of society—the ending of *The Alchemist, Volpone, Bartholomew Fair*. It is the conclusion of *Every Man In*, too, but here the fragments are unstably glued together in the hope that the traditional judgment, marriage, and banquet may retain their face value. Jonson continued to use them: marriage and banqueting (projected in the epilogue) conclude *The Alchemist;* judgment imposed from without, *Volpone;* a combination of the two, *Bartholomew Fair*. But in these, conventional comic form no longer compromises, but rather illuminates, the inner logic of Jonson's individual comic content: two of the three marriages are frankly utilitarian, the third emotionally insignificant (while the clear mandate for romance between Celia and Bonario is ignored); one banquet celebrates the success of manipulation ("laughter," but certainly not love or friendship), the other a recognition of general inability to amend—and in *The Silent Woman*, the banquet celebrates Morose's un-marriage. As for judgment, in *Volpone* it merely confirms the special isolation each character has selected for himself; in *Bartholomew Fair*, it is abandoned as unsuited to a society in which all human relationships turn out to be deceptive. The great Jonsonian ending is a parody of the traditional ending of interactive comedy: its symbols of unity become affirmations of fragmentation.

7

On a large scale as on a small (Volpone's morning hymn, Face's catechism), Jonson is a master of revelation through ironic form.

Although in *Every Man In* Jonson composes not ironically but straightforwardly, as if he were writing comedy of temporary, not permanent, non-interaction, the special nature of his characters and plot already exhibits itself everywhere. From the moment Knowell strikes the keynote in his opening lines by making Brainworm the bearer of his own paternal authority, each major character conducts his important relationships through a go-between. Brainworm shuttles back and forth between Knowell and Edward; Edward's courtship is conducted by Wellbred; Kitely sends his reprimand to Wellbred through Downright, whom he also uses as a stand-in at the connubial breakfast table; Kitely makes Cash his informant about his wife—and Cash delegates the position to Cob; Bobadill attacks Downright through a law clerk, whom he approaches through Matthew, and serves the resulting warrant by intermediary; even Justice Clement deals at one remove with the petitioner standing before him:

> *Clement.* Tell Oliver Cob he shall go to the jail, Formal.
>
> *Formal.* Oliver Cob: my master, Justice Clement, says you shall go to the jail.

Further, the most powerful fear of the characters is the development elsewhere of an unmediated relationship. All the primary action of the play springs from this anxiety. Knowell's trip to town is prompted by his dismay at the friendship of Edward and Wellbred; Wellbred, though with less animus, would like to pry Edward loose from his father: "change an old shirt for a whole smock with us. . . . Leave thy vigilant father alone to number over his green apricots." Kitely and Dame Kitely need no commentary. Brainworm, besides wishing to prevent a specific confrontation (between Knowell and Edward), is concerned to avoid confrontations in general (for example, between Downright and Stephen), since interaction is the natural enemy of manipulation. But the most striking exponent of non-interaction is kindly old Knowell, who first comes to town in vague hopes of somehow counteracting his son's friendship, then rushes to prevent his rendezvous, and finishes by exclaiming: "My son is not married, I hope!"

This intense recoil from any form of direct emotional contact appears more subtly in the later comedies, though Mosca's ingenuity in dividing families, Subtle's and Face's voluble resistance to their own "indenture tripartite," and Morose's obsessive self-insulation sufficiently show that it can still give direct impetus to plot developments. More typically it becomes a psychological quantity fused with and expressed by cruder forms of self-interest, but casts against the backdrop a shadow under which all action takes place. Structurally, it presents itself as that recoil in the action which I have before described as occurring when two or more plot lines meet. The shock of contact, instead of impelling the action in a new direction, brings it to a temporary or even permanent standstill. After the successful courtroom scene, as after the debacle of Volpone's attempt at seduction, Mosca and Volpone have to start the action going all over again; the accidental conjunction of all plots at the end of *The Alchemist* finishes Face's comic action; just as the appearance of half the cast at Cob's house in *Every Man In* leaves each person present powerless except to shift the responsibility for action to a magistrate. The need to interact is a challenge Jonson's characters cannot meet, and it is just this disability which really interests Jonson.

The successful pursuit of this interest raises formal problems of coherence in the play as artifact, which Jonson solves by the strictest economy and unity of structure. What he erects in the Prologue into a universal creed is really the intuitive perception by an individual artist of the form he needs. The formal Unities take over the role which in interactive comedy is played by motivation, while motivation performs the splintering which in interactive comedy can be accomplished by separation in time and space. The implications

9

as to what is the essence and what the accident in human behavior are, of course, precisely opposite. The frequent presence of a manipulator like Brainworm serves exactly the same purpose. Not only does his puppeteer-like control of the disparate actions tie them into an artistic whole—his feverish sleight-of-hand, without which there would be no plot at all, emphasizes the artificiality of simultaneous motion.

The characters themselves cohere by contrast—not only the general, and therefore structurally loose, contrast between a Downright and a Matthew, but the detailed and therefore structurally unifying contrast between, say, Matthew and Stephen. Whether or not the characters have met is immaterial; what is important is that Jonson, through parallels in their situations, puts them conceptually side by side. They throw psychological and moral light on one another by means of this non-personal unification, which in interactive comedy may reinforce the personal unification of emotional relationship, but in Jonsonian comedy replaces it. Jonson's balanced pairing sets off against one another those who seem identical and links those who seem opposite. Only when we meet the town gull, aping the fashion just coming in (rapier dueling) and praising the configuration of a friend's leg in a boot, can we comprehend the full idiotic pathos of the country gull, aping the fashion just going out (hawking) and praising the configuration of his own leg in a woolen stocking. Only beside his carefree "double" Wellbred can Edward be clearly seen as his father's serious-minded son, urging upon his counterpart temperance, abstention from oaths, and the gravity of their situation; Edward's sexual purity—or indifference—which keeps him from ever making an indecent remark stands out against Wellbred's penchant for bawdry as the latter seizes every opportunity for playing a heavy-handed Mercutio to Edward's anemic Romeo.

More telling still, because they reveal not so much character as the ultimate significance of character, are those surprising juxtapositions of the apparently unconnected or antithetical which pin-point a character's position in a universal pattern. In the great plays such unifying contrast is a major source of ironic illumination. Consider Corbaccio, the old man who obsessively pretends that he is young and vigorous, target of scorn for Volpone, the young man who obsessively pretends that he is old and impotent. Or Tribulation Wholesome, whom Subtle the Alchemist wittily baits for serving a false and self-seeking religion. Or Trouble-all and Quarlous, Bartholomew Fair's real and pretended madmen, of whom the real seeks a "warrant" for his every action and the pretended does whatever self-involvement directs. In *Every Man In*, Jonson is already intrigued with the structural balance to be obtained through such mirror images, but, as I have noted before, his sense of irony is not yet equal to his intuitive perception of ideal form. Whatever ironic insight could be provided by identification of Brainworm (the fake fake soldier) as a version of Bobadill (the real fake soldier) is denied by the straightforward view of Brainworm we are required to take; and Bobadill as a version of Brainworm is either obvious or untrue. What we do already get from this doubling is a forceful sense—forceful because of the surprise with which we recognize the likeness—that the play operates in a unified world, where the bases of unification lie in the realm of disguise and deception. The unexpected conjunction of Brainworm and Bobadill jolts us into the characteristic universe of Jonsonian comedy, though it is not yet, as by later conjunctions, brilliantly particularized.

Yet there are certain kinds of particularity and invitations to evaluate in this comedy which are in essence the same as the structural interplay of later work. These characters, while going about their unrelated business, parody one another's behavior in as effective, if not as far-reachingly significant, a way as they do in the great plays. Not only is Cob, in his jealousy, a burlesque of Kitely; both are travesties of the troubled, spying Knowell, distorted mirror images which come together in the grand superimposition before

Cob's house. Further, Knowell's acquaintanceship with the eccentric and easygoing Clement, the worried father's only reassurance, is an exact replica of the source of his worries: Edward's acquaintanceship with Wellbred—which is in its turn caricatured by that of Matthew with Bobadill (for Edward "is almost grown the idolator / Of this young Wellbred"). The cautious and unimaginative will always attach themselves respectfully to Pharaoh's foot. And so Stephen, who is even more cautious and less imaginative than Matthew, joins the pattern by giving his allegiance to that gentleman, and via him to Bobadill—for which Edward very rightly scoffs at him; while Edward's father muses in disbelief over Wellbred's letter, "Is this the man / My son hath sung so for the happiest wit, / The choicest brain the times hath sent us forth?" Everything depends on where one stands.

Knowell himself, despite his name, does not stand in the position of final authority. Personally he is appealing: the archetypal fond parent ("but why does he pick such inferior friends?"), he gives careful thought to his son's upbringing, exercises restraint and psychological insight in his discipline, puts himself to a good deal of trouble to follow his paternal course; a kindly and humane master, he risks an obviously poor investment in the begging Fitzsword, then forgives him immediately when he turns out to be Brainworm making a laughing stock of his employer; he is human enough in his customary moralism to stretch a moral point ("This letter is directed to my son; / Yet I am Edward Knowell, too . . ."), human enough in his customary generosity to be stung by the imputation of pettiness ("Why should he think I tell my apricots?"), and generous enough to recognize spontaneously that he deserves tricking, "to punish my impertinent search—and justly." But when he is placed in perspective, now with regard to this piece of similar behavior, now with regard to that, his actions lose their individuality and their coherence; he becomes depersonalized. The effect is just the opposite of that in interactive comedy, where the more links a character forms with others, the more personal qualities he displays. Knowell is instead subjected again and again to partial re-evaluation through people he has never met. His kinship with Kitely and Cob forces his reasoned solicitude to fall under the shadows of irrationality and possessiveness; his benign incomprehension of Brainworm's character must take its overall place beside Kitely's malign incomprehension of Cash's; his understandable outburst at Stephen's idiocy, " 'fore heaven, I am ashamed / Thou hast a kinsman's interest in me," is qualified by Downright's excessive outburst over Wellbred's pranks: "I am grieved it should be said he is my brother, and take these courses"—an unpleasantly similar refusal of indulgence on the grounds of personal dignity. Indeed, though Knowell has never set eyes on any member of Kitely's household, what he thinks he is doing is constantly compromised by what we know they are doing. How can we retain faith in his admirable theory of discipline when we hear it parroted by futile Kitely to incompetent Downright? Here is Knowell's original: "I am resolved I will not ... / ... practice any violent mean to stay / The unbridled course of youth in him; ... / ... / There is a way of winning more by love / And urging of the modesty, than fear: / ... / [he will] By softness and example, get a habit." And an act later, here is Kitely: "But, brother, let your reprehension, then, / Run in an easy current, not o'er-high / Carried ... / But rather use the soft persuading way, / Whose powers will work more gently, and compose / Th'imperfect thoughts you labor to reclaim: / More winning, than enforcing the consent." We know how to value Downright's "Aye, aye, let me alone for that, I warrant you"; and Knowell's psychological validities are integrated into a pattern of useless educational theory. These implied equivalences between Knowell and others—particularly his major counterpart, Kitely—produce an interesting complication of value judgment. We are forced to look at a piece of behavior first in isolation and then all over again in juxtaposition. The positive values projected by a Knowell seen as

complete in himself are as true as, but no truer than, the negative
values acquired by a Knowell divided into spiritual parts with
matching doubles. Who would not live in kindly, generous, soft-
hearted Knowell's household? And yet all over London men like
him are misunderstanding their servants, denying their relatives,
failing their juniors, and beating their wives.

This dramatic guilt by association is not yet the glittering web of
corruption woven by characters in the great plays, but it displays the
identical complex of personalities, totally disparate in type, unconnected by emotional relationship, yet held together by a single
spiritual disorder. But whereas *Volpone, The Alchemist,* and *The
Silent Woman* are tightly constructed, each around one central
spiritual disease, *Every Man In* resembles *Bartholomew Fair* in its
multiplicity of aberrations, without a connecting character like the
latter's Trouble-all to raise one overreaching question with his
refrain, "Have you a warrant?" Instead, Jonson here strings the
characters together like beads, on thematic threads which hold a
few at a time. So the central question of use and misuse of poetry
is touched upon by everyone except Wellbred and Brainworm;
Stephen, Matthew, Kitely, Edward, and Cob are, each in his own
way, ineffectual lovers; Stephen, Matthew, and Cob are foolishly
concerned with lineage, on which Knowell has the deciding say;
Stephen, Kitely, and Matthew all affect melancholy; and book-
learning is honored and dishonored by Knowell, Cob (who likes
to bring Roger Bacon and King Cophetua into the conversation),
Edward, Matthew, and Stephen—each of the three last being, in his
special sense, "at his book." Jonson, who dedicated this first product
of his own muse to Camden, the paragon of true learning, must have
enjoyed writing the mischievous counterpoint in Scene 1: "*Knowell.*
Myself was once . . . / Dreaming on naught but idle poetry, / . . . /
But since, time and the truth have waked my judgment, (*Enter
Stephen.*) / And reason taught me better to distinguish / The vain
from th'useful learnings.—Cousin Stephen!"—as gratifying in its

way as "the heaven's breath / Smells wooingly here: . . . / . . . / The air is delicate. (*Enter Lady Macbeth*.)"

Distortion of education, of poetry, of love, of social status—Jonson's favorite issues are all here; like the pairing of characters and the unities of time and place, they tie together the action in a delimited realm where the same problems come up over and over again. Taken together, they amount to an enumeration of abuses similar to that formed by the aggregate of Juvenal's satires, or, contemporaneously, Marston's. Jonson, who drew liberally on Juvenal in *Every Man In*, had in mind a similar anatomizing of a diseased society, though here the disease is so mild as to be merely the common cold. As Juvenal devotes one satire to dramatizing one vice, and Marston follows suit with one central representative character in each such satire, Jonson here assembles a sub-group of his characters around each separate folly and connects the groups into a play. The sum of all the parts is Society, or, more correctly, Humanity in a specific microcosm, built up out of a multitude of local references until the existence of the characters in time and place becomes indisputable.

This definition of an ethical whole by adducing all possible parts is the characteristic additive technique of Jonson's comedy. In *Every Man In* he still makes some use of the iterative technique favored by interactive comedy, in which a subplot repeats the situation of the main plot, but in the mature comedies he abandons it. Even here the iteration (Cob's and Kitely's jealousy, Edward's and Wellbred's images in their elders' eyes) is subordinate to the introduction of more and more individual examples of varied human folly. Characteristically, instead of a proliferation from one original source—of absurd passions, say, as in *A Midsummer Night's Dream*, or of hopeless adorations as in *Twelfth Night*, or of rulers and usurpers as in *The Tempest*—Jonson gives us one fox, one fruit-fly, one vulture, one crow, one raven, one parrot-turtle, and adds them together into a definitive summation of human animal life. The play's significance grows inductively, not deductively.

In *Every Man In* this typical profusion of unlike examples coheres structurally but not essentially. The absence of that pervasive symbolic imagery (e.g. of gold, of alchemy) so integral to the great plays is indicative of the absence of a pervasive metaphysical concern; the play lacks an ethical center. The attempt to make this center a loose, and moreover a practical, concept, society, is not artistically satisfying. Venice, Bartholomew Fair, an alchemical workshop—these set certain symbolic limits on the meaning of "society"; they postulate a select *kind* of society. The appearance in these settings of an apparently random sample of personages ceases to have sociological significance and instead becomes interpretable much as an emblem with separate constituents is interpretable. "Society" becomes a warped construct of warped spirits, and the accepted temporal values are so many clues to the eternal, world-controlling values which have been flouted. But London is a neutral setting in which society means merely a collocation of varied types; it cannot offer a hard ethical core. The constant insistence upon the locale, by providing a conceptual center, goes some way toward disguising the lack of an evaluative center, but it is no substitute.

In addition to this more or less artificial centralization, Jonson provides a tentative ethical norm in Justice Clement, which with sufficiently ingenious acting might prove palatable in performance. In theory Jonson is proposing a synthesis between excessive devotion to imagination (Brainworm, Wellbred, Kitely) and excessive devotion to practical concerns (Knowell, Downright) as the ordering principle in society. Clement, the orderer, is himself an older man of practical understanding, successful in the world of affairs, who recognizes the desirability of becoming "a staid man" but also sympathizes with youthful energy and excess (thus joining the two generations divided in the rest of the play), and both values and exhibits "mirth," eccentricity, and nimble wit—not to mention the nominal spiritual criterion of the play, poetry. He is the man of judgment as well as imagination. But Clement is only abstractly a satisfying character. His merry tricks are not among Jonson's happiest strokes. It is hard to be much tickled by his donning armor to meet Bobadill or by his natty scatological quatrain. His treatment of supplicant Cob borders on mild sadism ("I but fear the knave"), and his mechanical invocations of a drink of sack (four times), to signify that jollity has yet again conquered all, have the quality of slightly dipsomaniac reflex. As always, the supposedly constructive norm is by far the weakest part of Jonson's play.

The inadequacy of Justice Clement is typical of Jonson's drama because at bottom his plays are neither satire nor normative comedy, though they utilize some of the devices of each and Jonson believed them to be both. Satire, and especially social satire, constantly invokes the desirable norm whose violation it portrays. When Pope, for example, presents us with full-dress portraits of Atticus, Bufo, and Sporus in the "Epistle to Arbuthnot," he not only does it in order to advance our progressive comprehension of his own antithetical, normative self-portrait, but does it by means of allusion to ever-present and ever-recognizable norms of emotional and ethical behavior. "Damn with . . . praise," "civil leer," "timorous foe" are all phrases of crucial, deliberate paradox, which irresistibly invite the mind to contemplate their rationally and ethically coherent opposites. The pervasive technique is inversion of an established conjunction or an established standard: "Words we teach alone," "Placed at the door of Learning . . . / We never suffer it to stand too wide"—so in the *Dunciad* IV anti-education is defined by implicit appeal to the normally expected. The brilliance consists partly in the choice of just those principles which can be inverted to best effect, partly in inventing a totally unexpected form of inversion, and partly in matching the linguistic inversion to the conceptual. Jonson was very familiar with this technique, to be sure; he used it often for local effect. One thinks of the condemnation of youth in

The New Inn: "Instead of backing the brave steed, o' mornings, /
To mount the chambermaid," or of Knowell's indictment of upbringing: "only feared / His palate should degenerate, not his
manners," "Can it call 'whore'? cry, 'bastard'? Oh, then kiss it,"
or, for a compressed paradoxical phrase, "grey gluttony." But these
fine examples of concise sarcasm are, in Jonson, set pieces, not
illustrations of the basic principle of design. Jonson's great successes
are not posited on the functioning of antithesis, but on the inherent
fascination of the thing itself. Bufo's collection of poetic busts contains what might well be taken as an emblem of satirical antithesis:
"a true *Pindar* . . . without a head." A headless bust is funny because
the concept of a bust depends upon the head. But upon what conceptual norm does the funniness of Bobadill, or even of Stephen,
depend? Only upon the broad assumption that human beings behave with a degree of moderation, rationality, and adherence to
fact. Even Jonson's powerfully irradiated metaphysical norms operate
only as beacons from which to measure the distance to a character's
actual location. They illuminate grandly but generally. So Volpone's
religious invocation to his gold and Subtle's catechism of Face impart to these characters' actions the thrill of blasphemy, but make
them infinitely culpable without instilling any corresponding sense
of the desirability of conventional worship or, indeed, of any
particular mode of behavior except the avoidance of what we see.
Jonson's success, in such moments, is the combination of shudder
and laugh.

Just as Jonson's greatest strokes are independent of the support of
any precisely defined norm, so it is impossible to deduce a specific
norm from them by contrast, as one can deduce Pope from the
negation of Atticus, Bufo, and Sporus. This definition of a norm by
contrast is a technique satire shares with normative comedy. From
Twelfth Night's Duke and Olivia we can deduce the ideal of Viola;
from the midsummer-night's lovers, Theseus; from the couples in
the Forest of Arden, Rosalind. But Celia and Bonario are not de-

lineated by their opposition to the other characters except insofar as good is the opposite of bad—rather too broad a contrast to serve for integrated dramatic structure. It is not just that Celia and Bonario are unsuccessfully characterized, as Justice Clement is unsuccessfully characterized. True, they are bores, and Justice Clement is a bore, and Crites in *Cynthia's Revels* is a bore—but so, at times, is Milton's God, without invalidating his normative function. What is peculiar about Jonson's normative characters is that they are extraneous to the real dramatic activity of the play. They are not engaged in the same type of action as the others in a more desirable way (like Viola, Theseus, and Rosalind)—they are simply not engaged in the same type of action. The nature of Jonson's comedy precludes the integrated normative character. Justice Clement is a try at it; but he, too, remains dramatically irrelevant, though his eccentricity is certainly an attempt to show him behaving like the others in a more desirable way. He is intractably extraneous to Stephen and Matthew, if not to Brainworm and Wellbred, and, what is much worse, hopelessly extraneous to the chief ornaments of the play, Kitely and Bobadill. Jonson's attempt to proffer him symbolically as a normative version of Bobadill by making him dress up as a soldier is only embarrassing.

The truth is that Jonson's greatness is not the greatness of satire at all, except in the supremely general sense in which all great comedy is satire because it exposes neglected truths about human behavior. Nor is it the greatness of normative vision. Jonson, in his numerous manifesto-like utterances, has himself been the most diligent obfuscator of his creation. Evidently he regarded himself, and wished to regard himself, as a writer of corrective comedy and satire. Indeed, his compelling moral and ethical bias caused him to punish all his highly imaginative characters for deviation from spiritual and social equipoise—perhaps a form of self-flagellation for his own zest in portraying their feats. But no amount of beating or imprisonment can convince us that Bobadill is less worthwhile than Justice

Clement, or that Bonario should have been a model for Volpone. Jonson's devotion to the ideals of correction and satire pulls in a direction contrary to his bent for pure comedy, and creates an unevenness in the progress of his work. His social satire is by turns brilliant, dull, and incandescent: brilliant when it constitutes a beautifully composed aria; dull when it affords merely "an image of the times" (Cob on fasting days); incandescent when it plays into Jonson's comedy of solipsism by giving his characters recognizable objects of obsession. When it is incandescent it is not at all corrective. To lampoon the affectations of fencing or the popularity of tobacco is no more the real point of Bobadill than to decry the disproportionate concentration of wealth among the aristocracy is the point of *Volpone*. The road of normality from which Bobadill and Volpone have diverged is lost to view, and well lost, behind the picturesque landscape of the territory in which they have arrived.

On the grounds of successful presentation of a comic norm, we would have to give the palm to *Poetaster*, since Horace, if not lovable, is at least deducible. But this evaluation is manifest nonsense. It is evident that Jonson is writing a different sort of comedy: nonnormative comedy. Jonson's success is invariably to be gauged by the strength of the anti-norm. His greatest plays succeed not by enforcing a concept of balance but by impressing upon us the overwhelming force of imbalance. So *Every Man In* succeeds not insofar as Justice Clement succeeds but insofar as Bobadill and Kitely succeed. For Jonson is not writing about common agreement on the outside world at all. He is writing about diverse and unmergeable inner worlds, about the impossibility of common agreement, about the psychological artificiality of a commonly defined outer world, even when it is a moral necessity. We recognize him as a writer of genius when he exchanges the mandatory optimism of satire for the deep pessimism of comedy.

Jonson's comedy is of the type afforded by a really thoroughgoing marital quarrel or a United Nations debate. It is the comedy of

minds which never touch, of confinement within an insurmount-
able point of view. Jonson's so-called humor characters and his
later elaborations upon them are human beings whose minds have
become (or have been from the beginning) rigid in a certain position
—a phenomenon by no means uncommon. In fact it is the frustrat-
ing familiarity of the immovable mind in ordinary life that makes
its objectification on the stage so welcome. Anyone who has been
much concerned with logical demonstration—anyone who has
taught—has bowed to the inert strength of Stephen's type of mind,
as pliable and as resilient as rubber. Give him your best twenty-five
lines on the social, moral, and logical impossibility of standing upon
gentility, and he will yield you the following harvest: "Nay, we
do'not stand much on our gentility, friend; yet you are welcome,
and I assure you, mine uncle here is a man of a thousand a year,
Middlesex land; he has but one son in all the world, I am his next
heir (at the common law), Master Stephen, as simple as I stand here
. . . though I do not stand upon my gentility neither in't."

But it is not only specific types of fixity that we recognize in
Jonson. It is the inherent capacity of every mind to retreat, as it
does in extreme joy or extreme pain, deep into itself, and there to
relate every event to its own pleasure or suffering. It is the impulse
which upheld for thousands of years the natural assumption that the
sun revolves around the earth. It is the impulse which convinces us
that the automobile turning at the same corner with us contains
guests for the party to which we are going. When Knowell before
Cob's house absurdly mis-sees Kitely ("Soft, who is this? 'tis not
my son, disguised?")—when, unregenerately solipsistic in the very
utterance which proclaims his supposed comprehension, he nods
wisely, "I do taste this as a trick, put on me / To punish my impertinent search—and justly; / And half forgive my son for the device"
—he is the exact comic equivalent of Lear on the heath mis-seeing
Edgar: "Didst thou give all to thy two daughters? And art thou
come to this? . . . Nothing could have subdu'd nature to such a

lowness, but his unkind daughters. . . . Judicious punishment!" They are both upholding a sense of personal significance and mental control in the face of a universe suddenly incomprehensible. Since both have chosen to define themselves by their relationships to their children, if they are to see themselves as centrally important they must see outer events as similarly defined. Lear responds to Kent's "He hath no daughters, sir," with "Death, traitor!" while Knowell reacts to Clement's "Your son is old enough to govern himself" with total deafness. Who can bear to be tangential?

Jonsonian comedy constantly plays upon its participants the cosmic joke of encouraging each to think himself central, while its author knows that they are every one tangential. This is exactly the joke Wellbred and Edward play upon Matthew and Stephen, Volpone and Subtle upon their visitors, Mosca and Face upon Volpone and Subtle, and Jonson upon Mosca and Face. Furthermore, since the characters, being non-interactive, are all tangential to one another, the action is a continual revelation that centrality is delusion. *Volpone* and *The Alchemist* play out the joke most perfectly, for here Jonson produces with inexhaustible copiousness another and yet another variation on the deluded figure of The Chosen, within a situation itself dependent upon the concept. Each of Volpone's dupes believes that "Only you / Of all the rest, are he commands his love," just as Volpone believes this in regard to Mosca; each dupe believes that the inheritance "is yours without a rival, / Decreed by destiny," just as Mosca believes this for himself. Each of Subtle's gulls believes not only that Subtle is an initiate, but also that he himself is uniquely selected to share in supernatural benefits, as long as he does not "cause the blessing leave you." The paradigm case is certainly Dapper, persuaded that "a rare star / Reign'd at your birth" and made him nephew and favorite of the Queen of Fairies; the really important action crowds him into the privy, to drop utterly out of memory for an act and a half. The audience itself becomes an accomplice in the existential joke; we forget him, his gag, his blindfold, his hopes, his illusions—and his sudden return into our consciousness, sick to his stomach, totally irrelevant, unwaveringly committed to his long-obsolete centrality, makes his *cri de coeur*, "For God's sake, when will her Grace be at leisure?" one of the great triumphs of comedy.

The essence of Dapper is already incarnated in *Every Man In*: in Stephen, "a wight that (hitherto) his every step hath left the stamp of a great foot behind him, ... the true, rare, and accomplished monster—or miracle—of nature"; in Matthew, exemplar of "some peculiar and choice spirits to whom I am extraordinarily engaged"; in Bobadill, singled out for persecution by the multitude "Because I am excellent, and for no other vile reason on the earth"; all bear willingly the burden of unique importance. And the tangential privy is present, too, in the form of the buttery and courtyard to which these indispensable spirits are consigned—Matthew and Bobadill fasting, like Dapper, and urged to "pray there that we may be so merry within as to forgive or forget you."

Jonson's unwillingness or unreadiness to see his own implications in *Every Man In* makes him conceal the necessary ending of his joke behind the comforting charade of mutual centrality arranged by Justice Clement for the "worthy" characters; but though he is not yet prepared to admit that Clement himself, in a non-interactive universe, must be tangential in his attempt to impose order (an admission finally made in Justice Overdo of *Bartholomew Fair*), he is already drawing characters of stature whose claim to dignity is the degree of their delusion. For to accept tangentiality can only be a source of stature when the inner self is so strong and spiritually resourceful that it can afford to secede from what it has come to recognize as centrality, and to rely wholly on itself, or itself in combination with its few spiritual allies. It declares the central principles of the universe tangential to something of greater value which it possesses in itself. This is the condition of Lear in his final address to Cordelia, in which he welcomes their prison as a reflection of the tangentiality he desires. Jonson's "humor" characters counterfeit this condition of spiritual independence by ignoring the central principles of the universe and erecting whatever psychological principle is most crucial to their own inner lives into an objective truth or criterion of value. Having eschewed any painful confrontation with reality, they are subject to have their scheme of values destroyed by its intrusion, as Lear no longer is. Reality, in the very act of destroying what is dearest to Lear, can only confirm its importance. In destroying the humor character's psychological treasure, however, reality would simultaneously wipe out its significance. Consequently there is almost no limit to the amount of delusion Jonsonian characters are willing to accept or invent for themselves to fend off what would be—and in the end often is—psychological annihilation.

This clinging to a subjective construct is much closer to what most men do in real life than the behavior of Lear. Very few of us are willing to die and be born again; we would rather live with all our imperfections on our heads—preferably regarded as special versions of perfection. Who has not marveled at the extraordinary inner jugglings and compromises that human beings prefer to what an observer, with the smugness of detachment, can call "facing the facts"? Such self-delusion is the instinct of self-preservation dictating to the mind; despite all self-righteous superiority, we must recognize survival as victory—and especially survival with *panache*. Who could do other than applaud Bobadill's virtuoso recovery from the brutality of fact: "*Matthew*. . . . But what can they say of your beating? *Bobadill*. A rude part, a touch with soft wood, a kind of gross battery used, laid on strongly, borne most patiently: and that's all"—or refuse to admire that gallant vision of an ideal world especially constructed for him: "*Matthew*. Aye, but would any man have offered it in Venice—as you say? *Bobadill*. Tut, I assure you, no: you shall have there your *nobilis*, your *gentilezza*, come in bravely upon your reverse, stand you close, stand you firm, stand you fair, save your *retricato* with his left leg, come to the *assalto* with the right, thrust with brave steel, defy your base wood! But wherefore do I awake this remembrance?" *Nessun maggior dolore che ricordarsi del tempo felice nella miseria*—as they say in Venice.

This saving imbalance which invents its self-centralized Utopia ("*Knowell*. When I was young, he lived not in the stews, / Durst have conceived a scorn, and uttered it, / On a gray head; age was authority / Against a buffon"; "*Kitely*. See, what a drove of horns fly in the air, / . . . / Watch 'em, suspicious eyes, watch where they fall. / See, see! On heads that think th'have none at all!")—this imbalance was fitly imaged by contemporary medicine as physical incompatibility with the elements of the universe. The universe being, to the Elizabethan view, a balanced composition of the four elements—earth, air, fire, and water—the little world of man formed a corresponding amalgam of the four "humors," earth appearing as bile or melancholy (cold and dry), air as blood (hot and moist), fire as choler (hot and dry), and water as phlegm (cold and moist). Predominance of one element produced physical and thus psychological unbalance—the condition of a humor character. It is easy to see how this well-known medical theory would be symbolically suggestive for Jonson, interested as he was in the predominance of one element of the inner self and the ensuing lack of correspondence between the makeup of an individual and the makeup of his surroundings. It is equally easy to see how the simplistic concept of four humors would rapidly become inadequate for dramatic representation of mental convolutions in a character engaged in preserving his psychological existence. So even in *Every Man In* only Kitely is a true humor character, suffering from a recognizable medical condition of head-melancholy, while in the others "melancholy" is already a metaphor for a spiritual stance, and "humor" shorthand for "identifying aspect of self."

Jonson's cosmic joke is the disparity between the psychological need of human beings for this kind of significant identification and the inexorable demands of the universe or society. Refusing reduction of their unique selves to a balanced component of the impersonal universe; refusing the moral equivalent, a Christian self-abnegation for the common salvation; refusing the psychological analogue, yielding up a portion of the self to relationship with another human being—Jonson's comic characters revel in their delusion of freedom. Their solipsistic conviction of centrality renders them infinitely gullible and creates Jonson's special comedy of mutual deception. Sundered from the outside world by urgent attention to an inner clamor, these characters meet in a congenial setting (which fosters their illusions of a reality constructed around their needs) to assume the roles of dupe and manipulator-dupe. For the manipulators are merely solipsists with talent. Perceiving in their superior intelligence that other human beings render themselves cosmically ridiculous by a rigidity calculated as monumentality, they seek their escape into significance by way of volatility. Instead of one mask of self the manipulator assumes many, as though this were a difference in kind. But his varied masks prove to be only alternative ways of making a single statement about himself, for disguises in Jonson's mature plays are always as ironically revelatory of hidden springs of motivation as are the self-presentations of the dupes. The manipulator, though gifted with more consciousness of his surroundings than the people he manipulates, is still rigid in acting out his conviction that he defines the universe, that only the creations of his intellect are really real, and that events are arrangeable for his exclusive benefit. In the end his line of force, too, crosses another, and the collision overthrows him; he discovers that the action to which he is central is itself tangential to another which he did not comprehend. This is the fate of Brainworm. His disguises as manipulator, like the other typically Jonsonian elements in the play, are not ironically exploited, but they are already ironic in their deceptive offer of freedom. Not only is Brainworm entrapped by his disguise into the final accounting, but he has himself

had to recognize at the outset—when he was less self-enamored—
that disguise is a ruse by which the tangential character renders
himself apparently central: "now I, . . . to insinuate with my young
master (for so must we that are . . . men of hope and service, do . . .)
have got me afore in this disguise." Whether he be nominally dupe
or nominally manipulator, the Jonsonian character is ultimately
confronted with the fact that every man's action involves him in,
and subordinates him to, the action of others—whereupon Jonsonian man ceases to function.

This active and passive solipsism produces those moments of
collision which, together with the inspired portrayal of self-
delimited character, are the glory of Jonsonian comedy. Seen from
without, a moment of collision is a point at which two (or more)
consciousnesses, like billiard balls of different colors, touch surfaces
with a perceptible click and part. One might take as its type this
interchange between Mosca and Volpone:

> *Mosca.* You loathe the widow's or the orphan's tears
> Should wash your pavements, or their piteous cries
> Ring in your roofs, and beat the air for vengeance—
>
> *Volpone.* Right, Mosca, I do loathe it.

The pleasures of Volpone's reply are manifold. One is simply the
neatness of the collision itself, like a well-executed shot at billiards.
Beyond this lies the sudden perception that what appears to be
communication is only self-propulsion. Beyond this still, the intellectual pleasure of recognizing, in one sharp instant, the source of
the collision, the gap between the ruthless, bored aristocracy of
Volpone the Magnifico and the essentially conventional, bourgeois
orientation of social-climbing Mosca. And just as the points at which
moving objects collide with a stationary one define the outer limits
of the latter, so this collision defines the outer limits of Volpone's
human comprehension.

The defining collision is already one of the aural satisfactions of *Every Man In*:

> *Brainworm* [disguised as a soldier]. I assure you, the blade may become the side or thigh of the best prince in Europe.
> *Edward*. Aye, with a velvet scabbard, I think.
> *Stephen*. Nay, and't be mine, it shall have a velvet scabbard, cos, that's flat . . .

Here are fewer overtones, no doubt—less resonance; but that is in the nature of the body struck. Kitely gives off a deeper sound:

> *Kitely*.   if thou should'st
> Reveal it, but—
>   *Cash*.   How? I reveal it?
>   *Kitely*.   Nay,
> I do not think thou would'st; but if thou should'st:
> 'Twere a great weakness.
>   *Cash*.   A great treachery.
> Give it no other name.
>   *Kitely*.   Thou wilt not do't, then?
>   *Cash*. Sir, if I do, mankind disclaim me ever.
>   *Kitely*. [*Aside*.] He will not swear, he has some reservation.

Here the *non sequitur* bears more clearly the identifying marks of such a moment of collision. Seen from within, it is a point at which one human being (often, though not here, himself the fantasy hero in his own world) enters the delusion of another in a supporting role—a moment when the nearness of outer reality, in the shape of an independent presence, only lights up the cavernous reaches of the deluded self.

It is Jonson's special gift to embody this illumination in an instant, in a single clash of phrase against phrase. But the mental process, which in Jonson always remains implicit, may be clearer if we look at a more expansive treatment. Novelistically seen, the bitter comedy of non-interaction unrolls as follows:

"Remember, we are looking forward to a better sort of happiness even than this . . . Come, dear, tell me how soon you can be altogether mine."

There was a serious pleading in Lydgate's tone . . . Rosamond became serious too, and slightly meditative; in fact, she was going through many intricacies of lace-edging and hosiery and petticoat-tucking, in order to give an answer that would at least be approximative.

. . . "There would be the house-linen and the furniture to be prepared. Still, mamma could see to those while we were away."

"Yes, to be sure. We must be away a week or so."

"Oh, more than that!" said Rosamond, earnestly. She was thinking of her evening dresses for the visit to Sir Godwin Lydgate's, which she had long been secretly hoping for as a delightful employment of at least one quarter of the honeymoon . . . She looked at her lover with some wondering remonstrance as she spoke, and he readily understood that she might wish to lengthen the sweet time of double solitude.

(*Middlemarch*, Bk. IV, Ch. xxxvi)

Here is the impenetrability of mind to mind upon which relationship thrives. If Rosamond and Lydgate understood one another, they would instantly part; just so Volpone and Mosca. But each would have to give up a crucial character in his personal drama, or even the drama itself as plotted by the self-creating sensibility. Anything rather than that; so, in the Jonsonian world, fuller than Middlemarch of comedy and hopelessness, incomprehension becomes the only basis of relationship. All important relationships in the plays could be seen as collisions drawn out into the semblance of interaction.

The converse is also true: a moment of collision occurring within what passes itself off, to either or both of the participants, as a relationship reveals its essence, and heralds the inevitable disintegration of its bonds. But it is a failed revelation. It is the moment we remember in retrospect and understand when acrid experience has confirmed it. Jonson's entirely external representation of it shifts the burden of comprehension from actor to observer: as audience, we pre-experience what the speaker may never come to feel.

Kitely, who fears nothing so much as pseudo-relationship, is revealed in this moment as doomed to its creation; in his mental deflection from contact with Cash we can foresee the whole unraveling, from "He is a jewel, brother . . . in his place so full of faith that I durst trust my life into his hands" to "Oh, that villain dors me. . . . She's gone a'purpose, now, to cuckold me / With that lewd rascal, who, to win her favor, / Hath told her all." We can foresee it because, as in Volpone's reply, we have heard Kitely fix the limits of his comprehension. "Full of faith" can have no practical meaning for a man himself constitutionally incapable of faith, just as "sweet . . . solitude" can have no meaning for a woman who derives all sense of personal value from contact with others. Clement dimly perceives Kitely's plight when he offers his truism: "Horns in the mind are worse than on the head"; but Kitely never understands his disability at all, and so preserves his inner construct against the assault of Clement's good sense. Similarly, Stephen remains as impervious to Edward's indirect as to Clement's direct sarcasm, and to the implications of his final allotted place (with Cob and Tib in the buttery) for his gentlemanly pretensions. All his connections are laid open as false; but to Stephen the revelation does not signify, for he is equally happy with relationship or pseudo-relationship— a position self-sufficient in its irony, and typically Jonsonian. Self-absorption is the source of all vital energy; relationship must crumble before it.

The crudest dramatic version of this statement—the leave-taking between Mosca and deaf Corbaccio—serves best as symbolic pattern for these unnoticed collisions which prefigure disruption:

> *Mosca.*   You are he
> For whom I labor here.
>   *Corbaccio*   Ay, do, do, do.
> I'll straight about it.
>   *Mosca.*   Rook go with you, raven.
>   *Corbaccio.* I know thee honest.

Mosca.	You do lie, sir—
Corbaccio.	And—

Mosca. Your knowledge is no better than your ears, sir.
Corbaccio. I do not doubt to be a father to thee.

The closeness necessary to collision often masquerades as a high point of psychological intimacy. Deafness, of course, is essential, but then it is never lacking.

Rosamond thought no one could be more in love than she was; and Lydgate ... felt as if already breathed upon by exquisite wedded affection ... by an accomplished creature who venerated his high musings ... marriage would not be an obstruction but a furtherance.

These are the moments at which relationship becomes evidently hopeless.

Such collisions are undoubtedly the most ironic; yet there is another group of collisions which shares all their basic principles and is even more purely comic—those between people utterly unrelated to one another. Here the disparity between apparent intimate connection and actual indifference is absolute. Here the sole justification for a belief in connection is the construct of the individual mind. So intense is the craving for personal centrality that perception simply gulps down whole anyone who walks into range. One thinks of jealous Lady Wouldbe "unmasking" Peregrine as a harlot, or of pugnacious Kastril, interrupted in a deliberate breach of the peace— his attempt to start a fight with Surly—when Ananias brings Subtle the news of the Puritan capitulation to alchemy: "*Ananias.* Peace to the household. ... Casting of dollars is concluded lawful. *Kastril.* Is he the constable?" Here the hopelessness of relationship is not grounded in personal difference; it appears rather as a category of experience. Out of the chaotic happenstance of ordinary life the mind constructs an orderly set of relationships—painful perhaps, but also full of meaning. By the end of this latter scene, the accidental convergence of a number of unrelated customers upon the

Alchemist's house has been satisfactorily arranged into significant pattern in the mind of each—in each mind, a different significant pattern.

In these collisions the hopelessness of relationship and the mind's circumvention of it are represented dramatically in the sudden encounter between disparate actions. The great example in *Every Man In* is the scene before Cob's house, the play's climax. The fantasy of interaction can go no further than the mutual "recognition" of Kitely and Knowell, begun when Knowell identifies Dame Kitely ("Oh, this is the female copesmate of my son! / Now I shall meet him straight"), continuing with Knowell's assimilation of Kitely into his private world as Edward, and culminating in the moment of actual collision, as Kitely literally turns around and assimilates Knowell: "This hoary-headed lecher, this old goat, / ... / O, old incontinent, dost not thou shame, / When all thy powers' inchastity is spent, / To have a mind so hot?" This is the very parody of Aristotle's "discovery and peripeteia," the conjunction by which tragic action becomes meaningful to its protagonist. If action has no inherent meaning, but is only a product of individual bent or of manipulation, then pattern in events is the product of the mind's illusion. And under the circumstances co-existing before Cob's house, the logic of delusion is at least as persuasive as the real explanation. We have a choice, momentarily, only between the crazy conclusion of Kitely ("*Knowell.* What lunacy is this, that haunts this man?") and the obsessive insistence of Knowell ("*Tib.* The constable? The man is mad, I think"), wherein either derangement is aesthetically far more satisfying, in its imaginative unity, than the truth. Is it not wholly natural to prefer the organically meaningful, internally consistent plot of either of these imaginary actions to the forced, meaningless machinations of Brainworm? and to prefer to see oneself as the hub of the one rather than a cog in the other? The moment is uniquely Jonsonian in inducting us into the satisfactions of imaginative delusion. The characters have successfully escaped epiphany. Like chaotic *Bartholomew Fair*'s Trouble-All, also haunted by lunacy and also calling for the official representative of law and order, they preserve faith in the "warrant" behind action by retreat into the self. The moment of collision, with its proffer of reality, is a dangerous invitation refused.

The ultimate importance of collision, then, is that it provides the occasion upon which the self is enabled to confirm its refashioning of reality. At these moments the deluded mind ties together events in the outside world, and ties itself to the world by the illusion of human relationship. Since neither connection really exists, commitment to them means further and further progress into fantasy—the typical mode by which action in Jonsonian comedy advances.

Though Jonson professed himself to be writing in the spirit of the ancients, and cited Greek authority for his belief that "The parts of a Comedy are the same with a Tragedy, and the end is partly the same" (*Discoveries* 2625–26), the premises of his comedy are directly anti-Aristotelian. Aristotle recommends the choice of incidents which have "an appearance of design as it were in them; as for instance the statue of Mitys at Argos killed the author of Mitys' death by falling down on him . . .; for incidents like that we think to be not without meaning. A Plot, therefore, of this sort is necessarily finer than others" (*Poetics*, 1452a). But this sort of fine plot is limited to the imaginations of Jonson's characters. In Jonson's own plot coherence is formal and symbolic, but never personally meaningful. If final coherence is established, it is imposed from without in the name of ethically necessary order—a process not inherently different from manipulation, or from the imposition of psychologically necessary order, but aimed away from, rather than toward, individual freedom. The need for bondage is also very strong. Jonson's comic action appeals to the aspiration for significance; his moral endings, to the conviction of mediocrity—the belief that real strength is social strength, that real meaning is the meaning of the group, the company, the university, the church.

Without these saving structures we would live, in a Jonsonian universe, in the midst of the comedy of non-interaction forever. With them, we can join in composing a harmonious balance of which each element is equally unimportant.

Committed to both its comic action and its ending, *Every Man In* provides conflicting answers to that most basic Jonsonian question: is non-interaction the cause or the effect of the characters' delusions? Jonson the critic and satirist would like us to deduce that it is effect: that a beneficent universe is distorted by, then rescued from, abnormality. But Jonson the comic genius deduces for us, rather, from the premises of an indifferent universe, splendid abnormalities of the protesting imagination.

To the Most Learned,
and My Honored Friend,
Mr. Camden, Clarentiaux

Sir,

There are, no doubt, a supercilious race in the world, who will
esteem all office done you in this kind an injury: so solemn a vice
it is with them to use the authority of their ignorance to the crying
down of poetry, or the professors; but my gratitude must not leave   5
to correct their error, since I am none of those that can suffer the
benefits conferred upon my youth to perish with my age. It is a frail
memory, that remembers but present things; and, had the favor of
the times so conspired with my disposition as it could have brought
forth other, or better, you had had the same proportion and number   10
of the fruits, the first. Now I pray you to accept this: such, wherein

---

CAMDEN *N.*

CLARENTIAUX *N.*

3 IN THIS KIND *i.e. in the dedication of poetical works. N.*

5 PROFESSORS *practitioners, esp. those who make a profession of it. Cf.* I.1.19.

5–6 MY . . . ERROR *Jonson means that he must make plain the value of his plays
because he wants to show, with gratitude, how worthy an effect Camden's teaching
has had on him.*

6 SUFFER *permit.*

8–10 HAD . . . OTHER *The sense seems to be, "had the taste of the times wrought
upon my own particular bent in such a way that I had produced a different kind of
work." Jonson's plays were not always much to the current taste.*

10 HAD HAD *would have had.*

11 FIRST *Jonson is playing on the religious offering of the first-fruits of the harvest to
God; EI was the first play in the Folio.*

neither the confession of my manners shall make you blush; nor of my studies, repent you to have been the instructor. And, for the profession of my thankfulness, I am sure it will, with good men, find either praise, or excuse.

Your true lover,
Ben. Jonson

Though need make many poets, and some such
As art and nature have not bettered much,
Yet ours for want hath not so loved the stage
As he dare serve th'ill customs of the age
Or purchase your delight at such a rate   5
As, for it, he himself must justly hate:
To make a child, now swaddled, to proceed
Man, and then shoot up, in one beard and weed,
Past threescore years; or, with three rusty swords,
And help of some few foot-and-half-foot words,   10
Fight over York and Lancaster's long jars,
And in the tiring-house bring wounds to scars.
He rather prays you will be pleased to see
One such, today, as other plays should be:
Where neither Chorus wafts you o'er the seas;   15
Nor creaking throne comes down, the boys to please;
Nor nimble squib is seen, to make afeared

---

3 OURS . . . STAGE *our poet (Jonson) has not been forced by poverty to be such a lover of (i.e. regular contributor to) the stage.*

4 ILL CUSTOMS *N.*

7–9 *N.*

7 NOW *just now, a moment ago.* PROCEED *go on to become.*

8 ONE *one and the same.* WEED *garment.*

9 WITH . . . SWORDS *N.*

10 FOOT . . . WORDS *pompous polysyllabic expressions; a translation of Horace's "sesquipedalia verba" in the* Ars Poetica, *and therefore an implicit appeal to classical criteria of composition.*

11 JARS *discords. N.*

12 TIRING-HOUSE *actors' dressing room.* BRING . . . TO *turn . . . into.*

14 *N.*

15–16 CHORUS . . . DOWN *N.*

17 SQUIB *small explosive firework. N.*

The gentlewomen; nor rolled bullet heard
To say, it thunders; nor tempestuous drum

20 Rumbles to tell you when the storm doth come;
But deeds and language such as men do use,
And persons such as Comedy would choose
When she would show an image of the times,
And sport with human follies, not with crimes—

25 Except we make 'em such by loving still
Our popular errors, when we know they'are ill.
I mean such errors as you'll all confess
By laughing at them—they deserve no less;
Which when you heartily do, there's hope left, then,

30 You that have so graced monsters may like men.

18 BULLET *cannonball.*

21–24 N.

26 POPULAR *prevalent among people in general.* THEY'ARE *This punctuation of Jonson's indicates two adjoining syllables run together so that they are almost one. It will not be mentioned in the footnotes hereafter.*

30 *Either: 1. you who have shown favor, by laughing, to my "monstrous" characters, may come away with a taste for those who are truly men; or: 2. you who have shown such favor to the unnatural characters of other playwrights may show, by laughing, that you also like men (i.e. my characters). Reading 2 is favored by the line's groundwork, a statement in Martial which Jonson chose as motto for Sejanus: "You will not find here Centaurs, nor Gorgons and Harpies: our page is concerned with comprehending man."* MONSTERS *This, together with "tempestuous drum" (l. 19), has been taken as an allusion to Shakespeare's Tempest.*

The Persons of the Play

Knowell, an old gentleman
Ed[ward] Knowell, his son
Brainworm, the father's man
Mr. Stephen, a country gull [Edward's cousin]
[A Servingman]
Downright, a plain squire
Wellbred, his half-brother
Just[ice] Clement, an old merry magistrate
Roger Formal, his clerk
[Servants to Justice Clement]
Kitely, a merchant
Dame Kitely, his wife [Wellbred's sister]
Mrs. Bridget, his sister
Mr. Matthew, the town gull
Cash, Kitely's man
Cob, a water-bearer

MR. *Master; title denoting a certain degree of rank, and sometimes youth.*
GULL *simpleton, dupe; usually with pretensions to elegance and savoir-faire.*
SQUIRE *a gentleman of good birth, often a landed country gentleman; just below the minor nobility in rank. The name is probably a play on an old tune, "Downright Squire."*
JUSTICE CLEMENT *play on Clement's Inn, one of the Inns of Chancery, to which attorneys and solicitors belonged. N.*
MRS. *Mistress; courtesy title for either a married or an unmarried woman, but apparently used here to distinguish the latter—cf. Dame Kitely.*
WATER-BEARER *N.*

Tib, his wife
Cap[tain] Bobadill, a Paul's man

The Scene
LONDON

TIB *nickname for Isabel; standard stage-name for a lower-class woman; colloquial for a woman of easy virtue.*

BOBADILL *an actual Spanish name, probably from Boabdil, the Moorish king expelled from Spain; presumably picked to connote vast, empty claims to military prowess and power.*

PAUL'S MAN *one who habitually frequented St. Paul's Cathedral. N.*

Act I Scene 1

[*Outside Knowell's house.*]

(*Enter Knowell, Brainworm.*)

Knowell. A goodly day toward! And a fresh morning! Brain-
worm,
Call up your young master: bid him rise, sir.
Tell him I have some business to employ him.
  Brainworm. I will, sir, presently.
  Knowell. But hear you, sirrah,
If he be'at his book, disturb him not.
  Brainworm. Well, sir. (*Exit Brainworm.*)   5
  Knowell. How happy, yet, should I esteem myself,
Could I (by any practice) wean the boy
From one vain course of study he affects.
He is a scholar, if a man may trust
The liberal voice of fame, in her report   10

---

1 TOWARD *under way, in prospect.*
4 PRESENTLY *immediately.* SIRRAH *form of address used to a familiar or an inferior.*
6 YET *emphatic, used like "now" in such contexts.*
7 PRACTICE *device.*
10 LIBERAL *1. generous; 2. uncoerced; with a possible play on "directed to . . . intellectual enlargement and refinement" (OED).*

Act I Scene 1

Of good account in both our universities,
Either of which hath favored him with graces;
But their indulgence must not spring in me
A fond opinion that he cannot err.
15   Myself was once a student; and, indeed,
Fed with the self-same humor he is now,
Dreaming on naught but idle poetry,
That fruitless and unprofitable art,
Good unto none, but least to the professors,
20   Which then I thought the mistress of all knowledge;
But since, time and the truth have waked my judgment,

(*Enter Stephen.*)

And reason taught me better to distinguish
The vain from th'useful learnings.—Cousin Stephen!
What news with you, that you are here so early?
25   *Stephen.* Nothing, but e'en come to see how you do, uncle.
Knowell. That's kindly done; you are welcome, cos.
Stephen. Aye, I know that, sir, I would not ha' come else. How
do my cousin Edward, uncle?
Knowell. Oh, well, cos, go in and see; I doubt he be scarce stirring
30   yet.

11 UNIVERSITIES *Oxford and Cambridge. Jonson himself had honorary degrees from both.*
12 EITHER . . . HATH *both . . . have.* GRACES *either degrees, or—more likely—dispensation from some of the statutory requirements for the degree.*
13 SPRING *produce.*
14 FOND *1. doting; 2. foolish.*
15–19 N.
23 COUSIN *used of any relative not in the direct line of descent; here, nephew.*
26 COS *cousin.*
27–28 HOW DO *apparently an acceptable form.* N.
29 DOUBT *suspect, imagine.*

Stephen. Uncle, afore I go in, can you tell me an' he have e'er a book of the sciences of hawking and hunting? I would fain borrow it.

Knowell. Why, I hope you will not a-hawking now, will you?

Stephen. No, wusse; but I'll practice against next year, uncle: I 35 have bought me a hawk, and a hood, and bells, and all; I lack nothing but a book to keep it by.

Knowell. Oh, most ridiculous.

Stephen. Nay, look you now, you are angry, uncle; why you know, an' a man have not skill in the hawking- and hunting- 40 languages nowadays, I'll not give a rush for him. They are more studied than the Greek or the Latin. He is for no gallants' company without 'em. And by gads lid I scorn it, I, so I do, to be a consort for every humdrum hang 'em scroyles—there's nothing in 'em i' the world. What do you talk on it? Because I dwell at Hogsden, 45 I shall keep company with none but the archers of Finsbury? or the

31 AN' *whether.*

32 BOOK . . . HUNTING N. FAIN *gladly.*

34–35 *It is now April 24 (see III.1.104 and—since Bobadill always needs corroboration—I.3.37–38); the fashionable hunting season is about over. During the summer "unseasonable hawking" was forbidden by law (7 Jac. c. 11).*

35 WUSSE *iwis, certainly.* AGAINST *in anticipation of.*

36 A HOOD, AND BELLS *basic hawking equipment. The leather hood blindfolded the hawk when it was not hunting; bells on its legs betrayed its whereabouts when out of sight.*

40–41 HAWKING . . . LANGUAGES N.

41 RUSH *reed.*

43 GADS LID *fashionable, euphemistic adaptation of "God's eyelid."*

44 SCROYLES *wretches.*

45 WHAT . . . ON IT? *Why . . . of it?* HOGSDEN *Hoxton, a country-like suburb of London; Hoxton Fields was a favorite holiday resort for London citizens.*

46 ARCHERS OF FINSBURY *citizens practicing archery in Finsbury Fields, set aside for that purpose. Part of Finsbury Fields adjoined Hoxton.*

47 A-DUCKING *hunting ducks on a pond by letting water-spaniels pursue them.* ISLINGTON PONDS *ducking-ponds in the fields of Islington, another rural suburb, adjoining Hoxton.*

citizens that come a-ducking to Islington ponds? A fine jest, i'
faith! 'Slid, a gentleman mun show himself like a gentleman.
Uncle, I pray you be not angry, I know what I have to do, I trow,
50   I am no novice.

    Knowell. You are a prodigal absurd coxcomb; go to.
Nay, never look at me, it's I that speak,
Take 't as you will, sir, I'll not flatter you.
Ha' you not yet found means enow to waste
55   That which your friends have left you, but you must
Go cast away your money on a kite,
And know not how to keep it, when you ha' done?
Oh, it's comely! This will make you a gentleman!
Well, cousin, well! I see you are e'en past hope
Of all reclaim.

                         [Stephen hangs his head.]
60   Aye, so, now you are told on it
You look another way.

    Stephen.   What would you ha' me do?

    Knowell. What would I have you do? I'll tell you, kinsman:
Learn to be wise, and practice how to thrive,
That would I have you do; and not to spend
65   Your coin on every bauble that you fancy
Or every foolish brain that humors you.

---

48 'SLID *God's eyelid.* MUN *must. A northern and Midlands dialect verb.*
49 TROW *trust.*
51 GO TO *expression of contempt, impatience, or incredulity (originally meaning
"get to work, get along with you").*
54 ENOW *enough.*
56 KITE *an ignoble bird of prey;* "You can't make a hawk out of a kite" *was proverbial in various forms (see Camden, Proverb No. 5).*
58 COMELY *appropriate and attractive.*
60 ON *of.*

I would not have you to invade each place,
Nor thrust yourself on all societies,
Till men's affections, or your own desert,
Should worthily invite you to your rank.   70
He that is so respectless in his courses
Oft sells his reputation at cheap market.
Nor would I you should melt away yourself
In flashing bravery, lest while you affect
To make a blaze of gentry to the world,   75
A little puff of scorn extinguish it,
And you be left, like an unsavory snuff,
Whose property is only to offend.
I'd ha' you sober, and contain yourself;
Not, that your sail be bigger than your boat,   80
But moderate your expenses now (at first),
As you may keep the same proportion still;
Nor stand so much on your gentility,
           (*Enter a servingman.*)
Which is an airy and mere borrowed thing
From dead men's dust and bones: and none of yours   85
Except you make or hold it.—Who comes here?

69 AFFECTIONS *1. inclinations; 2. feelings of fondness.*
70 RANK *position in that society.*
71 RESPECTLESS . . . COURSES *uncontrolled . . . behavior.*
72 AT CHEAP MARKET *when the market is low; i.e. in exchange for trifles.*
73 MELT AWAY YOURSELF *like a candle, which perishes in creating a "blaze." The metaphor alludes backward to Stephen's reckless expenditure ("melting" of his substance).*
74 BRAVERY *1. ostentation; 2. finery.*
75 BLAZE *probably a play on "blazon," a coat of arms; as verbs, the two words were associated and used interchangeably.*
77 SNUFF *candle end.*
78 PROPERTY *quality, nature; with possible pun on "wealth."*
83 STAND . . . ON *assert, claim respect for.* GENTILITY *rank as a gentleman.*
83–86 *N.*

Act I Scene 2

Servant. Save you, gentlemen.

Stephen. Nay, we do'not stand much on our gentility, friend; yet you are welcome, and I assure you, mine uncle here is a man of a thousand a year, Middlesex land; he has but one son in all the world,

5   I am his next heir (at the common law), Master Stephen, as simple . as I stand here, if my cousin die (as there's hope he will)—I have a pretty living o' mine own, too, beside, hard by here.

Servant. In good time, sir.

Stephen. In good time, sir? Why! and in very good time, sir.

10   You do not flout, friend, do you?

Servant. Not I, sir.

Stephen. Not you, sir? You were not best, sir; an' you should, here be them can perceive it, and that quickly, too—go to. And they can give it again soundly, too, and need be.

15   *Servant.* Why, sir, let this satisfy you: good faith, I had no such intent.

Stephen. Sir, an' I thought you had, I would talk with you, and that presently.

Servant. Good Master Stephen, so you may, sir, at your pleasure.

---

1 SAVE YOU *God save you.*

4 THOUSAND . . . LAND *a thousand pounds as yearly income from his property in Middlesex, the county within which northwest London lies.*

5 SIMPLE *plain; with pun on "simple-minded."*

7 LIVING *piece of property.* HARD BY *very near by.*

8 IN GOOD TIME *certainly (often ironical).*

14 AND *if.*

17 TALK WITH YOU *with the implication "challenge you to fight."*

Stephen. And so I would, sir, good my saucy companion, an' you 20
were out o' mine uncle's ground, I can tell you; though I do not
stand upon my gentility neither in't.

Knowell. Cousin! Cousin! Will this ne'er be left?

Stephen. Whoreson base fellow! A mechanical servingman! By
this cudgel, and 't were not for shame, I would— 25

Knowell. What would you do, you peremptory gull?
If you cannot be quiet, get you hence.
You see the honest man demeans himself
Modestly towards you, giving no reply
To your unseasoned, quarreling, rude fashion; 30
And still you huff it, with a kind of carriage
As void of wit as of humanity.
Go, get you in; 'fore heaven, I am ashamed (*Exit Stephen.*)
Thou hast a kinsman's interest in me.

Servant. I pray you, sir. Is this Master Knowell's house? 35

Knowell. Yes, marry, is it, sir.

Servant. I should inquire for a gentleman here, one Master Edward
Knowell; do you know any such, sir, I pray you?

Knowell. I should forget myself else, sir.

Servant. Are you the gentleman? Cry you mercy, sir: I was 40

---

20 COMPANION *fellow.*

21 OUT O' *outside of. To challenge an accepted visitor on the premises was to affront
the host. (Cf. Romeo and Juliet I.5.67–79.)*

24 MECHANICAL *engaged in manual labor, menial.*

25 SHAME *disgrace (in fighting with a person of inferior rank).*

26 PEREMPTORY *utter; with pun on: 1. obstinate; 2. imperious. Stressed on the first
syllable.*

28 DEMEANS *conducts; probably with pun on "humbles."*

30 UNSEASONED *1. unseasonable; 2. immature.*

31 HUFF IT *1. bluster; 2. are in a huff.*

34 INTEREST IN *claim on.*

36 MARRY *mild expletive, originally "By Mary!"*

40 CRY YOU MERCY *beg your pardon.*

required by a gentleman i' the City, as I rode out at this end o' the town, to deliver you this letter, sir.

    Knowell. To me, sir! What do you mean? Pray you remember your courtesy. [*Knowell takes the letter and reads the superscription.*]

45 "To his most selected friend, Master Edward Knowell." [*To Servant.*] What might the gentleman's name be, sir, that sent it? Nay, pray you be covered.

    Servant. One Master Wellbred, sir.

    Knowell. Master Wellbred! A young gentleman, is he not?

50   *Servant.* The same, sir; Master Kitely married his sister: the rich merchant i' the old Jewry.

    Knowell. You say very true. [*Calls.*] Brainworm—

                    (*Enter Brainworm.*)

    Brainworm. Sir.

    Knowell. Make this honest friend drink here; [*To Servant.*] pray

55 you go in. (*Exeunt* [*Servant and Brainworm*].)

This letter is directed to my son;
Yet I am Edward Knowell, too, and may,
With the safe conscience of good manners, use
The fellow's error to my satisfaction.

60 Well, I will break it ope (old men are curious),
Be it but for the style's sake, and the phrase,
To see if both do answer my son's praises,
Who is almost grown the idolater
Of this young Wellbred.

                [*He opens the letter.*]
                What have we here? What's this?

---

41 THE CITY *physically, socially, and commercially central area of London (most of it within the old Roman city walls). It was politically independent.*

43–44 REMEMBER YOUR COURTESY *put on your hat.*

51 MERCHANT *i.e. Kitely.* OLD JEWRY *street in the City, in and near which most London Jews in reasonably good circumstances had lived before the expulsion of the Jews from England (1290).*

62 ANSWER *correspond to.*

"Why, Ned, I beseech thee: hast thou forsworn all thy   *The letter*   65
friends i' the old Jewry? Or dost thou think us all Jews that inhabit
there, yet? If thou dost, come over, and but see our frippery;
change an old shirt for a whole smock with us. Do not conceive
that antipathy between us and Hogsden as was between Jews and
hogs' flesh. Leave thy vigilant father alone to number over his green   70
apricots, evening and morning, o' the northwest wall; an' I had
been his son, I had saved him the labor long since; if taking in all
the young wenches that pass by at the back door, and coddling
every kernel of the fruit for 'em, would ha' served. But pr'y thee,
come over to me quickly this morning; I have such a present for   75
thee (our Turkey Company never sent the like to the Grand Signior)! One is a rhymer, sir, o' your own batch, your own leaven,
but doth think himself Poet-mayor o' the town: willing to be shown,
and worthy to be seen. The other—I will not venture his description
with you till you come, because I would ha' you make hither with   80
an appetite. If the worst of 'em be not worth your journey, draw

67 YET *still.* FRIPPERY *old clothes shop. Wellbred is playing on the fact that these
establishments were characteristic of Jewish quarters (selling second-hand clothes
was one of the few occupations not legally forbidden to Jews).*

68 CHANGE *exchange.* OLD SHIRT . . . WHOLE SMOCK *old man (Knowell) . . .
undiseased wench.*

73 CODDLING *stewing; with play on "codling," slang for scrotum.*

74 KERNEL *continues the* double entendre *with play on "gland."*

76 TURKEY COMPANY *an English company royally chartered to trade with the
Turkish Empire.*

76–77 GRAND SIGNIOR *Sultan. He received extremely valuable gifts from the British
crown through the Company.*

77 YOUR OWN BATCH . . . LEAVEN *baked simultaneously with you and identically
leavened.*

78 POET . . . TOWN *cf. V.5.37–40. "Mayor" is also a play on "major," from which
it is derived.*

78–79 WILLING . . . SEEN *an allusion to the Lord Mayor's Show, the traditional
procession through London in which a new mayor is exhibited in a gilded coach.*

your bill of charges as unconscionable as any Guildhall verdict will
give it you, and you shall be allowed your *viaticum.*

From The Windmill."

85 From the bordello it might come as well,
The Spittle, or Pict-hatch. Is this the man
My son hath sung so for the happiest wit,
The choicest brain the times hath sent us forth?
I know not what he may be in the arts,
90 Nor what in schools; but surely, for his manners,
I judge him a profane and dissolute wretch:
Worse by possession of such great good gifts,
Being the master of so loose a spirit.
Why, what unhallowed ruffian would have writ
95 In such a scurrilous manner to a friend!
Why should he think I tell my apricots?
Or play th' Hesperian dragon with my fruit,
To watch it? Well, my son, I'd thought
You'd had more judgment t' have made election
100 Of your companions, than t' have ta'en on trust
Such petulant, jeering gamesters, that can spare
No argument or subject from their jest.
But I perceive affection makes a fool

---

82 GUILDHALL *London's City Hall (originally a guild meeting hall). London juries
were notorious for prejudice and unjust decisions.*

83 VIATICUM *sum to cover traveling expenses.*

84 THE WINDMILL *a tavern in the old Jewry.*

86 SPITTLE *contraction of "hospital," a charitable institution offering hospitality;
this contraction generally signified a haven for the down-and-out, especially those
with venereal diseases.* PICT-HATCH *London area notorious as haunt of low
characters, especially prostitutes.*

87 HAPPIEST *most dexterous, most felicitous.*

96 TELL *count.*

97 HESPERIAN DRAGON *in Greek myth, an unsleeping dragon, guard of the golden
apples in the garden of the nymphs called the Hesperides.*

Of any man too much the father.—Brainworm!
　　　　　(*Enter Brainworm.*)
　Brainworm. Sir.　　　　　　　　　　　　　　　　　　　　105
　Knowell. Is the fellow gone that brought this letter?
　Brainworm. Yes, sir, a pretty while since.
　Knowell. And where's your young master?
　Brainworm. In his chamber, sir.
　Knowell. He spake not with the fellow, did he?　　　110
　Brainworm. No, sir, he saw him not.
　Knowell. Take you this letter and deliver it my son,
But with no notice that I have opened it, on your life.
　Brainworm. Oh lord, sir, that were a jest, indeed!
　　　　　　　　　　　　　　　(*Exit Brainworm.*)
　Knowell. I am resolved I will not stop his journey,　115
Nor practice any violent mean to stay
The unbridled course of youth in him; for that,
Restrained, grows more impatient; and in kind
Like to the eager but the generous greyhound,
Who, ne'er so little from his game withheld,　　　　　120
Turns head, and leaps up at his holder's throat.
There is a way of winning more by love
And urging of the modesty, than fear:
Force works on servile natures, not the free.
He that's compelled to goodness may be good,　　　125

107　SINCE *ago.*
115–27　N.
116　STAY *hinder.*
118　IN KIND *in its nature. The construction is ambiguous; "in kind . . . greyhound"
　　may be read as parallel with "more impatient" or as an independent statement
　　with "is" understood after "kind."*
119　GENEROUS *of good breed or stock.*
120　GAME *perhaps, in view of l. 101, with pun on "amusement."*
121　TURNS HEAD *turns to face the enemy, presents bold resistance (opposite of "turns
　　tail").*

But 'tis but for that fit; where others, drawn
By softness and example, get a habit.
Then, if they stray, but warn 'em: and the same
They should for virtue'have done, they'll do for shame. (*Exit.*)

Act I Scene 3

[In Knowell's house.]

(*Enter Edward [holding a letter], with Brainworm.*)

Edward. Did he open it, sayest thou?

Brainworm. Yes, o' my word, sir, and read the contents.

Edward. That scarce contents me. What countenance, pr'y thee, made he i' the reading of it? Was he angry or pleased?

5 *Brainworm.* Nay, sir, I saw him not read it, nor open it, I assure your Worship.

Edward. No? How know'st thou, then, that he did either?

Brainworm. Marry, sir, because he charged me on my life to tell nobody that he opened it; which unless he had done, he would
10 never fear to have it revealed.

Edward. That's true. Well, I thank thee, Brainworm.

[*Edward opens the letter. Brainworm starts to leave.*
Enter Stephen, meeting Brainworm near the door.]

Stephen. Oh, Brainworm, did'st thou not see a fellow here in a what-sha'-call-him doublet? He brought mine uncle a letter e'en now.

15 *Brainworm.* Yes, Master Stephen, what of him?

I.3.] scene misnumbered II in F₁.
1 *Edward.*] F₁ gives this name throughout as E. Kn. or Edw. Kno'well. My alteration will not be noted again.

---

2 CONTENTS *stressed on the second syllable.*

Stephen. Oh, I ha' such a mind to beat him—where is he? Canst thou tell?

Brainworm. Faith, he is not of that mind: he is gone, Master Stephen.

Stephen. Gone? Which way? When went he? How long since? 20

Brainworm. He is rid hence. He took horse at the street door.

Stephen. And I stayed i' the fields! Whoreson scander-bag rogue! Oh, that I had but a horse to fetch him back again.

Brainworm. Why, you may ha' my mistress's gelding, to save your longing, sir. 25

Stephen. But I ha' no boots, that's the spite on't.

Brainworm. Why, a fine wisp of hay rolled hard, Master Stephen.

Stephen. No, faith, it's no boot to follow him, now; let him e'en go and hang. Pray thee, help to truss me a little. He does so vex me—

Brainworm. You'll be worse vexed when you are trussed, Master 30 Stephen. Best keep unbraced and walk yourself till you be cold; your choler may founder you else.

16, 18 MIND *The senses "desire" and "opinion" were sufficiently distinct to lend themselves to word-play.*

21 IS RID *has ridden.*

22 WHORESON *pun on "horse-on."* SCANDER-BAG *swaggering; a common corruption of Iskander Beg (Prince Alexander), the name with which the Turks honored their greatest Albanian enemy, in allusion to Alexander the Great. N.*

27 WISP . . . HARD *in lieu of riding boots, workmen or farmers sometimes bound a firm bunch of hay to the inside of the leg to protect it. N.*

28 BOOT *avail.*

29 TRUSS *tie the laces fastening hose or breeches to doublet. Stephen has loosened his clothing for a fight; cf. Q: "nothing angers me, but I have waited such a while for him all unlaced and untrussed yonder . . ." (I.2.32–33).*

30 TRUSSED *a pun; probably on "strung up" (hanged), but possibly on "sent packing" (a rare usage, however).*

31 UNBRACED *unlaced.* COLD *i.e. cooled off.*

32 CHOLER MAY FOUNDER *a pun on the draught-horse's collar (a leather-covered roll around neck or breast, corresponding well enough to Stephen's laces), which, if too tight, would cause the horse to stagger or collapse.*

Stephen. By my faith and so I will, now thou tell'st me on 't.
[*He begins to walk up and down, and stops in front of Brainworm.*]
How dost thou like my leg, Brainworm?

35   *Brainworm.* A very good leg, Master Stephen! But the woolen
stocking does not commend it so well.

Stephen. Foh, the stockings be good enough, now summer is
coming on, for the dust; I'll have a pair of silk again' winter, that
I go to dwell i' the town. I think my leg would show in a silk hose.

40   *Brainworm.* Believe me, Master Stephen, rarely well.

Stephen. [*Surveying his leg.*] In sadness, I think it would; I have a
reasonable good leg.

Brainworm. You have an excellent good leg, Master Stephen, but
I cannot stay to praise it longer now, and I am very sorry for 't.

45   *Stephen.* Another time will serve, Brainworm. Gramercy for this.

(*Exit [Brainworm].*)

Edward. Ha, ha, ha!   [*Edward*]
                                                   Knowell laughs,
Stephen. 'Slid, I hope he laughs not at me; and he   *having read*
do—   *the letter.*

Edward. [*To himself.*] Here was a letter, indeed, to be
50   intercepted by a man's father, and do him good with him! He
cannot but think most virtuously both of me and the sender, sure,
that make the careful costermonger of him in our Familiar Epistles.
Well, if he read this with patience, I'll be gelt, and troll ballads for
Mr. John Trundle yonder the rest of my mortality. It is true, and

38 AGAIN' *against; when I prepare for.* THAT *in which.*
39 SHOW *show up.*
41 SADNESS *seriousness.*
45 GRAMERCY *French* grand merci, *much thanks.*
52 COSTERMONGER *fruitseller.* FAMILIAR EPISTLES *a popular current title for published collections of personal correspondence, modeled on the title of Cicero's
letters.*
53 GELT *castrated.* N.
54 MR. JOHN TRUNDLE *a contemporary publisher and bookseller, especially of popular
literature.*

likely, my father may have as much patience as another man; for 55
he takes much physic, and oft taking physic makes a man very
patient. But would your packet, Master Wellbred, had arrived at
him in such a minute of his patience; then we had known the end
of it, which now is doubtful, and threatens—

[*He notices Stephen. Still to himself.*]

What! My wise cousin! Nay, then I'll furnish our feast with one 60
gull more toward the mess. He writes to me of a brace, and here's
one, that's three; oh, for a fourth! Fortune, if ever thou'lt use thine
eyes, I entreat thee—

Stephen. Oh, now I see who he laughed at. He laughed at some-
body in that letter. By this good light, and he had laughed at me— 65

Edward. How now, cousin Stephen, melancholy?

Stephen. Yes, a little. I thought you had laughed at me, cousin.

Edward. Why, what an' I had, cos, what would you ha' done?

Stephen. By this light, I would ha' told mine uncle.

Edward. Nay, if you would ha' told your uncle, I did laugh at you, 70
cos.

Stephen. Did you, indeed?

Edward. Yes, indeed.

Stephen. Why, then—

Edward. What then? 75

Stephen. I am satisfied, it is sufficient.

Edward. Why, be so, gentle cos. And I pray you let me entreat a
courtesy of you. I am sent for this morning by a friend i' the old

69, 72 *Stephen.*] Serv. F₁.

---

56 PHYSIC *medicine, particularly a cathartic.*

57 PATIENT *pun on the medical sense.*

61 MESS *group of four (into which company at banquets was formerly divided).*

62–63 FORTUNE . . . EYES *Fortune, goddess of human accidents, was often conceived
of as being blind or having bound eyes. Finding a fourth gull is a worthy occasion
for her to exercise her eyesight.*

66 MELANCHOLY *a fashionable "humor."*

Jewry to come to him; it's but crossing over the fields to Moorgate
—will you bear me company? I protest it is not to draw you into
bond, or any plot against the state, cos.

80

Stephen. Sir, that's all one, and 't were: you shall command me
twice so far as Moorgate to do you good in such a matter. Do you
think I would leave you? I protest—

85

Edward. No, no, you shall not protest, cos.

Stephen. By my fackins, but I will, by your leave; I'll protest more
to my friend than I'll speak of at this time.

Edward. You speak very well, cos.

Stephen. Nay, not so neither, you shall pardon me; but I speak to

90

serve my turn.

Edward. Your turn, cos? Do you know what you say? A gentleman of your sort, parts, carriage, and estimation, to talk o' your
turn i' this company, and to me alone, like a tankard-bearer at a
conduit! Fie. A wight that (hitherto) his every step hath left the

95

stamp of a great foot behind him, as every word the savor of a
strong spirit! And he! This man! So graced, gilded, or (to use a
more fit metaphor) so tin-foiled by nature, as not ten housewives'
pewter (again' a good time) shows more bright to the world than
he! And he (as I said last, so I say again, and still shall say it), this

100

man! To conceal such real ornaments as these, and shadow their

79 MOORGATE *a gate in the city wall on the side nearest Hoxton.*

80 PROTEST *give (you) assurance. A fashionable turn of phrase.*

81 BOND *legal commitment to be responsible for another's debt.*

86 FACKINS *faith.*

92 SORT . . . ESTIMATION *rank, talents, bearing, and consequence.*

93 TURN *a trip to and from the conduit; water-bearers were paid by the "turn."*
   THIS COMPANY *the audience. (J. Dover Wilson, cited HS.)*

94 WIGHT *person; here probably an elevated term.*

98 AGAIN' . . . TIME *prepared for a holiday celebration.*

100 REAL *a pun on 1. genuine; 2. royal; 3. relating to ready money.*

glory, as a millaner's wife does her wrought stomacher with a smoky lawn or a black cypress? Oh, cos! It cannot be answered, go not about it. Drake's old ship at Deptford may sooner circle the world again. Come, wrong not the quality of your desert with looking downward, cos; but hold up your head, so; and let the 105
Idea of what you are be portrayed i' your face, that men may read i' your physnomy, "Here, within this place, is to be seen the true, rare, and accomplished monster—or miracle—of nature" (which is all one). What think you of this, cos?

Stephen. Why, I do think of it; and I will be more proud, and 110
melancholy, and gentleman-like, than I have been, I'll ensure you.

Edward. Why, that's resolute Master Stephen! [*Aside.*] Now, if I can but hold him up to his height, as it is happily begun, it will do well for a suburb-humor; we may hap have a match with the city, and play him for forty pound. [*To Stephen.*] Come, cos. 115

Stephen. I'll follow you.

101 MILLANER *seller of accessories such as gloves, ribbon, fancy fabrics, most of them originally imported from Milan.* WROUGHT STOMACHER *embroidered covering for the chest, worn under lacing of bodice.*

102 SMOKY LAWN *Jonson seems to mean that this delicate white fabric, used for ruffs, ruffles, and kerchiefs, resembled a cloud of smoke.* CYPRESS *a light, veil-like fabric.* ANSWERED *justified.*

103 GO . . . IT *don't try.* DRAKE'S . . . DEPTFORD *Sir Francis Drake's Golden Hind was a national monument and holiday resort, permanently docked in the royal naval dockyard south of London. It had returned from its voyage round the world— the first by an Englishman—in 1580.*

106 IDEA *in Plato, the perfect pattern of an earthly thing.*

107 PHYSNOMY *physiognomy.*

111 ENSURE *guarantee.*

113 HEIGHT *hauteur; probably also "high point."* HAPPILY *successfully.*

113–14 DO . . . SUBURB–HUMOR *provide an apt example of the form humor takes in the suburbs.* HAP *chance to.*

115 PLAY HIM *i.e. against a city gull.*

Edward. Follow me? You must go before.

Stephen. Nay, an' I must, I will. Pray you, show me, good cousin.

(*Exeunt.*)

117 GO BEFORE *Edward plays on* "*take the role of a servant*" (*cf.* TT *IV.4.8–9:* "*Pray you goe before her, | Serving-man-like*").

Act I Scene 4

[*The street, before Cob's house.*]

(*Enter Matthew.*)

Matthew. I think this be the house. [*Knocks and calls.*] What ho?

Cob. [*Within.*] Who's there? [*Opens the door.*] Oh, Master Matthew! Gi' your Worship good morrow.

Matthew. What! Cob! How dost thou, good Cob? Dost thou
5   inhabit here, Cob?

Cob. Aye, sir, I and my lineage ha' kept a poor house here in our days.

Matthew. Thy lineage, Monsieur Cob—what lineage? What lineage?

10   *Cob.* Why, sir, an ancient lineage and a princely. Mine ance'try came from a king's belly, no worse man; and yet no man neither (by your Worship's leave, I did lie in that), but Herring, the King of Fish (from his belly I proceed), one o' the monarchs o' the world, I assure you. The first red herring that was broiled in Adam and
15   Eve's kitchen do I fetch my pedigree from, by the harrot's books.

6 POOR HOUSE *modest inn; with play on* "*keep a good house,*" *provide generous food and drink.*

12–13 KING OF FISH *popularly so called on the basis that he* "*wears a coronet on his head*" (*Nashe,* LS, *p. 203*).

14 RED HERRING *smoked herring.*

15 HARROT's *herald's.*

His cob was my great-great-mighty-great-grandfather.

Matthew. Why mighty? Why mighty, I pray thee?

Cob. Oh, it was a mighty while ago, sir, and a mighty great cob.

Matthew. How know'st thou that?

Cob. How know I? Why, I smell his ghost, ever and anon.   20

Matthew. Smell a ghost? Oh, unsavory jest! And the ghost of a herring, Cob!

Cob. Aye, sir, with favor of your Worship's nose, Mr. Matthew, why not the ghost of a herring-cob, as well as the ghost of rasher-bacon?   25

Matthew. Roger Bacon, thou would'st say?

Cob. I say rasher-bacon. They were both broiled o' the coals? And a man may smell broiled meat, I hope? You are a scholar; upsolve me that, now.

Matthew. O raw ignorance!—Cob, canst thou show me of a   30 gentleman, one Captain Bobadill, where his lodging is?

Cob. Oh, my guest, sir, you mean!

Matthew. Thy guest! Alas! Ha, ha!

Cob. Why do you laugh, sir? Do you not mean Captain Bobadill?

Matthew. Cob, pray thee, advise thyself well; do not wrong the   35 gentleman, and thyself too. I dare be sworn he scorns thy house. He! He lodge in such a base, obscure place as thy house! Tut, I know his disposition so well—he would not lie in thy bed, if thou'dst gi' it him.

Cob. I will not give it him, though, sir. Mass, I thought somewhat   40 was in't—we could not get him to bed all night! Well, sir, though he lie not o' my bed, he lies o' my bench; an't please you to go up,

---

16 COB *head of a herring; with pun on the meaning "testicle."*

26–27 ROGER BACON ... COALS *The famous friar and philosopher was long imprisoned in his cell on suspicion of black magic; popular history may have reported him burnt at the stake.*

28 UPSOLVE *clear up, resolve. Cob's own coinage.*

30 RAW *unschooled; a pun, of course, on "broiled."*

sir, you shall find him with two cushions under his head and his
cloak wrapped about him, as though he had neither won nor lost,
45 and yet I warrant he ne'er cast better in his life than he has done
tonight.

    Matthew. Why? Was he drunk?

    Cob. Drunk, sir? You hear not me say so. Perhaps he swallowed
a tavern-token, or some such device, sir; I have nothing to do withal.
50 I deal with water, and not with wine. [*Calls in at the door.*] Gi' me
my tankard there, ho! [*To Matthew.*] God b'w'you, sir. It's six
o'clock; I should ha' carried two turns by this.—What ho? My
stopple? Come!

    Matthew. [*To himself.*] Lie in a water-bearer's house! A gentleman
55 of his havings! Well, I'll tell him my mind. (*Exit* [*into the house*].)

    Cob. [*Speaks in at the door.*] What, Tib, show this gentleman up
to the Captain.—Oh, an' my house were The Brazen Head, now!
Faith, it would e'en speak, "Mo fools yet." You should ha' some,
now, would take this Mr. Matthew to be a gentleman, at the least.
60 His father's an honest man, a worshipful fishmonger, and so forth;
and now does he creep and wriggle into acquaintance with all the
brave gallants about the town, such as my guest is (oh, my guest is a

---

44 AS THOUGH . . . NEITHER . . . LOST *proverbial for "in a daze" or "sunk in
melancholy."*

45 CAST *pun on* 1. *threw dice;* 2. *threw up.*

48–49 SWALLOWED . . . TOKEN *slang for "got drunk." Tokens worth about a
farthing were issued by tradesmen as change.*

53 STOPPLE *stopper. Between this speech and l. 56, Tib hands out stopple and tankard.*

57 THE BRAZEN HEAD *Roger Bacon was supposed to have constructed, with diabolical
aid, a head of brass which could speak.*

58 "MO FOOLS YET" *proverbial. N.*

60 WORSHIPFUL *a joke alluding to membership in the Worshipful Company of
Fishmongers. Every City guild or company had this form of title, but not the
individual members; "worshipful" was reserved for gentlemen in high positions.*

62 BRAVE *fine.*

fine man), and they flout him invincibly. He useth every day to a
merchant's house (where I serve water), one Master Kitely's, i' the
old Jewry; and here's the jest, he is in love with my Master's sister,   65
Mistress Bridget, and calls her mistress; and there he will sit you a
whole afternoon sometimes, reading o' these same abominable,
vile (a pox on 'em, I cannot abide them), rascally verses, "poyetry,
poyetry," and speaking of "interludes," 'twill make a man burst to
hear him. And the wenches, they do so jeer and tee-hee at him—   70
well, should they do so much to me, I'd forswear them all, by the
foot of Pharaoh. There's an oath! How many water-bearers shall you
hear swear such an oath? Oh, I have a guest (he teaches me), he
does swear the legiblest of any man christened: "By St. George!"
"The foot of Pharaoh!" "The body of me!" "As I am a gentleman   75
and a soldier!" Such dainty oaths! And withal he does take this
same filthy roguish tobacco the finest and cleanliest! It would do a
man good to see the fume come forth at's tunnels! Well, he owes
me forty shillings (my wife lent him out of her purse, by sixpence
a time) besides his lodging; I would I had it. I shall ha' it, he says,   80
the next action. Helter skelter, hang sorrow, care'll kill a cat, up
tails all, and a louse for the hangman. (*Exit.*)

75 am a gentleman] F₂; am gentleman F₁.

---

63 INVINCIBLY *a malapropism, appropriate to the situation, for* "invisibly." *N.*
    USETH *customarily goes.*
67 THESE SAME *intensive; no particular verses are referred to.*
69 "INTERLUDES" *stage plays, especially comedies or farces (originally given between
    acts of long mystery or morality plays).*
77 ROGUISH *rascally.*
78 FUME *smoke.* TUNNELS *nostrils.*
78–80 WELL . . . IT *Note that the indefatigable Bobadill has made eighty separate
    applications to his hostess's purse. For commentary on the relationship between
    Bobadill and his landlord, see N. to III.6.47–48.*
81 ACTION *?campaign; ?lawsuit. N.*
81–82 UP TAILS ALL *refrain of a popular song, often used in speech. It meant* "com-
    pletely topsy-turvy," *usually with sexual innuendo.*

Act I Scene 5

[*Bobadill's room.*]

Bobadill. Hostess, hostess!

[*Enter Tib.*]

Tib. What say you, sir?

Bobadill. A cup o' thy small beer, sweet hostess.

Tib. Sir, there's a gentleman below would speak with you.

5   *Bobadill.* A gentleman! 'Ods so, I am not within.

Tib. My husband told him you were, sir.

Bobadill. What a plague—what meant he?

Matthew. Captain Bobadill? (*Matthew within.*)

Bobadill. [*Calls.*] Who's there? [*To Tib.*] Take away the basin,

10   good hostess.—Come up, sir.

Tib. [*Calls out the door.*] He would desire you to come up, sir.
[*Enter Matthew.*] You come into a cleanly house, here.

Matthew. Save you, sir. Save you, Captain.

Bobadill. Gentle Master Matthew! Is it you, sir? Please you sit

15   down.

Matthew. [*Looks about, but finds no seat.*] Thank you, good Captain;
you may see I am somewhat audacious.

Bobadill. Not so, sir. I was requested to supper last night by a

---

3   SMALL BEER *weak beer; apparently considered a remedy for hangover.*

5   'ODS SO *fashionable, euphemistic form of "God!"*

7   A *the.*

9   BASIN *bowl. Bobadill has been vomiting.*

17   AUDACIOUS *in seeking out Bobadill's lodging.*

sort of gallants, where you were wished for, and drunk to, I assure
you.   20

Matthew. Vouchsafe me by whom, good Captain.

Bobadill. Marry, by young Wellbred and others. [*He notices the
lack of a seat.*] Why, hostess, a stool here for this gentleman! [*Exit
Tib.*]

Matthew. No haste, sir, 'tis very well.

Bobadill. Body of me! It was so late ere we parted last night, I   25
can scarce open my eyes yet; I was but new risen as you came. How
passes the day abroad, sir? You can tell.

Matthew. Faith, some half hour to seven. Now trust ^[Enter Tib, with stool.]
me, you have an exceeding fine lodging here, very neat, and private!

Bobadill. Aye, sir; sit down, I pray you. [*Matthew sits.*] Master   30
Matthew, in any case possess no gentleman of our acquaintance
with notice of my lodging.

Matthew. Who? I, sir? No.

Bobadill. Not that I need to care who know it, for the cabin is
convenient, but in regard I would not be too popular, and generally 35
visited, as some are.

Matthew. True, Captain, I conceive you.

Bobadill. For do you see, sir, by the heart of valor in me: except
it be to some peculiar and choice spirits to whom I am extraordinarily engaged, as yourself, or so, I could not extend thus far.   40

Matthew. Oh lord, sir, I resolve so.

Bobadill. I confess I love a cleanly and quiet privacy above all the

---

19 SORT *company.*

23 STOOL *the usual domestic seat at this time; an oblong box on legs, solid and often
ornamented.*

28 *s.d. Tib may exit after placing the stool. See footnote to ll. 113–14 below.*

31–32 POSSESS . . . NOTICE *provide . . . information.*

34 CABIN *military language: a soldier's temporary shelter.*

39 PECULIAR *special.*

41 RESOLVE *am convinced. A fashionable turn of phrase.*

tumult and roar of fortune.—What new book ha' you there? [*He examines it.*] What! "Go by, Hieronimo!"

45   *Matthew*. Aye; did you ever see it acted? Is't not well penned?

    Bobadill. Well penned? I would fain see all the poets of these times pen such another play as that was! They'll prate and swagger, and keep a stir of art and devices, when (as I am a gentleman), read 'em, they are the most shallow, pitiful, barren fellows that live upon

50 the face of the earth, again!

    Matthew. Indeed, here are a number of fine speeches in this book. [*Reads.*] "O eyes, no eyes, but fountains fraught with tears!" There's a conceit! Fountains fraught with tears! "O life, no life, but lively form of death!" Another! "O world, no world, but mass of

55 public wrongs!" A third! "Confused and filled with murder and misdeeds!" A fourth! Oh, the Muses! Is't not excellent? Is't not simply the best that ever you heard, Captain? Ha? How do you like it?

    Bobadill. 'Tis good.

    Matthew. [*He takes out a piece of paper and reads from it.*]

60   "To thee, the purest object to my sense,
        The most refinèd essence heaven covers,
        Send I these lines, wherein I do commence
        The happy state of turtle-billing lovers.
           If they prove rough, unpolished, harsh, and rude,
65   Haste made the waste. Thus, mildly, I conclude."

43–44 NEW . . . HIERONIMO "*Go by, Hieronimo!*" *is the most famous line in* The Spanish Tragedy. *Originally presented in the second half of the 1580s, this play was an old chestnut even when EI was first acted, and went through seven editions before the revision of EI appeared. Jonson had played the part of Hieronimo.*

46 I . . . FAIN *I would like to.*

50 AGAIN *intensifying exclamation.*

53 CONCEIT *ingenious metaphor.*

63 TURTLE-BILLING *kissing like turtle doves.*

Bobadill. Nay, proceed, proceed. Where's this? Bobadill is mak-
ing him ready
Matthew. This, sir? A toy o' mine own, in my non- all this while.
age: the infancy of my muses! But when will you come and see my
study? Good faith, I can show you some very good things I have
done of late—That boot becomes your leg passing well, Captain, 70
methinks!
Bobadill. So, so; it's the fashion gentlemen now use.
Matthew. Troth, Captain, an' now you speak o' the fashion,
Master Wellbred's elder brother and I are fall'n out exceedingly:
this other day I happened to enter into some discourse of a hanger, 75
which, I assure you, both for fashion and workmanship, was most
peremptory-beautiful and gentlemanlike! Yet he condemned and
cried it down for the most pied and ridiculous that ever he saw.
Bobadill. Squire Downright? The half-brother, was't not?
Matthew. Aye, sir, he. 80
Bobadill. Hang him, rook, he! Why, he has no more judgment
than a malt-horse. By Saint George, I wonder you'd lose a thought
upon such an animal: the most peremptory absurd clown of Christendom this day, he is holden. I protest to you, as I am a gentleman
and a soldier, I ne'er changed words with his like. By his discourse, 85
he should eat nothing but hay. He was born for the manger, pan-

67 TOY *trifle.*
67–68 NONAGE *minority; hence, period of immaturity.*
73 TROTH *in truth.*
74 ARE FALL'N OUT *have quarreled.*
75 HANGER *loop or strap, often decorated, by which the sword hung from the sword-
belt.*
77 PEREMPTORY-BEAUTIFUL *utterly beautiful. "Peremptory" as adverb was a fa-
shionable affectation of speech.*
78 PIED *gaudy.*
81 ROOK *simpleton.*
82 MALT-HORSE *heavy horse used by malt-makers, knowing only its one daily
round.*
84 HOLDEN *considered.*

nier, or pack-saddle! He has not so much as a good phrase in his belly, but all old iron and rusty proverbs! A good commodity for some smith to make hobnails of.

90   *Matthew.* Aye, and he thinks to carry it away with his manhood still, where he comes. He brags he will gi' me the *bastinado*, as I hear.

   Bobadill. How! He the *bastinado*! How came he by that word, trow?

   Matthew. Nay, indeed, he said cudgel me; I termed it so, for my 95 more grace.

   Bobadill. That may be; for I was sure it was none of his word. But when? When said he so?

   Matthew. Faith, yesterday, they say; a young gallant, a friend of mine, told me so.

100   *Bobadill.* By the foot of Pharaoh, and't were my case, now, I should send him a *chartel* presently. The *bastinado*! A most proper and sufficient dependence, warranted by the great Caranza. Come hither. You shall *chartel* him. I'll show you a trick or two you shall kill him with at pleasure: the first *stoccata*, if you will, by this air.

105   *Matthew.* Indeed, you have absolute knowledge i' the mystery, I have heard, sir.

   Bobadill. Of whom? Of whom ha' you heard it, I beseech you?

89 HOBNAILS *for protecting the soles of heavy boots; hence used to convey rusticity and boorishness.*

90 CARRY IT AWAY *sweep all before him.* MANHOOD *manly valor.*

91 STILL *always.* WHERE *wherever.* BASTINADO *beating with a cudgel. From Spanish* bastonada.

93 TROW *think you.*

101 CHARTEL *challenge. French* (cartel). N.

102 DEPENDENCE *ground for a duel, according to the rules. From the French.* CARANZA *Jeronimo de Carranza, author of the first Spanish treatise on the etiquette of dueling.*

104 STOCCATA *thrust. Italian.*

105 MYSTERY *craft, art; probably with play on the modern meaning. N.*

Matthew. Troth, I have heard it spoken of divers that you have very rare and un-in-one-breath-utterable skill, sir.

Bobadill. By heaven, no, not I; no skill i' the earth: some small 110 rudiments i' the science, as to know my time, distance, or so. I have professed it more for noblemen and gentlemen's use than mine own practice, I assure you.—Hostess, accommodate us with another bed-staff here, quickly!—Lend us another bed-staff! [*Exit Tib.*] [*To Matthew.*] The woman does not understand the words of action. 115

[*Takes up the available bed-staff and with it
illustrates the following speech.*]

Look you, sir. Exalt not your point above this state, at any hand, and let your poniard maintain your defense, thus. [*Enter Tib with bed-staff.*] Give it the gentleman, and leave us. [*Exit Tib.*] So, sir. Come on! Oh, twine your body more about, that you may fall to a more sweet comely gentleman-like guard. [*Matthew imitates* 120 *him.*] So, indifferent. Hollow your body more, sir, thus. Now, stand fast o' your left leg, note your distance, keep your due proportion of time—Oh, you disorder your point most irregularly!

Matthew. [*Adjusting the bed-staff.*] How is the bearing of it now, sir?

Bobadill. Oh, out of measure ill! A well-experienced hand would 125 pass upon you at pleasure.

110–13 N.

112 PROFESSED *made (myself) expert in.*

113–14 *If Tib has gone out ca. l. 28, Bobadill is here calling; but given the brevity of the interval in which he decides he is not communicating, she is probably standing motionless in the room and exits as indicated.*

113 ACCOMMODATE *one of "the perfumed terms of the time" (Jonson, D 2275).*

114 BED-STAFF *stick used to help make up a bed.*

115 WORDS OF ACTION *"Accommodate" was fashionably considered "a soldier-like word." (2 H IV III.2.75–81; cited Whalley.)*

116 STATE *position.* AT ANY HAND *whatever you do.*

117 PONIARD *held in the left hand to deflect thrusts.*

121 INDIFFERENT *fair.*

126 PASS UPON *make a successful pass at; but Matthew is confused by the colloquial sense, "deceive, impose upon."*

Act I Scene 5

Matthew. How mean you, sir, pass upon me?

Bobadill. Why, thus, sir (make a thrust at me): come in upon the answer, control your point, and make a full
130 career at the body. The best-practiced gallants of the time name it the *passada*: a most desperate thrust, believe it!

[Matthew lunges at Bobadill, who deflects the staff and with his own pushes Matthew backward.]

Matthew. [*Puts himself in position.*] Well, come, sir.

Bobadill. Why, you do not manage your weapon with any
135 facility or grace to invite me; I have no spirit to play with you. Your dearth of judgment renders you tedious.

Matthew. But one *venue*, sir.

Bobadill. "*Venue!*" Fie. Most gross denomination as ever I heard. Oh, the *stoccata*, while you live, sir. Note that. Come, put on your
140 cloak, and we'll go to some private place where you are acquainted, some tavern or so—and have a bit—I'll send for one of these fencers, and he shall breathe you, by my direction; and then I will teach you your trick. You shall kill him with it at the first, if you please. Why, I will learn you by the true judgment of the eye, hand, and
145 foot to control any enemy's point i' the world. Should your adversary confront you with a pistol, 't were nothing, by this hand, you should by the same rule control his bullet in a line—except it were hail-shot, and spread. What money ha' you about you, Mr. Matthew?

150 *Matthew.* Faith, I ha' not past a two shillings or so.

Bobadill. 'Tis somewhat with the least; but come. We will have a bunch of radish and salt, to taste our wine; and a pipe of tobacco,

---

129 ANSWER *answering thrust.*

130 CAREER *lunge.*

137 VENUE *thrust. This French term was out of fashion.*

141 BIT *bite.*

142 BREATHE *exercise.*

144 LEARN *teach. Grammatically acceptable at the time.*

152 RADISH *believed to stimulate appetite and digestion.* TASTE *give taste to.*

to close the orifice of the stomach; and then we'll call upon young Wellbred. Perhaps we shall meet the Corydon his brother there, and put him to the question. (*Exeunt.*) 155

154 CORYDON *rustic fellow (name of a shepherd in Vergil's* Eclogues*).*
155 PUT . . . QUESTION *call him to account; perhaps with play on "apply torture to him," i.e. physically force him to confess his misdeed.*

Act II Scene 1

[Before Kitely's house.]

(Enter Kitely, Downright, Cash.)

Kitely. Thomas, come hither:
There lies a note within upon my desk—
Here, take my key—*[He offers, then withdraws, a key.]*
          It is no matter, neither.
Where is the boy?
Cash.   Within, sir, i' the warehouse.
5   *Kitely.* Let him tell over, straight, that Spanish gold,
And weigh it, with th' pieces of eight. Do you
See the delivery of those silver stuffs
To Mr. Lucar. Tell him, if he will,
He shall ha' the grosgrains, at the rate I told him,
10 And I will meet him on the Exchange anon.

---

5 TELL OVER *count.* STRAIGHT *straightway, immediately.*

6 PIECES OF EIGHT *Spanish pesos, pieces of eight reales' worth each; about 8s. 6d. in Jonson's money.*

7 SEE *see to.* STUFFS *fabrics.*

10 EXCHANGE *The Royal Exchange, so called at the order of Queen Elizabeth, was "a burse, or place for merchants to assemble in" (Stow,* Survey, *I.193). It was also a popular lounging place for idlers and gossipers.* ANON *shortly.*

Cash. Good, sir. (*Exit Cash.*)

Kitely.   Do you see that fellow, brother Downright?

Downright. Aye, what of him?

Kitely.   He is a jewel, brother.
I took him of a child up at my door,
And christened him, gave him mine own name, Thomas,
Since bred him at the Hospital; where proving   15
A toward imp, I called him home, and taught him
So much, as I have made him my cashier,
And giv'n him, who had none, a surname, Cash;
And find him in his place so full of faith
That I durst trust my life into his hands.   20

Downright. So would not I in any bastard's, brother—
As it is like he is—although I knew
Myself his father. But you said you'd somewhat
To tell me, gentle brother; what is't? What is't?

Kitely. Faith, I am very loth to utter it,   25
As fearing it may hurt your patience:
But that I know your judgment is of strength
Against the nearness of affection—

Downright. What need this circumstance? Pray you be direct.

---

11 BROTHER *i.e. brother-in-law.*

13 OF *as.*

15 THE HOSPITAL *Christ's Hospital, an orphanage "of a new foundation* [1552] *in the Grey Friars church by* [*Edward VI*]: *poor fatherless children be there brought up and nourished at the charges of the citizens"; "in the year 1553 . . . a school was also ordained there, at the citizens' charges." (Stow,* Survey, *II.145, I.74.)*

16 TOWARD *promising. Disyllabic.* IMP *lad (most probably not yet used in sense o "rascal").*

17 CASHIER *treasurer.*

22–23 ALTHOUGH . . . FATHER *"to be" is understood after "myself."*

26 PATIENCE *three syllables.*

28 AFFECTION *four syllables.*

29 CIRCUMSTANCE *roundabout approach.*

Act II Scene 1

30   *Kitely.* I will not say how much I do ascribe
Unto your friendship; nor, in what regard
I hold your love; but let my past behavior
And usage of your sister but confirm
How well I'ave been affected to your—
35   *Downright.* You are too tedious, come to the matter, the matter.
   Kitely. Then (without further ceremony) thus.
My brother Wellbred, sir (I know not how),
Of late is much declined in what he was,
And greatly altered in his disposition.
40 When he came first to lodge here in my house,
Ne'er trust me if I were not proud of him:
Methought he bare himself in such a fashion,
So full of man, and sweetness in his carriage,
And (what was chief) it showed not borrowed in him,
45 But all he did became him as his own,
And seemed as perfect, proper, and possessed
As breath with life, or color with the blood.
But now his course is so irregular,
So loose, affected, and deprived of grace,
50 And he himself withal so far fall'n off
From that first place, as scarce no note remains
To tell men's judgments where he lately stood.
He's grown a stranger to all due respect,
Forgetful of his friends, and not content
55 To stale himself in all societies,
He makes my house here common as a mart,

30 ASCRIBE *consider due.*
34 AFFECTED *disposed.*
42 METHOUGHT *it seemed to me.* BARE *bore.*
43 CARRIAGE *bearing, manner.*
47 WITH . . . WITH *by . . . by.*
51 SCARCE NO *scarcely any. Double negatives were emphatic.*
55 STALE *make cheap.*

A theater, a public receptacle
For giddy humor and diseasèd riot;
And here (as in a tavern or a stews)
He and his wild associates spend their hours   60
In repetition of lascivious jests,
Swear, leap, drink, dance, and revel night by night,
Control my servants: and indeed what not?

    Downright. 'Sdeynes, I know not what I should say to him, i' the
whole world! He values me at a cracked three-farthings, for aught   65
I see: it will never out o' the flesh that's brèd i' the bone! I have told
him enough, one would think, if that would serve; but counsel
to him is as good as a shoulder of mutton to a sick horse. Well! He
knows what to trust to, 'fore George. Let him spend, and spend,
and domineer, till his heart ache; an' he think to be relieved by me,   70
when he is got into one o' your city pounds, the Counters, he has
the wrong sow by the ear, i' faith, and claps his dish at the wrong

---

57 RECEPTACLE *stressed on the third syllable.*

59 STEWS *brothel, or quarter occupied by brothels.*

62 LEAP *Leaping, a sport whose built-in double* entendre *evidently unnerves
Kitely, was much practiced by young men; it included execution of handsprings,
cartwheels, somersaults, and other forms of agile jumping. Such skill was highly
prized, and formally taught by masters.*

64 'SDEYNES *euphemistic exclamation, probably from " God's dignesse (dignity)."*

65 THREE-FARTHINGS *a silver piece coined only in Queen Elizabeth's reign; very
thin, and so apt to crack.*

66 IT . . . BONE *proverbial.*

68 AS GOOD . . . HORSE *proverbial, denoting total inappropriateness.*

69 GEORGE *St. George.*

70 DOMINEER *lord it.*

71 COUNTERS *the debtors' prisons attached to the sheriffs' courts. (From the sense
" a means of keeping accounts.")*

71–72 HE . . . EAR *proverbial.*

72–73 CLAPS . . . DOOR *proverbial. Beggars carried wooden almsdishes with movable
covers which they clapped to attract notice.*

man's door. I'll lay my hand o' my halfpenny ere I part with't to
fetch him out, I'll assure him.

75   *Kitely.* Nay, good brother, let it not trouble you thus.

    Downright. 'Sdeath, he mads me, I could eat my very spur-
leathers for anger! But why are you so tame? Why do you not
speak to him, and tell him how he disquiets your house?

    Kitely. Oh, there are divers reasons to dissuade, brother.

80 But would yourself vouchsafe to travail in it
(Though but with plain and easy circumstance),
It would both come much better to his sense,
And savor less of stomach or of passion.
You are his elder brother, and that title

85 Both gives and warrants you authority,
Which (by your presence seconded) must breed
A kind of duty in him, and regard;
Whereas, if I should intimate the least,
It would but add contempt to his neglect,

90 Heap worse on ill, make up a pile of hatred
That, in the rearing, would come tott'ring down,
And in the ruin bury all our love.
Nay, more than this, brother, if I should speak,
He would be ready from his heat of humor

---

73 LAY . . . HALFPENNY *i.e. keep a tight hold on my money. Proverbial.*

76–77 SPUR-LEATHERS *leather straps for securing spurs to the feet.*

79 DIVERS *various.*

81 CIRCUMSTANCE *manner of approach.*

83 STOMACH *resentment.*

85 WARRANTS *1. guarantees; 2. furnishes good grounds for.*

94 HEAT OF HUMOR *both metaphorical and literal, since Wellbred's predominant
humor, if he is easily angered, would be choler, a "hot and dry" humor (Burton,
I.I.2.2).*

And overflowing of the vapor in him   95
To blow the ears of his familiars
With the false breath of telling what disgraces
And low disparagements I had put upon him.
Whilst they, sir, to relieve him in the fable,
Make their loose comments upon every word,   100
Gesture, or look I use; mock me all over,
From my flat cap unto my shining shoes;
And, out of their impetuous rioting fant'sies,
Beget some slander that shall dwell with me.
And what would that be, think you? Marry, this.   105
They would give out (because my wife is fair,
Myself but lately married, and my sister
Here sojourning a virgin in my house)
That I were jealous! Nay, as sure as death,
That they would say. And how that I had quarreled   110
My brother purposely, thereby to find
An apt pretext to banish them my house.
   Downright. Mass, perhaps so: they'are like enough to do it.
   Kitely. Brother, they would, believe it; so should I
(Like one of these penurious quack-salvers)   115

95 VAPOR *medically, a hot humor taking the form of an exhalation from the internal*
organs: "Of humors some are more gross and cold, some are subtle and hot, and
are called vapors." (Elyot, Bk. III, Cap. 2, p. 53r. I have modernized the spelling
of all quotations from Elyot.) Note the precision of Kitely's terminology, which
culminates in his self-diagnosis in II.3.58ff.
96 BLOW *whisper into.*
99 RELIEVE HIM *"spell" him.*
102 FLAT . . . SHOES *apparel worn by citizens rather than courtly gentlemen.*
104 DWELL WITH *stick to.*
110 QUARRELED *could be transitive in Elizabethan English.*
115 QUACK-SALVERS *traveling quack doctors who sold cure-alls to crowds gathered*
to hear their harangues. Most reaped little success and much ridicule.

Act II Scene 2

But set the bills up to mine own disgrace,
And try experiments upon myself:
Lend scorn and envy opportunity
To stab my reputation and good name—

116 BILLS *advertisements (in this case, for the promised cures). These were "set up,"
or posted, on walls and pillars.*

Act II Scene 2

(Enter Bobadill and Matthew.)

Matthew. I will speak to him—
Bobadill. Speak to him? Away, by the foot of Pharaoh, you shall
not, you shall not do him that grace. [*To Kitely.*] The time of day
to you, gentleman o' the house. Is Mr. Wellbred stirring?
5   *Downright.* How then? What should he do?
Bobadill. [*To Kitely.*] Gentleman of the house, it is to you: is he
within, sir?
Kitely. He came not to his lodging tonight, sir, I assure you.
Downright. Why, do you hear? You!
10   *Bobadill.* The gentleman-citizen hath satisfied me, I'll talk to no
scavenger.
Downright. How, scavenger? Stay, sir, stay!
(Exeunt [Bobadill and Matthew. Downright moves to follow them].)
Kitely. [*Steps in front of him.*]   Nay, brother Downright.

6 TO YOU *"that I address myself" is understood.*
11 SCAVENGER *literally, a streetcleaner; hence, abusive term for one concerned with
low matters.*

76

Downright. Heart! Stand you away, and you love me.

Kitely. You shall not follow him now, I pray you, brother. Good faith you shall not: I will overrule you.   15

Downright. Ha! Scavenger? Well, go to, I say little; but by this good day (God forgive me I should swear), if I put it up so, say I am the rankest cow that ever pissed. 'Sdeynes, and I swallow this, I'll ne'er draw my sword in the sight of Fleet Street again while I live; I'll sit in a barn with Madge Owlet, and catch mice first.   20 Scavenger? Heart, and I'll go near to fill that huge tumbril-slop of yours with somewhat, and I have good luck: your Garagantua breech cannot carry it away so.

Kitely. Oh, do not fret yourself thus, never think on't.

Downright. These are my brother's consorts, these! These are his   25 comrades, his walking-mates! He's a gallant, a *cavaliero* too, right hangman cut! Let me not live, and I could not find in my heart to swinge the whole ging of 'em, one after another, and begin with him first. I am grieved it should be said he is my brother, and take these courses. Well, as he brews, so he shall drink, 'fore George, again.   30

---

13 HEART! *God's heart!* AND *if.*

16 GO TO *here expresses grudging acquiescence as well as a vague threat.*

17 PUT IT UP *pocket it; equivalent to "swallow it."*

18 RANKEST *most offensive in smell through being in sexual heat—perhaps a pun on "most absolute," but probably a self-sufficient allusion, for the cow provided a prototype of incontinence. N.*

19 FLEET STREET *a prime location for brawls.*

20 MADGE *popular name for the owl.*

21 TUMBRIL-SLOP *large, puffed-out breeches, very much in fashion. "Slop" (literally, "loose-fitting garment") was a genuine word for breeches, but "tumbril" is Downright's insult. N.*

22 GARAGANTUA *the amiable giant made famous by Rabelais. N.*

23 CARRY IT AWAY *carry off the victory.*

26–27 RIGHT HANGMAN CUT *just the right style, or make, for the hangman.*

28 SWINGE *thrash; possibly with play on "swing" (hang).* GING *gang.*

30 AS . . . DRINK *proverbial.*

Yet he shall hear on't, and that tightly too, and I live, i' faith.

    Kitely. But, brother, let your reprehension, then,
Run in an easy current, not o'er-high
Carried with rashness or devouring choler;
But rather use the soft persuading way,
Whose powers will work more gently, and compose
Th'imperfect thoughts you labor to reclaim:
More winning, than enforcing the consent.

    Downright. Aye, aye, let me alone for that, I warrant you.

    Kitely. How now? Oh, the bell rings to breakfast.   *Bell rings.*
Brother, I pray you go in, and bear my wife
Company till I come; I'll but give order
For some dispatch of business, to my servants—(*Exit Downright.*)

35

40

31 TIGHTLY *roundly.*
34 DEVOURING CHOLER "*the nature of choler is . . . of a fretting and biting quality*";
   when heated, it is "*turned . . . into a sharp lye.*" (*Bright, pp. 100, 101.*)
39 WARRANT *assure.*

Act II Scene 3

(*Enter Cob.*)

    Kitely. What, Cob? Our maids will have you by the back (i'faith)
For coming so late this morning.

    Cob. Perhaps so, sir, take heed somebody have not   *He passes by*
them by the belly, for walking so late in the evening.   *with his tankard.*
(*Exit.*)

    Kitely. Well, yet my troubled spirit's somewhat eased,

5

F_1 has *To them.* in margin next to act, scene numbers. N.

———

1 HAVE . . . BACK *lay hold of you, catch you.*

Though not reposed in that security
As I could wish; but I must be content.
How e'er I set a face on't to the world,
Would I had lost this finger at a venture,
So Wellbred had ne'er lodged within my house.   10
Why, 't cannot be, where there is such resort
Of wanton gallants and young revelers,
That any woman should be honest long.
Is't like that factious beauty will preserve
The public weal of chastity unshaken,   15
When such strong motives muster, and make head
Against her single peace? No, no. Beware
When mutual appetite doth meet to treat,
And spirits of one kind and quality
Come once to parley, in the pride of blood: 20
It is no slow conspiracy that follows.
Well (to be plain), if I but thought the time
Had answered their affections, all the world
Should not persuade me but I were a cuckold.
Marry, I hope they ha' not got that start,   25

9 AT A VENTURE *by chance.*
11 RESORT *repair, visitation.*
13 HONEST *virtuous.*
14 LIKE *likely.*
15 PUBLIC WEAL *commonwealth; from "public (general) good," a meaning here played on.*
16 MUSTER . . . HEAD *gather forces and rebel.*
17 HER *beauty's.* SINGLE *1. lone, as opposed to the "armies" of motives; 2. weak; 3. not matched with with any suitor.* PEACE *pun on 1. freedom from war; 2. tranquillity of mind; and possibly 3. piece.*
18 TREAT *negotiate (carrying on the image of war and statecraft).*
20 PRIDE OF BLOOD *high point of passion or excitement; probably with pun on "pride" as sexual desire, especially of a female animal in heat.*
23 ANSWERED *corresponded to.* AFFECTIONS *inclinations; with pun on "loves."*

For opportunity hath balked 'em yet,
And shall do still, while I have eyes and ears
To attend the impositions of my heart.
My presence shall be as an iron bar
30 'Twixt the conspiring motions of desire;
Yea, every look or glance mine eye ejects
Shall check occasion, as one doth his slave,
When he forgets the limits of prescription.

(*Enter Dame Kitely, with Mistress Bridget.*)

Dame Kitely. Sister Bridget, pray you fetch down the rose-water
35 above in the closet. [*To Kitely.*] Sweetheart, will you come in to
breakfast? (*Exit Bridget.*)

Kitely. [*Aside.*] An' she have overheard me now?

Dame Kitely. I pray thee, good Musse, we stay for you.

Kitely. [*Aside.*] By heaven, I would not for a thousand angels.

40 *Dame Kitely.* What ail you, sweetheart, are you not well? Speak,
good Musse.

Kitely. Troth, my head aches extremely, on a sudden.

Dame Kitely. [*Feeling his forehead.*] Oh, the Lord!

Kitely. How now? What?

45 *Dame Kitely.* Alas, how it burns! Musse, keep you warm; good
truth, it is this new disease! There's a number are troubled withal!
For love's sake, sweetheart, come in out of the air.

Kitely. [*Aside.*] How simple and how subtle are her answers!

---

28 ATTEND *1. pay heed to; 2. minister to; 3. be present at the scene of.* IMPOSITIONS
1. commands; 2. accusations; probably with pun on 3. falsehoods. N.

30 MOTIONS *impulses, promptings.*

34 ROSE-WATER *frequently served with fruit, along with sugar.*

38 MUSSE *a favorite term of endearment; probably from "muss," playful baby talk
for "mouth."* STAY *wait.*

39 ANGELS *gold coins worth ca. 10s. apiece.*

46 NEW DISEASE *an uncertainly diagnosed fever, called "new" for over seventy-five
years. Severe headache was a prime symptom. N.*

A new disease, and many troubled with it!
Why, true: she heard me, all the world to nothing.   50
   Dame Kitely. I pray thee, good sweetheart, come in; the air will
do you harm, in troth.
    Kitely. [Aside.] The air! She has me i' the wind! [*To her.*] Sweet-
    heart!
I'll come to you presently; 'twill away, I hope.
   Dame Kitely. Pray heaven it do. (*Exit.*)   55
   Kitely. A new disease? I know not, new or old,
But it may well be called poor mortals' plague:
For, like a pestilence, it doth infect
The houses of the brain. First it begins
Solely to work upon the fantasy,   60
Filling her seat with such pestiferous air
As soon corrupts the judgment, and from thence
Sends like contagion to the memory—
Still each to other giving the infection.
Which, as a subtle vapor, spreads itself   65
Confusedly through every sensive part,

---

52 harm, in troth] F₂; harme in, troth F₁.
55 *Dame Kitely.*] Dame. F₂; Dow. F₁.

---

50 TO NOTHING *notwithstanding; the sense is, "not the whole world could convince
me otherwise."*

53 HAS . . . WIND *knows what I am up to; literally used of a hunted animal scenting
his pursuers.*

54 PRESENTLY *shortly.*

58–73 N.

59 HOUSES . . . BRAIN *The three cells or ventricles into which contemporary anatomy
divided the brain from front to back; often (as here, ll. 59–63) the fantasy was
placed in the foremost cell, the judgment in the next, the memory in the hindmost.*

59–64 N.

66 SENSIVE *capable of sensation. "Now this humor . . . is sometimes in the substance
of the brain, sometimes contained in the membranes and tunicles that cover the
brain, sometimes in the passages of the ventricles of the brain, or veins of those
ventricles." (Burton, I.II.5.3.)*

Till not a thought or motion in the mind
Be free from the black poison of suspect.
Ah, but what misery'is it to know this?
70　Or, knowing it, to want the mind's erection
In such extremes? Well, I will once more strive
(In spite of this black cloud) myself to be,
And shake the fever off, that thus shakes me. (*Exit.*)

68　BLACK POISON *The choler which caused melancholy was black. (Burton, I.I.3.1.)*
70　ERECTION *steadfast strength, firmness. "If choler have yielded matter to this sharp*
　　kind of melancholy, then . . . the whole body is carried with that storm, contrary
　　to persuasion of reason: which hath no farther power over these affections, than
　　by way of counsel to give other direction . . ." (Bright, pp. 111–12.)

Act II Scene 4

[*Moorfields.*]

(*Enter Brainworm disguised like a soldier.*)

Brainworm. 'Slid, I cannot choose but laugh to see myself translated thus from a poor creature to a creator; for now must I create
an intolerable sort of lies, or my present profession loses the grace;
and yet the lie to a man of my coat is as ominous a fruit as the *fico.*
5　O sir, it holds for good polity ever, to have that outwardly in vilest

1–2　TRANSLATED *transformed.*
3　SORT *set.* GRACE *virtue which renders it effective.*
4　OMINOUS *portending disaster.* FRUIT *pun on "outcome."* FICO *fig; name of an*
　　obscene gesture originating in Spain or Italy. Like the imputation of lying, it
　　would be a mortal insult to a soldier's honor.
5　SIR *Brainworm pretends to address a member of the audience.* POLITY *policy.*

estimation that inwardly is most dear to us. So much for my borrowed shape. Well, the troth is, my old master intends to follow
my young, dry foot, over Moorfields to London, this morning;
now I, knowing of this hunting match, or rather conspiracy, and to
insinuate with my young master (for so must we that are blue-   10
waiters, and men of hope and service, do, or perhaps we may wear
motley at the year's end, and who wears motley, you know),
have got me afore in this disguise, determining here to lie in
ambuscado and intercept him in the mid-way. If I can but get his
cloak, his purse, his hat, nay, anything, to cut him off—that is, to   15
stay his journey—*Veni, vidi, vici*, I may say with Captain Caesar, I
am made forever, i'faith. Well, now must I practice to get the true
garb of one of these lance-knights: my arm here, [*Enter Edward and
Stephen, at a distance.*] and my—young master! And his cousin, Mr.
Stephen, as I am true counterfeit man of war, and no soldier!   20

[*Stephen stops, feeling in his pockets.*]

Edward. So, sir, and how then, cos?

Stephen. 'Sfoot, I have lost my purse, I think.

Edward. How? Lost your purse? Where? When had you it?

Stephen. I cannot tell—Stay.

---

8 DRY FOOT *a hunting term; without any tracks as guidance—by the scent alone.
In the revision, this happily lent itself to a play on the notoriously marshy Moorfields, impossible to cross "dry foot."*

9 CONSPIRACY *plot (not necessarily with more than one participant).*

10–11 BLUE-WAITERS *servants ("waiters" on their masters) wore blue livery.*

11–12 WEAR ... END *N.*

13 AFORE *ahead.*

14 MID-WAY *middle of his journey.*

15 CUT HIM OFF *a pun, perhaps on "bring to an untimely end"; but more likely on
"cut" as meaning "castrate."*

18 GARB *style, manner.* LANCE-KNIGHTS *mercenary foot-soldiers. N.*

22 'SFOOT *God's foot.*

25   *Brainworm.* 'Slid, I am afeared they will know me; would I could get by them.

   Edward. What? Ha' you it?

   Stephen. No, I think I was bewitched, I—

   Edward. Nay, do not weep the loss, hang it, let it go.

30   *Stephen.* Oh, it's here! No, and it had been lost, I had not cared, but for a jet ring Mistress Mary sent me.   *[They walk on;*

   Edward. A jet ring? Oh, the posy, the posy?   *as they approach,*
                                           Brainworm

   Stephen. Fine, i'faith! "Though fancy sleep, my love *slips off stage.]*
is deep." Meaning that though I did not fancy her, yet she loved me

35 dearly.

   Edward. Most excellent!

   Stephen. And then I sent her another, and my posy was: " 'The deeper, the sweeter,' I'll be judged by St. Peter."

   Edward. How, by St. Peter? I do not conceive that!

40   *Stephen.* Marry, St. Peter, to make up the meter.

   Edward. Well, there the Saint was your good patron; he helped you at your need. Thank him, thank him!

   Brainworm. I cannot take leave on 'em so: I will *He is come back.*
venture, come what will.—Gentlemen, please you change a few

45 crowns for a very excellent good blade, here? [*He shows his sword.*]
I am a poor gentleman, a soldier, one that (in the better state of my
fortunes) scorned so mean a refuge; but now it is the humor of

---

43 F₁ gives s.d. before referent *Brainworm.*

---

31 JET *a favorite material for cheap rings (HS); but also thought to have mysterious powers (perhaps because of its electrical attraction—cf. III.3.25 and fn.).*

32 POSY *motto (from "poesy"). They were engraved on rings intended to have sentimental significance. Stephen may have a circle of jet lined with silver, or a bit of jet set in a metal ring.*

37–38 THE . . . SWEETER *a common proverb of numerous uses, here utilizing the obviously available sexual overtones. N.*

46–51 *N.*

47 HUMOR *whim.*

necessity to have it so. You seem to be gentlemen well affected to
martial men, else I should rather die with silence, than live with
shame; however, vouchsafe to remember it is my want speaks, not 50
myself. This condition agrees not with my spirit—

Edward. Where hast thou served?

Brainworm. May it please you, sir, in all the late wars of Bohemia,
Hungaria, Dalmatia, Poland—where not, sir? I have been a poor
servitor, by sea and land, any time this fourteen years, and followed 55
the fortunes of the best commanders in Christendom. I was twice
shot at the taking of Aleppo, once at the relief of Vienna; I have been
at Marseilles, Naples, and the Adriatic Gulf, a gentleman-slave in
the galleys thrice, where I was most dangerously shot in the head,
through both the thighs—and yet, being thus maimed, I am void 60

48 AFFECTED *disposed.*

49–50 DIE . . . SHAME. *N.*

53 LATE WARS *of the countries mentioned, only Hungary had had "late wars."*
BOHEMIA *involved in battles against the Turks in 1526 and 1537.*

54 HUNGARIA *conquered by the Turks in 1526, and the scene of subsequent warfare
with them.* DALMATIA *scene of local conflicts between Venetian mercenaries and
Ottoman begs in the 1530s. A combined Christian force was sent in 1538.*
POLAND *prosecuted wars against Russia from 1512 to 1519, and again inter-
mittently from the 1560s to 1582; also fought the Livonian Order of Teutonic
Knights 1519–21.*

54–62 *N.*

55 ANY TIME *at any time you choose, i.e. constantly.* FOURTEEN YEARS *utterly at
variance, of course, with the dates given above; the revised play is specifically
Elizabethan, and Elizabeth's reign began in 1558.*

57 ALEPPO *taken in 1516 by the Ottoman Turks. Since this was a battle of Turks
against Egyptians on Syrian soil, it makes a pleasantly idiotic example of following "the best commanders in Christendom."* RELIEF *raising of the siege; in 1529
Vienna was besieged by the Turks.*

58 MARSEILLES *unsuccessfully besieged in 1524 by the Duke of Bourbon, siding with
Henry VIII against the King of France.* NAPLES *unsuccessfully besieged in 1528
by the Genoese, Venetians, and French (allied with England at the time); held by
the forces of Charles V.* ADRIATIC GULF. *N.*

of maintenance, nothing left me but my scars, the noted marks of my resolution.

Stephen. How will you sell this rapier, friend?

Brainworm. Generous sir, I refer it to your own judgment; you
65 are a gentleman, give me what you please.

Stephen. True, I am a gentleman, I know that, friend: but what though? I pray you say, what would you ask?

Brainworm. [*Offers Stephen the rapier.*] I assure you, the blade may become the side or thigh of the best prince in Europe.

70 *Edward.* [*Examining it.*] Aye, with a velvet scabbard, I think.

Stephen. Nay, and't be mine, it shall have a velvet scabbard, cos, that's flat; I'd not wear it as 'tis, and you would give me an angel.

Brainworm. At your Worship's pleasure, sir; nay, 'tis a most pure Toledo.

75 *Stephen.* I had rather it were a Spaniard! But tell me, what shall I give you for it? An' it had a silver hilt—

Edward. Come, come, you shall not buy it; [*To Brainworm.*] hold, there's a shilling, fellow, take thy rapier. [*Brainworm takes it.*]

Stephen. Why, but I will buy it now, because you say so, and
80 there's another shilling, fellow. [*He gives Brainworm a coin and takes the rapier.*] I scorn to be outbidden. What, shall I walk with a cudgel, like Higginbottom? And may have a rapier for money?

Edward. You may buy one in the City.

Stephen, Tut, I'll buy this i' the field, so I will; I have a mind to't,
85 because 'tis a field rapier. [*To Brainworm.*] Tell me your lowest price.

70 VELVET SCABBARD *impractical and therefore very elegant fashion of the time.*

74 TOLEDO *Sword blades made in this Spanish city were renowned throughout Europe from Roman times for the exceptional temper of their steel, attributed to some quality in the Tagus water into which the newly forged blade was plunged.*

77 COME, COME *Edward probably takes the rapier from Stephen at this juncture, though he may have done so earlier.*

82 HIGGINBOTTOM *not certainly identified. N.*

85 FIELD RAPIER *pun on "rapier used on the battlefield."*

Edward. You shall not buy it, I say.

Stephen. [*Shaking his purse.*] By this money, but I will, though I give more than 'tis worth.

Edward. Come away, you are a fool.   90

Stephen. Friend, I am a fool, that's granted; but I'll have it, for that word's sake. [*To Brainworm.*] Follow me for your money.

Brainworm. At your service, sir. (*Exeunt.*)

Act II Scene 5

[*Moorfields.*]

(*Enter Knowell.*)

Knowell. I cannot lose the thought, yet, of this letter
Sent to my son; nor leave t'admire the change
Of manners and the breeding of our youth
Within the kingdom, since myself was one.
When I was young, he lived not in the stews,   5
Durst have conceived a scorn, and uttered it,
On a gray head; age was authority
Against a buffon; and a man had, then,
A certain reverence paid unto his years,
That had none due unto his life. So much   10

2 ADMIRE *wonder at.*
5 HE *i.e. a youth.*
5–9 N.
6 DURST *the "not" of l. 5 carries its meaning over to this verb.*
7 AUTHORITY *warrant, protection.*
8 BUFFON *buffoon, jester.*

The sanctity of some prevailed for others.
But now we all are fall'n: youth from their fear,
And age from that which bred it, good example.
Nay, would ourselves were not the first, even parents,

15 That did destroy the hopes in our own children;
Or they not learned our vices in their cradles
And sucked in our ill customs with their milk.
Ere all their teeth be born, or they can speak,
We make their palates cunning! The first words

20 We form their tongues with are licentious jests!
Can it call, "whore"? cry, "bastard"? Oh, then kiss it —
A witty child! Can't swear? The father's dearling!
Give it two plums. Nay, rather than 't shall learn
No bawdy song, the mother'herself will teach it!

25 But this is in the infancy, the days
Of the long coat; when it puts on the breeches,
It will put off all this. Aye, it is like;
When it is gone into the bone already.
No, no: this dye goes deeper than the coat,

30 Or shirt, or skin. It stains unto the liver,
And heart, in some. And rather than it should not,
Note what we fathers do! Look how we live!
What mistresses we keep! At what expense,
In our sons' eyes! Where they may handle our gifts,

12 FEAR *reverence.*

12–36 *N.*

23 PLUMS *probably sugarplums or tidbits.*

26 COAT *petticoat, skirt; worn by young children.*

28 IT . . . ALREADY *alludes to proverbial saying (cf. II.1.66), but also prepares for the image of 29–31.*

30 LIVER *believed the seat of violent passion, especially sexual.*

Hear our lascivious courtships, see our dalliance,   35
Taste of the same provoking meats with us,
To ruin of our states! Nay, when our own
Portion is fled, to prey on their remainder,
We call them into fellowship of vice!
Bait 'em with the young chambermaid, to seal!   40
And teach 'em all bad ways to buy affliction!
This is one path! But there are millions more
In which we spoil our own with leading them.
Well, I thank heaven, I never yet was he
That travailed with my son, before sixteen,   45
To show him the Venetian courtesans.
Nor read the grammar of cheating I had made
To my sharp boy, at twelve: repeating still
The rule, "Get money"; still, "Get money, boy;
"No matter, by what means; money will do   50
"More, boy, than my Lord's letter." Neither have I
Dressed snails or mushrooms curiously before him,
Perfumed my sauces, and taught him to make 'em—
Preceding still, with my gray gluttony,
At all the ordinaries; and only feared   55

41 affliction] Gifford; affiction F₁; affection F₂.
49 still] Ff incorporate in quotation; HS separate out.

---

36 PROVOKING *stimulating, especially sexually. Highly spiced food was thought to have this effect.*

37 STATES *pun on 1. bodily conditions; 2. estates.*

40 SEAL *slang for "have intercourse."*

42–43 *N.*

45 TRAVAILED *1. journeyed; 2. labored.*

46 VENETIAN COURTESANS *famous for beauty, licentiousness, and craftiness.*

47–51 *N.*

52 CURIOUSLY *in exotic ways.*

52–56 *N.*

55 ORDINARIES *eating-houses or taverns offering public, fixed-price meals. Fashionable ones usually had gambling after dinner.*

His palate should degenerate, not his manners.
These are the trade of fathers now! However,
My son, I hope, hath met within my threshold
None of these household precedents, which are strong
60 And swift to rape youth to their precipice.
But let the house at home be ne'er so clean-
Swept, or kept sweet from filth—nay, dust and cobwebs—
If he will live abroad with his companions
In dung and lay-stalls, it is worth a fear.
65 Nor is the danger of conversing less
                    (*Enter Brainworm.*)
Than all that I have mentioned of example.

    Brainworm. My master? Nay, faith, have at you; I am fleshed now,
I have sped so well.—Worshipful sir, I beseech you, respect the
estate of a poor soldier; I am ashamed of this base course of life
70 (God's my comfort), but extremity provokes me to't, what remedy?

    Knowell. I have not for you now.

    Brainworm. By the faith I bear unto truth, gentleman, it is no
ordinary custom in me, but only to preserve manhood. I protest
to you, a man I have been, a man I may be, by your sweet bounty.
75 *Knowell.* Pray thee, good friend, be satisfied.

57–64 N.

60 RAPE *carry off, sweep along.* THEIR *i.e. of the precedents, on which "precipice" is an aural play.*

63 ABROAD *away from home.*

64 LAY-STALLS *dumping places for refuse and dung.*

65–66 N.

65 CONVERSING *associating familiarly.*

67 FLESHED *animated by a taste of success; with play on a more precise meaning, "initiated into warfare."*

68 SPED *fared, succeeded.* RESPECT *heed (with added sense of "have consideration for").* ESTATE *1. condition; 2. profession.*

73 MANHOOD *existence in man's shape; perhaps also the dignity of man.*

75 BE SATISFIED *with what you have said—i.e. leave me.*

Brainworm. Good sir, by that hand, you may do the part of a kind gentleman, in lending a poor soldier the price of two cans of beer (a matter of small value), the King of Heaven shall pay you, and I shall rest thankful; sweet Worship—

Knowell. Nay, and you be so importunate—   80
                    [*Moves to push him aside.*]

Brainworm. Oh, tender sir, need will have his course; I was not made to this vile use! Well, the edge of the enemy could not have abated me so much. It's hard when a man hath served *He weeps.*
in his prince's cause, and be thus— Honorable Worship, let me derive a small piece of silver from you, it shall not be given in the   85
course of time, by this good ground, I was fain to pawn my rapier last night for a poor supper, I had sucked the hilts long before, I am a pagan else; sweet Honor.

Knowell. Believe me, I am taken with some wonder,
To think a fellow of thy outward presence   90
Should (in the frame and fashion of his mind)
Be so degenerate and sordid-base!
Art thou a man? And sham'st thou not to beg?
To practice such a servile kind of life?
Why, were thy education ne'er so mean,   95
Having thy limbs, a thousand fairer courses

77 PRICE . . . BEER *twopence.* CANS *mugs.*

79 REST *here in weakened sense, equivalent to "be."*

82 EDGE *sword-edge.*

83 ABATED *cast down.*

85–86 IT . . . TIME *either: in the course of time it will become not a gift, but a loan, for God will repay you; or: it will be not an earthly gift, but a gift out of the course of time—immortal, bringing you a heavenly reward.*

86 FAIN *obliged.*

87 HAD *would have.* HILTS *The plural refers to the two projections of the crossbar.* BEFORE *i.e. before taking such a course as this.*

95 MEAN *poor, inferior.*

96 FAIRER *1. more attractive; 2. more reputable; 3. more just.*

Offer themselves to thy election.
Either the wars might still supply thy wants,
Or service of some virtuous gentleman,
100 Or honest labor; nay, what can I name,
But would become thee better than to beg?
But men of thy condition feed on sloth,
As doth the beetle on the dung she breeds in,
Not caring how the metal of your minds
105 Is eaten with the rust of idleness.
Now, afore me, what e'er he be that should
Relieve a person of thy quality
While thou insist's in this loose desperate course,
I would esteem the sin not thine, but his.
110 *Brainworm.* Faith, sir, I would gladly find some other course,
if so—
Knowell. Aye, you'd gladly find it, but you will not seek it.
Brainworm. Alas, sir, where should a man seek? In the wars there's
no ascent by desert in these days, but— And for service, would it
115 were as soon purchased as wished for—the air's my comfort—I
know what I would say—
Knowell. What's thy name?
Brainworm.   Please you, Fitzsword, sir.
Knowell.   Fitzsword?

---

97 ELECTION *four syllables.*
103 BEETLE *The scarab was believed to breed in and feed upon dung.*
104 METAL *pun on "mettle," originally a figurative use of "metal" but by now a
sense sufficiently independent to be played on.*
106 AFORE ME *a mild oath.*
108 INSIST'S *persist; the second person singular "est" ending was often contracted
(Kökeritz).*
114 SERVICE *i.e. domestic service.*
115 PURCHASED *procured.*
117 FITZSWORD *"Son of the sword."*

Say that a man should entertain thee, now,
Would'st thou be honest, humble, just, and true?
   Brainworm. Sir, by the place and honor of a soldier—   120
   Knowell. Nay, nay, I like not those affected oaths;
Speak plainly, man: what think'st thou of my words?
   Brainworm. Nothing, sir, but wish my fortunes were as happy as
my service should be honest.
   Knowell. Well, follow me; I'll prove thee, if thy deeds   125
Will carry a proportion to thy words.
   Brainworm. Yes, sir, straight, I'll but garter my hose. [*Exit
Knowell.*] Oh that my belly were hooped now, for I am ready to
burst with laughing! Never was bottle or bagpipe fuller. 'Slid, was
there ever seen a fox in years to betray himself thus? Now shall I be   130
possessed of all his counsels; and, by that conduit, my young master.
Well, he is resolved to prove my honesty; faith, and I am resolved
to prove his patience: oh, I shall abuse him intolerably. This small
piece of service will bring him clean out of love with the soldier
forever. He will never come within the sign of it, the sight of a   135
cassock or a musket-rest, again. He will hate the musters at Mile-end

118 ENTERTAIN *retain in one's service.*
125 FOLLOW ME *pun on "be a servant of mine."* PROVE *test.*
126 CARRY *bear.*
128 HOOPED *like a barrel, to hold it together.*
131 BY . . . MASTER *The construction has as its primary sense: by me, my young
master shall be possessed of all his counsels; but it can also carry a secondary
sense: by that avenue, I shall be possessed of (have in my power) my young
master.*
133–34 SMALL . . . SERVICE *The word-play yields three distinct meanings: 1. this
small bit of domestic service; 2. this small sample of soldiership; 3. this small
figure (Brainworm) of soldiership (or, of servantship).*
134 CLEAN *quite, wholly.*
136 CASSOCK *a soldier's cloak or long coat.* MUSKET-REST *strong wooden pole, with
metal spike in the bottom for fixing in the ground, and semicircular piece of metal
on top to support the musket.* MUSTERS *periodical gatherings of London's Trained
Bands of citizens for military drill.* MILE-END *Mile-end Green, a common on
one of the main roads out of London.*

for it to his dying day. It's no matter, let the world think me a bad counterfeit if I cannot give him the slip at an instant. Why, this is better than to have stayed his journey! Well, I'll follow him: oh, 140 how I long to be employed! (*Exit.*)

138 SLIP *pun on "counterfeit coin."*
140 EMPLOYED *pun on 1. engaged in activity; 2. taken into service.*

Act III Scene 1

[*A street.*]

(*Enter Wellbred, Bobadill, and Matthew.*)

Matthew. Yes, faith, sir, we were at your lodging to seek you, too.
Wellbred. Oh, I came not there tonight.
Bobadill. Your brother delivered us as much.
Wellbred. Who? My brother Downright?
Bobadill. He. Mr. Wellbred, I know not in what kind you hold   5
me, but let me say to you this: as sure as honor, I esteem it so much
out of the sunshine of reputation to throw the least beam of regard
upon such a—
Wellbred. Sir, I must hear no ill words of my brother.
Bobadill. I protest to you, as I have a thing to be saved about me,   10
I never saw any gentleman-like part—

[A STREET.] *Matthew and Bobadill, coming from Kitely's house in the old Jewry
(I.2.50–51), have just met Wellbred on his way to The Windmill from the north
end of town (I.2.40–42). Since Matthew and Bobadill have only twopence
between them (IV.9.37–41), they are not likely to be in The Windmill when they
encounter Wellbred. Edward, and subsequently Brainworm, also making for The
Windmill, duly come upon the growing group, which is plainly standing in the
street at III.2.55–56.*

3 DELIVERED *reported.*
5–6 IN . . . ME *what estimation you have of me.*
11 PART *quality.*

95

Wellbred. Good Captain, faces about, to some other discourse.

Bobadill. With your leave, sir, and there were no more men living upon the face of the earth, I should not fancy him, by St.
15 George.

Matthew. Troth, nor I, he is of a rustical cut, I know not how: he doth not carry himself like a gentleman of fashion—

Wellbred. Oh, Mr. Matthew, that's a grace peculiar but to a few; *quos aequus amavit Jupiter.*

20 *Matthew.* I understand you, sir.

Wellbred. No question, you do— [*Aside.*] or you do *Young Knowell* not, sir.—Ned Knowell! By my soul, welcome; how *enters. [Stephen enters a little* dost thou, sweet spirit, my genius? 'Slid, I shall love *behind him.]* Apollo and the mad Thespian girls the better while I live, for this;
25 my dear Fury! Now I see there's some love in thee! Sirrah, these be the two I writ to thee of—nay, what a drowsy humor is this, now? Why dost thou not speak?

Edward. Oh, you are a fine gallant, you sent me a rare letter!

Wellbred. Why, was't not rare?

30 *Edward.* Yes, I'll be sworn I was ne'er guilty of reading the like;

12 FACES ABOUT *about face.*

19 QUOS . . . JUPITER *those whom impartial Jupiter has loved. (From the* Aeneid, *VI.129–30, where the phrase describes those who have been able to return from the underworld.)*

23 GENIUS *familiar or guiding spirit (alluding to the pagan belief that every human being has an attendant "genius" allotted him at birth).*

24 APOLLO *god of poetry and song, leader of the Muses.* MAD THESPIAN GIRLS *the Muses, goddesses of the arts, often called " Thespiades" by Latin writers, from the festival in their honor at Thespiae, at the foot of Mount Helicon, traditionally one of their favorite haunts. "Mad" is a joking allusion to their inspiration.*

25 FURY *Wellbred's joking epithet takes account of the name "Eumenides," or "kind ones," euphemistically assigned to these avenging spirits from the underworld.*

match it in all Pliny or Symmachus' epistles, and I'll have my
judgment burned in the ear for a rogue; make much of thy vein,
for it is inimitable. But I mar'l what camel it was, that had the
carriage of it? For doubtless he was no ordinary beast that brought
it!   35

Wellbred. Why?

Edward. Why, sayest thou? Why, dost thou think that any
reasonable creature, especially in the morning (the sober time of the
day, too), could have mista'en my father for me?

Wellbred. 'Slid, you jest, I hope?   40

Edward. Indeed, the best use we can turn it to is to make a jest
on't, now; but I'll assure you, my father had the full view o' your
flourishing style some hour before I saw it.

Wellbred. What a dull slave was this? But, sirrah, what said he
to it, i'faith?   45

Edward. Nay, I know not what he said; but I have a shrewd guess
what he thought.

Wellbred. What? What?

Edward. Marry, that thou art some strange dissolute young fellow,
and I a grain or two better, for keeping thee company.   50

Wellbred. Tut, that thought is like the moon in her last quarter,
'twill change shortly. But, sirrah, I pray thee be acquainted with my

31 PLINY *the Younger; Roman author and administrator of the first and second
centuries* A.D. *His private letters, published in ten books (nine by him), are of
great literary polish and stylistic sophistication.* SYMMACHUS *Roman scholar,
statesman, and orator of the fourth and fifth centuries* A.D. *He modeled his epis-
tolary style on Pliny's, and like him published nine books of letters.*

32 BURNED . . . ROGUE *By Elizabethan law, rogues and vagabonds over 14 were,
as punishment, "burned through the gristle of the right ear with a hot iron of the
compass of an inch . . ." (14 El. c.5). This law was repealed in 1593 but, since
it had been in force for nearly 20 years, continued to provide an easily comprehensible reference.* FOR *as.*

33 MAR'L *marvel.* CAMEL *popular term for a dull creature.*

44 THIS *i.e. the messenger.*

97

two hang-bys, here; thou wilt take exceeding pleasure in 'em if thou
hear'st 'em once go: my wind-instruments. I'll wind 'em up—
55 [*He notices Stephen standing a little apart.*] But what strange piece of
silence is this? The sign of The Dumb Man?

Edward. Oh, sir, a kinsman of mine, one that may make your
music the fuller, and he please; he has his humor, sir.

Wellbred. Oh, what is't? What is't?

60 *Edward.* Nay, I'll neither do your judgment nor his folly that
wrong, as to prepare your apprehension: I'll leave him to the mercy
o' your search; if you can take him, so.

Wellbred. Well, Captain Bobadill, Mr. Matthew, pray you know
this gentleman here, he is a friend of mine, and one that will
65 deserve your affection. —I know not your name, sir, *To Master*
Stephen.
but I shall be glad of any occasion to render me more familiar to
you.

Stephen. My name is Mr. Stephen, sir, I am this gentleman's own
cousin, sir, his father is mine uncle, sir, I am somewhat melancholy,
70 but you shall command me, sir, in whatever is incident to a gentleman.

Bobadill. Sir, I must tell you this, I am no general *To [Edward]*
Knowell.
man, but for Mr. Wellbred's sake (you may embrace it at what
height of favor you please) I do communicate with you; and con-
75 ceive you to be a gentleman of some parts—I love few words.

53 HANG-BYS *hangers-on.*

54 WIND . . . WIND *The noun and the verb were both pronounced like the modern*
verb.

56 THE DUMB MAN *alluding to tavern signs painted with a picture illustrating the*
tavern's name—e.g. The Green Man.

61 APPREHENSION *understanding.*

62 TAKE *pun on "capture" and "find (him) out."* SO *well and good.*

72 GENERAL *affable to everyone; a play on "gen'ral man" and the immediately*
preceding pronunciation "gen'lman"; perhaps with pun on the common phrase
"general man" meaning "widely accomplished man."

73 EMBRACE *accept.*

Edward. And I fewer, sir. I have scarce enow to thank you.

Matthew. But are you indeed, sir? So given to it? ^{To Master} ^{Stephen.}

Stephen. Aye, truly, sir, I am mightily given to melancholy.

Matthew. Oh, it's your only fine humor, sir, your true melancholy breeds your perfect fine wit, sir; I am melancholy myself 80 divers times, sir, and then do I no more but take pen and paper presently, and overflow you half a score or a dozen of sonnets at a sitting.

Edward. [*To Wellbred.*] Sure, he utters them then by the gross.

Stephen. Truly, sir, and I love such things out of measure. 85

Edward. [*To Wellbred.*] Aye, faith, better than in measure, I'll undertake.

Matthew. Why, I pray you, sir, make use of my study, it's at your service.

Stephen. I thank you, sir, I shall be bold, I warrant you; have you 90 a stool there, to be melancholy upon?

Matthew. That I have, sir, and some papers there of mine own doing at idle hours, that you'll say there's some sparks of wit in 'em when you see them.

Wellbred. [*To Edward.*] Would the sparks would kindle once, and 95

77 indeed, sir?] F₂; indeed. Sir? F₁.

---

76 ENOW *enough.*

79–80 *This contemporary idea derived from Aristotle:* "*Why is it that all men who are outstanding in philosophy, poetry or the arts are melancholic . . .? . . . because this heat is near to the seat of the mind . . .*" *(*Problems, *30.1, 953a, ll. 10–12; 954a, 34ff.)*

82 PRESENTLY *on the spot.*

84 UTTERS *pun on the commercial meaning "puts on the market," supported by the commercial unit "gross."*

85 OUT OF MEASURE *boundlessly; with play on Edward's "measure" of the quantity of poems.*

86 IN MEASURE *pun on "metrically accurate."*

91 STOOL *a play on the meaning "toilet."*

become a fire amongst 'em; I might see self-love burnt for her heresy.

    Stephen. [*To Edward.*] Cousin, is it well? Am I melancholy enough?

100   *Edward.* Oh, aye, excellent!

    Wellbred. Captain Bobadill: why muse you so?

    Edward. [*To Wellbred.*] He is melancholy, too.

    Bobadill. Faith, sir, I was thinking of a most honorable piece of service, was performed tomorrow, being St. Mark's Day—shall

105 be some ten years, now?

    Edward. In what place, Captain?

    Bobadill. Why, at the beleag'ring of Strigonium, where, in less than two hours, seven hundred resolute gentlemen as any were in Europe lost their lives upon the breach. I'll tell you, gentlemen, it

110 was the first, but the best, league that ever I beheld with these eyes, except the taking in of—what do you call it, last year, by the Genowayes; but that (of all other) was the most fatal and dangerous exploit that ever I was ranged in since I first bore arms before the face of the enemy, as I am a gentleman and soldier.

115   *Stephen.* [*Aside.*] 'So, I had as lief as an angel I could swear as well as that gentleman!

    Edward. Then you were a servitor at both, it seems! At Strigonium? And what do you call't?

    Bobadill. Oh lord, sir! By St. George, I was the first man that

120 entered the breach; and, had I not effected it with resolution, I had been slain, if I had had a million of lives.

104 ST. MARK'S DAY *April 25.*
104–05 SHALL BE . . . YEARS *would it be about ten years ago . . . ?*
107 STRIGONIUM *Graan in Hungary, retaken from the Turks in 1595. N.*
109 BREACH *gap in the fortifications, created by the assault.*
110 LEAGURE *siege.*
111 TAKING IN *capture.*
112 GENOWAYES *Genoese. There appears to have been no such battle.*
115 'SO *Odso or Godso, euphemism for God.* LIEF *gladly.*

Edward. [*To Wellbred.*] 'Twas pity you had not ten: a cat's and your own, i'faith. [*To Bobadill.*] But was it possible?

Matthew. [*To Stephen.*] Pray you, mark this discourse, sir.

Stephen. So I do.   125

Bobadill. I assure you (upon my reputation) 'tis true, and yourself shall confess.

Edward. [*To Wellbred.*] You must bring me to the rack first.

Bobadill. Observe me judicially, sweet sir: they had planted me three demi-culverings just in the mouth of the breach; now, sir   130 (as we were to give on), their master gunner (a man of no mean skill and mark, you must think) confronts me with his linstock, ready to give fire; I spying his intendment, discharged my petronel in his bosom, and with these single arms, my poor rapier, ran violently upon the Moors that guarded the ordnance, and put 'em   135 pell-mell to the sword.

Wellbred. To the sword? To the rapier, Captain?

Edward. [*To Wellbred.*] Oh, it was a good figure observed, sir! [*To Bobadill.*] But did you all this, Captain, without hurting your blade?   140

Bobadill. Without any impeach o' the earth; [*He displays the blade.*]

140 blade ?] F₂; blade. F₁.

---

129 JUDICIALLY *judiciously.*

130 DEMI-CULVERINGS *one of the smaller cannon, with shot weighing about 10 pounds.*

131 GIVE ON *charge.*

132 MARK *quality, with pun on "marksmanship."* LINSTOCK *staff about a yard long, with a lighted match in its forked end to touch off the cannon.*

133 INTENDMENT *intention.* PETRONEL *a kind of large pistol or carbine.*

134 SINGLE *1. sole; 2. petty.*

135 MOORS *There seem to have been no hostilities involving Moors at this period, but they were a good old stand-by to cast in the role of the enemy.*

138 A GOOD . . . OBSERVED *a tried-and-true image kept to.*

141 IMPEACH *damage.*

you shall perceive, sir. It is the most fortunate weapon that ever rid on poor gentleman's thigh; shall I tell you, sir? You talk of Morglay, Excalibur, Durindana, or so? Tut, I lend no credit to that
145 is fabled of 'em, I know the virtue of mine own, and therefore I dare the boldlier maintain it.

Stephen. I mar'l whether it be a Toledo, or no?

Bobadill. A most perfect Toledo, I assure you, sir.

Stephen. I have a countryman of his here.

150 *Matthew.* [*Takes it.*] Pray you, let's see, sir; yes, faith, it is!

Bobadill. [*Takes it.*] This a Toledo? Pish.

Stephen. Why do you pish, Captain?

Bobadill. A Fleming, by Heaven! I'll buy them for a guilder apiece an' I would have a thousand of them.

155 *Edward.* How say you, cousin? I told you thus much?

Wellbred. Where bought you it, Mr. Stephen?

Stephen. Of a scurvy rogue soldier—a hundred of lice go with him—he swore it was a Toledo.

Bobadill. A poor provant rapier, no better.

160 *Matthew.* Mass, I think it be, indeed, now I look on't better.

Edward. Nay, the longer you look on't, the worse. [*To Stephen.*] Put it up, put it up.

Stephen. Well, I will put it up, but by— (I ha' forgot the Captain's oath, I thought to ha' sworn by it) an' e'er I meet him—

165 *Wellbred.* Oh, it is past help now, sir, you must have patience.

142 FORTUNATE *blessed with luck, or luck-bringing.*

143 RID *rode.*

144 MORGLAY, EXCALIBUR, DURINDANA *swords famous in legend for their extra-ordinary, even magical, properties—belonging respectively to Sir Bevis of Hampton, King Arthur, and Roland.* THAT *that which.*

153 FLEMING *the kind of sword issued for the fighting in the Low Countries; hence the valuation in Dutch money.* GUILDER *Netherlandish silver coin worth about 3s 4d in Jonson's money.*

159 PROVANT *government issue.*

162 PUT IT UP *sheathe it.*

Stephen. Whoreson cony-catching rascal! I could eat the very hilts for anger!

Edward. A sign of good digestion! You have an ostrich stomach, cousin.

Stephen. A stomach? Would I had him here, you should see an' 170 I had a stomach.

Wellbred. It's better as 'tis. Come, gentlemen, shall we go?

166 CONY-CATCHING *swindling. A cony was a rabbit (metaphorically a dupe); rabbits were often stolen from warrens by robbers who lured them out of their holes.*
168 DIGESTION *probably a pun on* "*endurance, ability to put up with an affront.*" OSTRICH STOMACH *The ostrich was popularly believed to refuse no sort of food, and to be especially good at digesting metal, iron for preference.*
171 STOMACH *pun on 1. resentment; 2. eagerness to fight.*

Act III Scene 2

(*Enter Brainworm* [*still disguised*].)

Edward. A miracle, cousin, look here! Look here!

Stephen. Oh, God's lid! [*To Brainworm.*] By your leave, do you know me, sir?

Brainworm. Aye, sir, I know you by sight.

Stephen. You sold me a rapier, did you not? 5

Brainworm. Yes, marry, did I, sir.

Stephen. You said it was a Toledo, ha?

Brainworm. True, I did so.

Stephen. But it is none?

Brainworm. No, sir, I confess it, it is none. 10

Stephen. Do you confess it? Gentlemen, bear witness, he has confessed it. By God's will, and you had not confessed it—

    Edward. Oh, cousin, forbear, forbear.

    Stephen. Nay, I have done, cousin.

15   *Wellbred.* Why, you have done like a gentleman, he has confessed it, what would you more?

    Stephen. Yet, by his leave, he is a rascal, under his favor, do you see?

    Edward. Aye, by his leave, he is, and under favor: a pretty piece

20 of civility! [*Aside to Wellbred.*] Sirrah, how dost thou like him?

    Wellbred. Oh, it's a most precious fool, make much on him; I can compare him to nothing more happily than a drum, for everyone may play upon him.

    Edward. No, no, a child's whistle were far the fitter.

25   *Brainworm.* [*To Edward.*] Sir, shall I entreat a word with you?

    Edward. With me, sir? You have not another Toledo to sell, ha' you?

    Brainworm. You are conceited, sir; [*He draws Edward aside.*] your name is Mr. Knowell, as I take it?

30   *Edward.* You are i' the right; you mean not to proceed in the catechism, do you?

    Brainworm. No, sir, I am none of that coat.

    Edward. Of as bare a coat, though? Well, say, sir.

    Brainworm. Faith, sir, I am but servant to the drum extraordinary,

---

30 right;] F₂; right? F₁.

17 UNDER HIS FAVOR *if he is agreeable (to the idea).*

22 HAPPILY *aptly.*

24 FITTER *more suitable (comparison); because of the shrill, undignified sound, and the triviality and childishness of the toy.*

28 CONCEITED *disposed to jest—full of conceits, witticisms.*

31 CATECHISM *The Child's Catechism (used at confirmation) in the Book of Common Prayer (1549) begins: "What is your name? . . . Who gave you this name?"*

33 BARE *threadbare (like a poor clergyman's).*

34 SERVANT . . . DRUM *soldier.* EXTRAORDINARY *outside the regular staff; with a sense of special employment on a temporary mission.*

and indeed (this smoky varnish being washed off, and *[He removes* 35
three or four patches removed) I appear your Wor- *some of his*
ship's in reversion, after the decease of your good father— Brain- *makeup.]*
worm.

Edward. Brainworm! 'Slight, what breath of a conjurer hath
blown thee hither in this shape? 40

Brainworm. The breath o' your letter, sir, this morning; the same
that blew you to The Windmill, and your father after you.

Edward. My father?

Brainworm. Nay, never start, 'tis true, he has followed you over
the fields by the foot, as you would do a hare i' the snow. 45

Edward. Sirrah, Wellbred, what shall we do, sirrah? My father
is come over after me.

Wellbred. Thy father? Where is he?

Brainworm. At Justice Clement's house here in Colman Street,
where he but stays my return; and then— 50

Wellbred. Who's this? Brainworm?

Brainworm. The same, sir.

Wellbred. Why, how i' the name of wit com'st thou transmuted
thus?

Brainworm. Faith, a device, a device; nay, for the love of reason, 55
gentlemen, and avoiding the danger, stand not here, withdraw, and
I'll tell you all.

Wellbred. But art thou sure he will stay thy return?

Brainworm. Do I live, sir? What a question is that?

Wellbred. We'll prorogue his expectation, then, a little: Brain- 60
worm, thou shalt go with us. Come on, gentlemen—nay, I pray

40 shape ?] F₂; shape. Q, F₁.

35 SMOKY VARNISH *dark-colored coating.*
37 REVERSION *legal right of succession to a property after the present owner's death.*
49 HERE . . . STREET *The company is probably not in Colman Street; cf. III.3.119.
Here = over here, very near by.*
60 PROROGUE *prolong.*

105

Is a most main attractive! Our great heads
35 Within the city never were in safety
Since our wives wore these little caps; I'll change 'em,
I'll change 'em straight, in mine. Mine shall no more
Wear three-piled acorns to make my horns ache.
Nor will I go. I am resolved for that.
                    [*Enter Cash, with Kitely's cloak.*]
40 Carry'in my cloak again— Yet, stay— Yet do, too.
I will defer going, on all occasions.
        Cash. Sir. Snare, your scrivener, will be there with th' bonds.
        Kitely. That's true! Fool on me! I had clean forgot it;
I must go. What's o'clock?
        Cash.   Exchange time, sir.
        Kitely. [*Aside.*]
45 Heart, then will Wellbred presently be here, too,
With one or other of his loose consorts.
I am a knave if I know what to say,
What course to take, or which way to resolve.

34 MAIN *play on 1. potent; 2. centrally important.* ATTRACTIVE *attraction.* OUR
    GREAT HEADS *our important men; with pun on "the large heads of such men as I
    am," the joke being the usual allusion to the danger of acquiring cuckold's horns.
    There may be a further play on "head" meaning a stag's antlers.*
36 CAPS *Diminutive round velvet caps were a current fashion.* N.
38 THREE-PILED *velvet with a triply thick pile, i.e. of the richest kind.* ACORNS *allud-
    ing to the shape of the cap, resembling the small cup on the end of the acorn. The
    word seems chosen for the sake of the pun.* HORNS ACHE *Besides the obvious pun,
    there is probably a play on the "velvet" covering the new horns of a stag.*
41 ON ALL OCCASIONS *in any case, whatever I do.*
42 SCRIVENER *one who draws up documents in legal form.*
44 EXCHANGE TIME *given in Q as "past ten"; the Exchange apparently opened at
    10 a.m.*
46 CONSORTS *stressed on the second syllable.*

My brain (methinks) is like an hourglass,
Wherein my'imaginations run like sands,   50
Filling up time; but then are turned, and turned,
So that I know not what to stay upon,
And less, to put in act. It shall be so.
Nay, I dare build upon his secrecy,
He knows not to deceive me.—Thomas?
   Cash.   Sir.   55
   Kitely. [*Aside.*] Yet now I have bethought me, too, I will not.
—Thomas, is Cob within?
   Cash.   I think he be, sir.
   Kitely. [*Aside.*] But he'll prate, too; there's no speech of him.
No, there were no man o' the earth to Thomas,
If I durst trust him; there is all the doubt.   60
But should he have a chink in him, I were gone,
Lost i' my fame for ever: talk for th' Exchange.
The manner he hath stood with, till this present,
Doth promise no such change! What should I fear, then?
Well, come what will, I'll tempt my fortune once.—   65
Thomas—you may deceive me, but I hope—
Your love to me is more—
   Cash.   Sir, if a servant's
Duty, with faith, may be called love, you are

49 HOURGLASS *three syllables.*
52 STAY UPON *stop at, with pun on "trust to, have confidence in."*
53 AND . . . ACT *The construction understands "know" before "less," and "what" before "to put."*
58 HE'LL *i.e. Cob. This word may be disyllabic, or the line may be headless like III.3. 5.* THERE'S . . . HIM *there's no talking to him (if I want secrecy).*
59 TO *compared to.*
61 HAVE A CHINK *i.e. be leaky. N.*
62 FAME *reputation.*
63 STOOD WITH *consistently maintained.*
66ff. *N.*

More than in hope—you are possessed of it.

70   *Kitely.* I thank you heartily, Thomas; gi' me your hand:

                          [They clasp hands.]

With all my heart, good Thomas. I have, Thomas,

A secret to impart unto you—but

When once you have it, I must seal your lips up:

So far I tell you, Thomas.

    Cash.   Sir, for that—

75   *Kitely.* Nay, hear me out. Think I esteem you, Thomas,

When I will let you in, thus, to my private.

It is a thing sits nearer to my crest

Than thou art 'ware of, Thomas. If thou should'st

Reveal it, but—

    Cash.   How? I reveal it?

    Kitely.   Nay,

80 I do not think thou would'st; but if thou should'st:

'Twere a great weakness.

    Cash.   A great treachery.

Give it no other name.

    Kitely.   Thou wilt not do't, then?

    Cash. Sir, if I do, mankind disclaim me ever.

    Kitely. [*Aside.*] He will not swear, he has some reservation.

85 Some concealed purpose, and close meaning, sure;

Else (being urged so much) how should he choose

But lend an oath to all this protestation?

H'is no precisian, that I am certain of.

---

76 PRIVATE *personal concerns; with pun on* "*private parts.*"

77 CREST *an identifying part of the coat-of-arms, used here for* "*the honor of my house*" (*cf.* "*a blot on the escutcheon*"); *with pun on* "*upright growth on top of the head*"—*the inevitable allusion to horns.*

88 PRECISIAN *popular term for Puritan (rigidly precise in details of religious observance).*

Nor rigid Roman Catholic. He'll play
At Fails and Tick-tack—I have heard him swear.   90
What should I think of it? Urge him again,
And by some other way? I will do so.
—Well, Thomas, thou hast sworn not to disclose—
Yes, you did swear?
   Cash.   Not yet, sir, but I will,
Please you—
   Kitely.   No, Thomas, I dare take thy word.   95
But: if thou wilt swear, do—as thou think'st good;
I am resolved without it—at thy pleasure.
   Cash. By my soul's safety, then, sir, I protest:
My tongue shall ne'er take knowledge of a word
Delivered me in nature of your trust.   100
   Kitely. It's too much, these ceremonies need not,
I know thy faith to be as firm as rock.
Thomas, come hither, near: we cannot be
Too private in this business. So it is—
[*Aside.*] Now he has sworn, I dare the safelier venture—   105
[*To Cash.*] I have of late, by divers observations—
[*Aside.*] But whether his oath can bind him, yea, or no,
Being not taken lawfully? Ha? Say you?
I will ask counsel, ere I do proceed—
[*To Cash.*] Thomas, it will be now too long to stay;   110
I'll spy some fitter time soon, or tomorrow.

---

107 no] Q, F₂; no' F₁ [query: for "not" ?]

89–90 HE'LL . . . SWEAR *both Puritans and Catholics abstained from games of chance and oaths.*
90 FAILS AND TICK-TACK *both forms of backgammon, played by moving men on a board according to throws of the dice. N.*
101 NEED NOT *are not necessary.*
108 SAY YOU? *What do you say?*

 Cash. Sir, at your pleasure.
 Kitely.   I will think. And, Thomas,
I pray you search the books 'gainst my return,
For the receipts 'twixt me and Traps.
 Cash.   I will, sir.
115 *Kitely.* And, hear you, if your mistress' brother, Wellbred,
Chance to bring hither any gentlemen
Ere I come back, let one straight bring me word.
 Cash. Very well, sir.
 Kitely.   To the Exchange—do you hear?
Or here in Colman Street, to Justice Clement's.
120 Forget it not, nor be not out of the way.
 Cash. I will not, sir.
 Kitely.   I pray you have a care on't.
Or whether he come or no, if any other—
Stranger, or else—fail not to send me word.
 Cash. I shall not, sir.
 Kitely.   Be't your special business,
Now, to remember it.
125 *Cash.*   Sir. I warrant you.
 Kitely. But, Thomas, this is not the secret, Thomas,
I told you of.
 Cash.   No, sir. I do suppose it.
 Kitely. Believe me, it is not.
 Cash.   Sir. I do believe you.
 Kitely. By heaven, it is not, that's enough. But, Thomas,
130 I would not you should utter it, do you see?
To any creature living—yet, I care not.
Well, I must hence. Thomas, conceive thus much.

117 ONE *someone.*
123 ELSE *otherwise.*
127 SUPPOSE *believe (not to be the secret).*

It was a trial of you, when I meant
So deep a secret to you—I mean not this,
But that I have to tell you—this is nothing, this.   135
But, Thomas, keep this from my wife, I charge you,
Locked up in silence, midnight, buried here.
[*Aside.*] No greater hell, than to be slave to fear. (*Exit Kitely.*)
    Cash. "Locked up in silence, midnight, buried here."
Whence should this flood of passion (trow) take head? Ha?   140
Best dream no longer of this running humor,
For fear I sink! The violence of the stream
Already hath transported me so far
That I can feel no ground at all! (*Enter Cob* [*from the house*].) But
    soft—
Oh, 'tis our water-bearer; somewhat has crossed him, now.   145

133   MEANT *intimated.*
140   TROW *do you think?* TAKE HEAD *spring from, find its source.*

Act III Scene 4

   Cob. Fasting days? What tell you me of fasting days? 'Slid,
would they were all on a light fire, for me. They say the whole
world shall be consumed with fire one day, but would I had these
Ember Weeks and villainous Fridays burnt, in the meantime, and
then—   5

1 FASTING DAYS *On Fridays, Saturdays, Ember days (see fn. to l. 4), eves of holy
    days, and during Lent, no meat could be sold or consumed, according to a strin-
    gently enforced law "intended and meant politicly for the increase of fishermen
    and mariners, and repairing of port-towns and navigation" (5 El. c.5).*
2 ON . . . FIRE *in a blaze.*
4 EMBER WEEKS *four weeks, one in each season of the year, within each of which
    Wednesday, Friday, and Saturday are observed as fast days, or "ember days." N.*

Cash. Why, how now, Cob, what moves thee to this choler?
Ha?

Cob. Collar, Master Thomas? I scorn your collar, I, sir, I am none
o' your cart-horse, though I carry and draw water. An' you offer
10 to ride me, with your collar, or halter either, I may hap show you a
jade's trick, sir.

Cash. Oh, you'll slip your head out of the collar? Why, Good-
man Cob, you mistake me.

Cob. Nay, I have my rheum, and I can be angry as well as another,
15 sir.

Cash. Thy rheum, Cob? Thy humor, thy humor! Thou
mistak'st.

Cob. Humor? Mack, I think it be so, indeed; what is that humor?
Some rare thing, I warrant.

20 *Cash.* Marry, I'll tell thee, Cob: it is a gentleman-like monster,
bred, in the special gallantry of our time, by affectation; and fed by
folly.

Cob. How? Must it be fed?

Cash. Oh, aye, humor is nothing if it be not fed. Did'st thou
25 never hear that? It's a common phrase, "Feed my humor."

Cob. I'll none on it: humor, avant, I know you not, begone.
Let who will make hungry meals for your monster-ship, it shall

---

9 DRAW *pun on 1. get from the tap; 2. pull.*

10 RIDE *tyrannize over, insolently dominate.* HALTER *perhaps a play on the threat
of the hangman's noose; but probably Cob is merely grumpy here, and it is Cash
who quibbles on escaping the hangman, in l. 12.*

11 JADE'S TRICK *action characteristic of a poor (in this case, unmanageable) horse.*

14 RHEUM *meaning "humor," but no longer a fashionable term.*

18 MACK *euphemistic distortion of Mass.*

25 "FEED MY HUMOR" *cater to my disposition. The phrase was a fashionable
affectation.*

26 AVANT *be off!*

27 MAKE HUNGRY MEALS *eat sparingly (to save the wherewithal to feed "humor").*

not be I. Feed you, quoth he? 'Slid, I ha' much ado to feed myself;
especially on these lean rascally days, too; and't had been any other
day but a fasting day—a plague on them all, for me— By this light,   30
one might have done the commonwealth good service and have
drowned them all i' the flood, two or three hundred thousand years
ago. Oh, I do stomach them hugely! I have a maw now, and't
were for Sir Bevis his horse, against 'em.

Cash. I pray thee, good Cob, what makes thee so out of love with   35
fasting days?

Cob. Marry, that which will make any man out of love with 'em,
I think: their bad conditions, and you will needs know. First, they
are of a Flemish breed, I am sure on't, for they raven up more
butter than all the days of the week beside; next, they stink of fish   40
and leek-porridge miserably; thirdly, they'll keep a man devoutly
hungry all day, and at night send him supperless to bed.

Cash. Indeed, these are faults, Cob.

Cob. Nay, and this were all, 'twere something, but they are the
only known enemies to my generation. A fasting day no sooner   45
comes, but my lineage goes to rack; poor cobs, they smoke for it,

28 QUOTH HE *did he say?*
33 STOMACH *resent; with punning allusion to hunger.* MAW *appetite (literally
"stomach").*
34 SIR . . . HORSE *Cob makes quite a pithy assertion out of "I could eat a horse,"
turning it into large-scale defiance of the edicts, as well as a sign of intrepidity in
disobedience (Sir Bevis's horse was a redoubtable fighter in its own right).*
39 FLEMISH *?a pun on "phlegm-ish," possessing a disposition dominated by the
humor phlegm. Eating of fish was believed to engender phlegm. (Elyot, Bk. I,
Cap. 2, Dv.)*
40 BUTTER *The great fondness of the Netherlanders for butter was well known and
considered very odd.*
41 DEVOUTLY *pun on 1. fervently, heartily; 2. piously; many fast days had a religious origin.*
45 GENERATION *breed.*
46 RACK *pun on 1. destruction; 2. broiling rack; 3. torture rack (for religious
martyrs).* SMOKE FOR IT *colloquial, equivalent to "smart for it"; with pun on
smoked herring.*

they are made martyrs o' the gridiron, they melt in passion; and
your maids, too, know this, and yet would have me turn Hannibal,
and eat my own fish and blood. My princely cos, *He pulls out a*
red herring.
50 fear nothing; I have not the heart to devour you, and I might be
made as rich as King Cophetua. Oh, that I had room for my
tears, I could weep salt water enough, now, to preserve the lives of
ten thousand of my kin. But I may curse none but these filthy
almanacs, for an't were not for them, these days of persecution
55 would ne'er be known. I'll be hanged an' some fishmonger's son
do not make of 'em; and puts in more fasting days than he should
do, because he would utter his father's dried stock-fish and stinking
conger.

    Cash. 'Slight, peace, thou'lt be beaten like a stock- *(Enter Matthew,*
Wellbred, Ed-
60 fish else; here is Mr. Matthew. Now must I look out *ward, Bobadill,*
for a messenger to my master. (*Exeunt Cob and Cash* *Stephen, Brain-*
worm.)
[*into the house*].)

---

47 MARTYRS . . . GRIDIRON *an allusion to St. Lawrence, Roman martyr, roasted to*
death on a gridiron in 258. MELT IN PASSION *play on the stock love-description*
and "passion" as "suffering," with its religious overtones.

48 HANNIBAL *"Cannibal" was a still a relatively recent word at this time, and Cob*
is not quite secure in the changes of verbal fashion (cf. "rheum" above). N.

51 COPHETUA *a legendary African king who married a beggar maid; Cob may have*
deduced his riches from this fact. More likely his mythology is as shaky as his
history and he means Midas. N. ROOM *scope.*

52 PRESERVE *pun on 1. save (by providing an ocean for); 2. pickle in brine (pickled*
herring was so prepared).

55–57 FISHMONGER'S SON . . . SHOULD DO. N.

57 UTTER *dispose of.* STOCK-FISH *dried cod.*

58 CONGER *large salt-water eel.*

59–60 BEATEN . . . STOCKFISH *a common expression. The cod was beaten before*
it was boiled.

60 MR. MATTHEW *a fishmonger's son. (Sale.)*

Act III Scene 5

Wellbred. Beshrew me, but it was an absolute good jest, and exceedingly well carried!

Edward. Aye, and our ignorance maintained it as well, did it not?

Wellbred. Yes, faith, but was't possible thou should'st not know him? I forgive Mr. Stephen, for he is stupidity itself! 5

Edward. 'Fore God, not I, and I might have been joined patten with one of the Seven Wise Masters for knowing him. He had so writhen himself into the habit of one of your poor infantry, your decayed, ruinous, worm-eaten gentlemen of the round: such as have vowed to sit on the skirts of the city, let your Provost and his 10 half-dozen of halberdiers do what they can, and have translated begging out of the old hackney pace to a fine easy amble, and made it run as smooth of the tongue as a shove-groat shilling. Into the

1 BESHREW *curse.*

6 AND *even if.* JOINED PATTEN *made a sharer, by letters patent, in a privilege or position.*

7 SEVEN WISE MASTERS. *N.*

8 HABIT *appearance, guise.*

9 GENTLEMEN . . . ROUND *members of a military patrol (going the rounds).*

10 SIT . . . SKIRTS *pun on* 1. *take up residence on the outskirts;* 2. *harass, hinder the activities of.* PROVOST *officer charged with keeping public order, with power to arrest, imprison, and punish offenders, and particularly to "repair with a convenient company to all common highways near London to apprehend all vagrant and suspected persons." (Rymer, quoted Harrison II, p. 39.)*

11 HALBERDIERS *civic guards, who carried halberds as a sign of office.*

12 HACKNEY *characteristic of a horse for public hire, i.e. awkward and graceless; probably with play on " trite."*

13 SHOVE-GROAT SHILLING *smooth shilling—often specifically an Edward VI shilling—used in table version of shuffleboard, played with a coin.*

likeness of one of these *reformados* had he molded himself so per-
15 fectly, observing every trick of their action, as varying the accent,
swearing with an *emphasis*, indeed all, with so special and exquisite
a grace that (had'st thou seen him) thou would'st have sworn he
might have been Sergeant Major, if not Lieutenant-Coronel, to the
regiment.
20   *Wellbred.* Why, Brainworm, who would have thought thou
had'st been such an artificer?
        Edward. An artificer! An architect! Except a man had studied
begging all his lifetime, and been a weaver of language from his
infancy for the clothing of it, I never saw his rival!
25   *Wellbred.* Where got'st thou this coat, I mar'l?
        Brainworm. Of a Houndsditch man, sir. One of the devil's near
kinsmen, a broker.
        Wellbred. That cannot be, if the proverb hold; for "a crafty knave
needs no broker."
30   *Brainworm.* True, sir, but I did need a broker, *ergo.*
        Wellbred. Well put off! No crafty knave, you'll say.
        Edward. Tut, he has more of these shifts.
        Brainworm. And yet where I have one, the broker has ten, sir.
                        (*Enter Cash.*)

---

14 REFORMADOS *officers of a "re-formed" (i.e. disbanded) company (originally,
"re-formed" meant broken up to form other companies).*
18 CORONEL *original form of "colonel," from early French.*
21 ARTIFICER *artful fellow, trickster.*
22 ARTIFICER . . . ARCHITECT *play on "artificer" in the sense of "craftsman."
The antithesis is comparable to that between "artisan" and "artist."*
24 IT *i.e. begging.*
26 HOUNDSDITCH *a disreputable London street noted for pawnbrokers specializing
in old clothes.*
26–27 DEVIL'S . . . BROKER *proverbial (see HS for examples); pawnbrokers were
famous for craftiness and dishonesty.*
31 PUT OFF *parried.*
32 SHIFTS *dodges; Brainworm puns on the meaning "changes of clothing."*

Cash. Francis, Martin!—Ne'er a one to be found, now? What a spite's this? 35

Wellbred. How now, Thomas? Is my brother Kitely within?

Cash. No, sir, my master went forth e'en now; but Master Down-right is within. —Cob! What, Cob? Is he gone, too?

Wellbred. Whither went your master, Thomas, canst thou tell?

Cash. I know not, to Justice Clement's, I think, sir.—Cob! (*Exit* 40 *Cash* [*into the house*].)

Edward. Justice Clement—what's he?

Wellbred. Why, dost thou not know him? He is a City magis-trate, a justice here, an excellent good lawyer and a great scholar; but the only mad, merry old fellow in Europe! I showed him you the other day. 45

Edward. Oh, is that he? I remember him now. Good faith, and he has a very strange presence, methinks; it shows as if he stood out of the rank from other men; I have heard many of his jests i' the university. They say he will commit a man for taking the wall of his horse. 50

Wellbred. Aye, or wearing his cloak of one shoulder, or serving of God: anything, indeed, if it come in the way of his humor.

Cash. Gasper, Martin, Cob! Heart, where should *Cash goes in and out calling.* they be, trow?

Bobadill. Master Kitely's man, pray thee vouchsafe us the lighting 55 of this match.

Cash. [*Takes it.*] Fire on your match, no time but now to vouch-safe? —Francis! Cob! (*Exit.*)

48–49 i' the university] F₂; i' university F₁.

44 ONLY *peerless, so outstanding as to be the only one worth counting.*

49 TAKING THE WALL *walking on the inside of the street, the cleaner and safer part. To take or give the wall was equivalent to claiming or yielding social precedence.*

55–56 LIGHTING . . . MATCH *Matches at this time were long pieces of easily com-bustible material which had been dipped into melted sulphur so as to be readily ignited by a spark, usually from a tinderbox.*

Bobadill. [*Takes out a tobacco box.*] Body of me! Here's the re-
60 mainder of seven pound, since yesterday was sevennight. 'Tis your
right Trinidado! Did you never take any, Master Stephen?

Stephen. No, truly, sir; but I'll learn to take it now, since you
commend it so.

Bobadill. Sir, believe me (upon my relation), for what I tell you,
65 the world shall not reprove. I have been in the Indies (where this
herb grows), where neither myself, nor a dozen gentlemen more
(of my knowledge), have received the taste of any other nutriment
in the world for the space of one and twenty weeks, but the fume
of this simple only. Therefore, it cannot be but 'tis most divine!
70 Further, take it in the nature, in the true kind so, it makes an antidote
that, had you taken the most deadly poisonous plant in all Italy,
it should expel it, and clarify you, with as much ease as I speak.
And, for your green wound, your Balsamum and your St. John's
wort are all mere gulleries and trash to it, especially your Trinidado!

62 sir;] F₂; sir ? Q, F₁

---

59 *Between this point and l. 86, Bobadill fills his pipe. He presumably then passes
the tobacco to Matthew, who fills his; for Matthew has the box at l. 117, and
seems to have begun smoking by then.*
60 YESTERDAY WAS SEVENNIGHT *a week ago yesterday.*
61 TRINIDADO *The best tobacco was believed to come from Trinidad.*
65 REPROVE *refute.*
65–80 *N.*
69 SIMPLE *medicinal herb.*
70 IN . . . KIND *in its natural form.*
71 MOST . . . ITALY *Italy was considered the home of poisoning; the most effective
ingredients would grow there.*
72 CLARIFY *purge of impure matter.*
73 GREEN *fresh.* BALSAMUM *the Middle Eastern fir tree producing Balm of Gilead
or "true Balsam," the earliest known kind of medicinal resin; or any balsam tree
or shrub yielding such "balm."*
74 WORT *herb. St. John's wort was considered good for all wounds and bruises,
internal and external.* GULLERIES *cheats.*

Your Nicotian is good, too. I could say what I know of the virtue   75
of it for the expulsion of rheums, raw humors, crudities, obstructions, with a thousand of this kind; but I profess myself no quack-
salver. Only, thus much: by Hercules, I do hold it and will affirm it
before any prince in Europe to be the most sovereign and precious
weed that ever the earth tendered to the use of man.   80

    Edward. [*To Wellbred.*] This speech would ha' done decently in a
tobacco trader's mouth!

(Enter Cash and Cob.)

    Cash. [*To Cob.*] At Justice Clement's, he is: in the middle of Col-
man Street.

    Cob. Oh, oh?   85

    Bobadill. Where's the match I gave thee? Master Kitely's man?

    Cash. Would his match, and he, and pipe, and all were at Sancto
Domingo! I had forgot it. (*Exit* [*Cash*].)

    Cob. By God's me, I mar'l what pleasure or felicity they have in
taking this roguish tobacco! It's good for nothing but to choke a   90
man, and fill him full of smoke and embers—there were four died
out of one house, last week, with taking of it, and two more the bell
went for yesternight; one of them, they say, will ne'er 'scape it:

75 NICOTIAN *generic name for tobacco (J. Nicot, French ambassador at Lisbon,*
    introduced tobacco into France). Bobadill is blundering.

76 RHEUMS *colds, catarrhs, or any "dropping down of a liquid matter out of the head,*
    and falling either into the mouth, or into the nostrils, or into the eyes, and some-
    time into the cheeks and ears" (Elyot, Bk. IV, Cap. 2, p. 78r). RAW HUMORS
    humors not broken down and absorbed, but lying in the stomach in their original
    liquid form. CRUDITIES *"a vicious concoction [digestion—or in this case, mis-*
    digestion] of things received, they not being wholly or perfectly altered" (Elyot,
    Bk. IV, Cap. 1, p. 74v).

76–77 OBSTRUCTIONS *blockages of any bodily passage; especially constipation.*

79 SOVEREIGN *supremely efficacious; with pun on "monarchic."*

90–98 N.

90 ROGUISH *rascally, vile.*

92 BELL *usually rung after someone has died, but here apparently for a person on the*
    point of death.

121

he voided a bushel of soot yesterday, upward and downward. By
95 the stocks, an' there were no wiser men than I, I'd have it present
whipping, man or woman, that should but deal with a tobacco
pipe; why, it will stifle them all in the end, as many as use it; it's
little better than ratsbane or rosaker.

All. Oh, good Captain, hold, hold!   *Bobadill beats*
him with a
100 *Bobadill.* You base cullion, you!   *cudgel.*

[*Enter Cash, with the lighted match.*]

Cash. Sir, here's your match; [*To Cob.*] come, thou must needs be
talking, too, tho'art well enough served.

Cob. Nay, he will not meddle with his match, I warrant you.
Well, it shall be a dear beating, and I live.

105 *Bobadill.* Do you prate? Do you murmur?

Edward. Nay, good Captain, will you regard the humor of a fool?
[*To Cob.*] Away, knave.

Wellbred. Thomas, get him away. (*Exit Cash, and Cob.*)

Bobadill. A whoreson filthy slave, a dung-worm, an excrement!
110 Body o' Caesar, but that I scorn to let forth so mean a spirit, I'd ha'
stabbed him to the earth!

Wellbred. Marry, the law forbid, sir.

Bobadill. By Pharaoh's foot, I would have done it.

Stephen. [*Aside.*] Oh, he swears admirably! "By Pharaoh's
115 foot—" "Body of Caesar—" I shall never do it, sure— "Upon
mine honor, and by Saint George—" no, I ha' not the right grace.

Matthew. [*Offers the tobacco.*] Master Stephen, will you any? By
this air, the most divine tobacco that ever I drunk!

95 PRESENT *instant.*
98 RATSBANE *rat poison, specifically arsenic.* ROSAKER *red arsenic.*
100 CULLION *low rascal.*
101 SIR . . . MATCH *Bobadill lights his pipe during the next few lines, then pre-*
sumably gives the match to Matthew, who does the same.
104 DEAR *costly.*
118 DRUNK *" To drink tobacco" was a frequent expression.*

Stephen. None, I thank you, sir. [*Aside.*] Oh, this gentleman does it rarely, too! But nothing like the other. [*He walks apart.*] By this air, as I am a gentleman; by—(*Exit Bobadill and Matthew [into the house].*) 120

Brainworm. [*To Edward.*] Master, glance, glance! Master Wellbred!

Master Stephen is practicing to the post.

Stephen. As I have somewhat to be saved, I protest—

Wellbred. [*Sotto voce.*] —you are a fool; it needs no affidavit. 125

Edward. Cousin, will you any tobacco?

Stephen. I, sir! Upon my reputation—

Edward. How now, cousin!

Stephen. I protest, as I am a gentleman, but no soldier, indeed—

Wellbred. No, Master Stephen? As I remember, your name is entered in the Artillery Garden? 130

Stephen. Aye, sir, that's true. Cousin, may I swear "as I am a soldier" by that?

Edward. Oh, yes, that you may. It's all you have for your money.

Stephen. Then, as I am a gentleman and a soldier, it is divine tobacco! 135

Wellbred. But soft, where's Mr. Matthew? Gone?

Brainworm. No, sir, they went in here. [*Indicates house door.*]

Wellbred. Oh, let's follow them; Master Matthew is gone to salute his mistress in verse. We shall ha' the happiness to hear some 140

131 ARTILLERY GARDEN *the Artillery Yard, practice ground of the Honorable Artillery Company, an organization of citizens incorporated by Henry VIII. It had produced men of real training for the crisis of 1588; but they had seen no action for years, and their meetings "every Thursday in the year, practising all the usual points of war" (Raikes, p. 33) were open to mild ridicule. Stephen has probably joined for social reasons—most of the aldermen, and even the Lord Mayor, were members.*

134 MONEY *Besides his entrance money, a member of the Company paid quarterings, a fee toward the servants' wages, and perhaps fines for lateness or non-attendance.*

140 SALUTE *greet formally.*

of his poetry now. He never comes unfurnished. Brainworm?

Stephen. Brainworm? Where— Is this Brainworm?

Edward. Aye, cousin, no words of it, upon your gentility.

Stephen. Not I, body of me, by this air, St. George, and the foot
145 of Pharaoh!

Wellbred. [*To Edward.*] Rare! Your cousin's discourse is simply
drawn out with oaths.

Edward. 'Tis larded with 'em. A kind of French dressing, if you
love it. (*Exeunt [all, into the house].*)

141 UNFURNISHED *unsupplied.*

147 DRAWN OUT *increased in quantity by admixture. N. The phrase perhaps suggests Edward's reply because in cookery it meant to remove the entrails, a process
in preparing a fowl which would precede the larding.*

148 LARDED ... DRESSING *The French were celebrated for both swearing and
cookery; Edward puns on their manner of dressing lean meat by inserting pieces
of fat under the surface before roasting it, to make the dish juicy, like Stephen's
discourse.*

Act III Scene 6

[*In Justice Clement's house.*]

(*Enter Kitely with Cob.*)

Kitely. Ha? How many are there, sayest thou?

Cob. Marry, sir, your brother, Master Wellbred—

Kitely. Tut, beside him: what strangers are there, man?

Cob. Strangers, let me see: one, two— Mass, I know not well,
5 there are so many.

Kitely. How? So many?

Cob. Aye, there's some five, or six of them at the most.

Kitely. [*Aside.*] A swarm, a swarm,

Spite of the devil, how they sting my head
With forkèd stings, thus wide and large!
[*He holds up his fingers to indicate horns upon his head.*]
                                        But, Cob,   10
How long hast thou been coming hither, Cob?
  Cob. A little while, sir.
  Kitely.   Didst thou come running?
  Cob.   No, sir.
  Kitely. Nay, then I am familiar with thy haste!
[*Aside.*] Bane to my fortunes! What meant I to marry?
I, that before was ranked in such content,   15
My mind at rest, too, in so soft a peace,
Being free master of mine own free thoughts—
And now become a slave? What? Never sigh,
Be of good cheer, man: for thou art a cuckold—
'Tis done, 'tis done! Nay, when such flowing store,   20
Plenty itself, falls in my wivès lap,
The *cornu-copiae* will be mine, I know.—But, Cob,
What entertainment had they? I am sure
My sister—and my wife—would bid them welcome! Ha?
  Cob. Like enough, sir, yet I heard not a word of it.   25
  Kitely. [*Aside.*] No: their lips were sealed with kisses, and the voice
Drowned in a flood of joy at their arrival
Had lost her motion, state, and faculty.

10 LARGE *broad.*
15 RANKED *established.*
20–21 FLOWING . . . LAP *an allusion to the archetypal seduction, that of Danae by Zeus, who transformed himself into a shower of gold that poured into Danae's lap through the skylight of the room in which she was confined. Kitely's formulation emphasizes the sexual symbolism nearly to the point of punning.*
22 CORNU-COPIAE *horns of plenty.*
23 ENTERTAINMENT *manner of reception.*

—Cob, which of them was't that first kissed my wife?

30 —My sister, I should say—my wife, alas,
I fear not her—ha? Who was it, say'st thou?

   Cob. By my troth, sir, will you have the truth of it?

   Kitely. Oh, aye, good Cob; I pray thee heartily.

   Cob. Then I am a vagabond, and fitter for Bridewell than your
35 Worship's company, if I saw anybody to be kissed, unless they
would have kissed the post in the middle of the warehouse; for
there I left them all at their tobacco, with a pox.

   Kitely. How? Were they not gone in, then, ere thou cam'st?

   Cob. Oh, no, sir.

40   *Kitely.* Spite of the devil! What do I stay here, then?
Cob, follow me. (*Exit Kitely.*)

   Cob. Nay, soft and fair, I have eggs on the spit; I cannot go yet,
sir. Now am I for some five and fifty reasons hammering, hammering revenge; oh, for three or four gallons of vinegar to sharpen
45 my wits. Revenge! Vinegar revenge! Vinegar and mustard revenge! Nay, and he had not lyen in my house, 'twould never have
grieved me; but being my guest, one that I'll be sworn my wife has
lent him her smock off her back while his one shirt has been at

---

34 BRIDEWELL "*an Hospital (or house of correction) founded . . . to be a workhouse
for the poor and idle persons of the city, wherein a great number of vagrant persons
be now set a work, and relieved at the charges of the citizens.*" (*Stow*, Survey,
II.145.)

36 KISSED THE POST *play on the colloquial meaning*, "*been shut out because of
arriving too late*" (*in allusion to the doorpost*).

37 WITH A POX *a plague on them.*

42 EGGS ON THE SPIT *proverbial: urgent business at hand. Roasting eggs (pre-
viously hard-boiled) required constant turning.*

46 LYEN *lain; i.e. lodged.*

47–48 MY . . . BACK *Since "smock" (petticoat) was the operative word in* double
entendres *too numerous to count, this suggestive phrase no doubt fell easily into
place. N.*

washing, pawned her neckerchers for clean bands for him, sold almost all my platters to buy him tobacco; and he to turn monster of ingratitude, and strike his lawful host! Well, I hope to raise up an host of fury for't; here comes Justice Clement. 50

49 NECKERCHERS *neckerchiefs.* BANDS *neckbands: ornamental collars or ruffs.*

Act III Scene 7

(*Enter* [*at one door*] *Clement, Knowell*[; *at another*], *Formal.*)

Clement. What, 's Master Kitely gone? Roger?
Formal. Aye, sir.
Clement. Heart of me! What made him leave us so abruptly? [*He notices Cob.*] How now, sirrah? What make you here? What would you have, ha? 5
Cob. And't please your Worship, I am a poor neighbor of your Worship's—
Clement. A poor neighbor of mine? Why, speak, poor neighbor.
Cob. I dwell, sir, at the sign of The Water Tankard, hard by The Green Lattice: I have paid scot and lot there any time this eighteen years. 10
Clement. To The Green Lattice?
Cob. No, sir, to the parish; marry, I have seldom 'scaped scot free at the Lattice.
Clement. Oh well! What business has my poor neighbor with me? 15

4 MAKE YOU *are you doing.*
10 GREEN LATTICE *Alehouses commonly had painted lattices over their window openings; the fixture was so general that its name "became synonymous with alehouse" (Larwood and Hotten, quoted Carter).* SCOT AND LOT *municipal taxes.*

127

Act III Scene 7

Cob. And't like your Worship, I am come to crave the peace of your Worship.

Clement. Of me, knave? Peace of me, knave? Did I e'er hurt
20 thee? or threaten thee? or wrong thee? ha?

Cob. No, sir, but your Worship's warrant, for one that has wronged me, sir; his arms are at too much liberty; I would fain have them bound to a treaty of peace, an' my credit could compass it with your Worship.

25 *Clement.* Thou goest far enough about for't, I'm sure.

Knowell. Why, dost thou go in danger of thy life for him, friend?

Cob. No, sir; but I go in danger of my death, every hour, by his means; an' I die within a twelvemonth and a day, I may swear by
30 the law of the land that he killed me.

Clement. How? How, knave? Swear he killed thee? And by the law? What pretense? What color hast thou for that?

Cob. Marry, and't please your Worship, both black [*He shows his bruises.*]
and blue; color enough, I warrant you. I have it here to show your
35 Worship.

Clement. What is he that gave you this, sirrah?

Cob. A gentleman and a soldier he says he is, o' the City here.

Clement. A soldier o' the City? What call you him?

Cob. Captain Bobadill.

40 *Clement.* Bobadill? And why did he bob and beat you, sirrah?

17 CRAVE THE PEACE *ask, in due legal form, for a warrant of peace-keeping.*

23–24 COMPASS IT *bring it about.*

25 THOU . . . ABOUT *You are certainly taking the long way around; a pun on Cob's "compass it" as meaning "encircle it," go all around it.*

29–30 AN' . . . ME *Prosecution for murder could be instituted within a year and a day of the deed. If the victim of a beating died within that period, therefore, there would still be time to indict the killer. N.*

32 COLOR *justification.*

40 BOB *strike with the fist.*

How began the quarrel betwixt you, ha? Speak truly, knave, I advise you.

Cob. Marry, indeed, and please your Worship, only because I spake against their vagrant tobacco, as I came by 'em when they were taking on't—for nothing else.   45

Clement. Ha? You speak against tobacco? Formal, his name.

Formal. What's your name, sirrah?

Cob. Oliver, sir, Oliver Cob, sir.

Clement. Tell Oliver Cob he shall go to the jail, Formal.

Formal. Oliver Cob: my master, Justice Clement, says you shall   50
go to the jail.

Cob. Oh, I beseech your Worship—for God's sake—dear Master Justice!

Clement. Nay, God's precious: and such drunkards, and tankards, as you are come to dispute of tobacco once— I have done! Away   55
with him.

Cob. Oh, good Master Justice—sweet old gentleman!

Knowell. Sweet Oliver, would I could do thee any good! Justice Clement, let me entreat you, sir.

Clement. What? A threadbare rascal! A beggar! A slave that never   60
drunk out of better than piss-pot metal in his life! And he to deprave and abuse the virtue of an herb so generally received in the courts of princes, the chambers of nobles, the bowers of sweet

41 you, ha?] you? ha: Q, F₁.

---

44 VAGRANT *rascally, low and vile.*

54 GOD'S PRECIOUS *euphemistic contraction of "God's precious body."*

54–55 AND SUCH . . . ONCE *if . . . ever. The sense is: if things have reached such a pass that the rabble are entering the debate about tobacco . . .*

58 SWEET OLIVER *a current joke on the name Oliver. The phrase was colloquial for "high liver, carouser, boon companion"; "O sweet Oliver" was the opening of a popular ballad; and the phrase also became a stock epithet for Roland's faithful friend in the Charlemagne legends. N.*

61 PISS-POT METAL *pewter; the usual metal for tavern mugs, too.*

ladies, the cabins of soldiers! Roger, away with him, by God's
65 precious— [*Cob makes a gesture of appeal.*] I say, go to.

Cob. Dear Master Justice! Let me be beaten again, I have deserved
it—but not the prison, I beseech you!

Knowell. Alas, poor Oliver!

Clement. Roger, make him a warrant—he shall not go—I but
70 fear the knave.

Formal. Do not stink, sweet Oliver, you shall not go; my master
will give you a warrant.

Cob. Oh, the Lord maintain his Worship, his worthy Worship.

Clement. Away, dispatch him. [*Exeunt Formal and Cob.*] How
75 now, Master Knowell! In dumps? In dumps? Come, this becomes
not.

Knowell. Sir, would I could not feel my cares—

Clement. Your cares are nothing! They are like my cap,
soon put on, and as soon put off. What? Your son is old enough to
80 govern himself: let him run his course, it's the only way to make him
a staid man. If he were an unthrift, a ruffian, a drunkard, or a licentious liver, then you had reason; you had reason to take care; but,
being none of these, mirth's my witness, an' I had twice so many
cares as you have, I'd drown them all in a cup of sack. Come,
85 come, let's try it—I muse your parcel of a soldier returns not all this
while. (*Exeunt.*)

64 CABINS *tents.*

70 FEAR *frighten.*

78 CAP *A justice, when dressed for his office, wore a special cap (a close coif covering
the whole skull). Clement seems to mean that Knowell's melancholy arises from a
disposition to sit in judgment—an expendable "humor."*

81 STAID *settled (stayed). Not a pejorative word.* UNTHRIFT *spendthrift, wastrel.*

84 SACK *a class of white wines from Spain, Portugal, and the Canary Islands; often
specifically sherry.*

85 MUSE *wonder.* PARCEL *piece, bit.*

Act IV Scene 1

[*A room in Kitely's house.*]

(*Enter Downright, with Dame Kitely.*)

Downright. Well, sister, I tell you true: and you'll find it so in the
end.

Dame Kitely. Alas, brother, what would you have me to do?
I cannot help it: you see my brother brings 'em in here, they are his
friends.   5

Downright. His friends? His fiends. 'Slud, they do nothing but
haunt him up and down like a sort of unlucky sprites, and tempt
him to all manner of villainy that can be thought of. Well, by this
light, a little thing would make me play the devil with some of
'em; and 'twere not more for your husband's sake than anything   10
else, I'd make the house too hot for the best on 'em: they should say,
and swear, hell were broken loose, ere they went hence. But, by
God's will, 'tis nobody's fault but yours: for, an' you had done as
you might have done, they should have been parboiled, and
baked too, every mother's son, ere they should ha' come in, e'er   15
a one of 'em.

6 'SLUD *variant of* 'slid *or* 'sblood.
7 SPRITES *spirits.*
14 PARBOILED *thoroughly boiled.*

Dame Kitely. God's my life! Did you ever hear the like? What a strange man is this! Could I keep out all them, think you? I should put myself against half a dozen men? Should I? Good faith, 20 you'd mad the patient'st body in the world, to hear you talk so, without any sense, or reason!

Act IV Scene 2

(*Enter Matthew with Bridget, Bobadill,*

Stephen, Edward, Wellbred, Brainworm.)

Bridget. Servant (in troth) you are too prodigal
Of your wit's treasure, thus to pour it forth,
Upon so mean a subject as my worth.
    Matthew. You say well, mistress; and I mean as well.
5   *Downright.* Hoy-day, here is stuff!
    Wellbred. [*To Edward.*] Oh, now stand close; pray heaven, she can get him to read; he should do it of his own natural impudency.
    Bridget. [*Indicates a paper in Matthew's hand.*] Servant, what is this same, I pray you?
10   *Matthew.* Marry, an elegy, an elegy, an odd toy—
    Downright. To mock an ape withal. Oh, I could sew up his mouth, now.

1 SERVANT *authorized admirer, professing to "serve" his lady-love.*
4 MISTRESS *lady loved and served by an admirer.* MEAN *play on "mean" in l. 3.*
6 CLOSE *1. quiet; 2. to one side (literally, secret). Perhaps also 3. near by.*
10 ELEGY *short lyric, not necessarily mournful (originally any species of poetry for which the ancients used the elegiac meter).* ODD TOY *whimsical trifle.*
10–11 TOY . . . WITHAL *proverbial for a trick to dupe a fool; cf. Nashe, LS, "As good a toy to mock an ape was it of him that showed a country fellow the Red Sea, where all the red herrings were made" (p. 212; cited Wheatley).*

Dame Kitely. Sister, I pray you let's hear it.

Downright. Are you rhyme-given, too?

Matthew. Mistress, I'll read it, if you please. 15

Bridget. Pray you do, servant.

Downright. Oh, here's no foppery! Death, I can endure the stocks better. (*Exit.*)

Edward. [*To Wellbred.*] What ails thy brother? Can he not hold his water at reading of a ballad? 20

Wellbred. Oh, no: a rhyme to him is worse than cheese or a bagpipe. But mark, you lose the protestation.

Matthew. Faith, I did it in an humor; I know not how it is; [*To Bobadill.*] but please you come near, sir. [*To Bridget.*] This gentleman has judgment, he knows how to censure of a— [*To* 25 *Stephen.*] Pray you, sir, you can judge.

Stephen. Not I, sir: upon my reputation, and by the foot of Pharaoh.

Wellbred. [*To Edward.*] Oh, chide your cousin for swearing.

Edward. Not I, so long as he does not forswear himself. 30

Bobadill. Master Matthew, you abuse the expectation of your dear mistress, and her fair sister; fie! While you live, avoid this prolixity.

Matthew. I shall, sir: well, *incipere dulce.*

Edward. [*To Wellbred.*] How! *Insipere dulce?* A sweet thing to be 35 a fool, indeed.

Wellbred. What, do you take *incipere* in that sense?

37 incipere] Incipere Q; Insipere Ff.

19–22 CAN ... BAGPIPE N.

34 INCIPERE DULCE *To begin is sweet. The "c" was soft, inviting Edward's pun.*

35 INSIPERE DULCE *immediately translated by Edward. Jonson seems to have in the back of his mind Horace's "dulce est desipere in loco": "it is sweet to behave foolishly at the appropriate time" (Odes 4.12, last line).*

Edward. You do not, you? This was your villainy, to gull him with a *motte.*

40   *Wellbred.* Oh, the benchers' phrase: *pauca verba, pauca verba.*

Matthew. [*He reads.*]

> "Rare creature, let me speak without offense;
> Would God my rude words had the influence
> To rule thy thoughts, as thy fair looks do mine,
> Then should'st thou be his prisoner, who is thine."

45   *Edward.* [*To Wellbred.*] This is in "Hero and Leander"?

Wellbred. Oh, ay! Peace, we shall have more of this.

Matthew. "Be not unkind and fair; misshapen stuff
> Is of behavior boisterous and rough:"

Wellbred. [*To Stephen.*] How like you that, sir?

50   *Edward.* [*To Wellbred.*] 'Slight, he shakes his head like a bottle, to feel and there be any brain in it!

                                               Master Stephen answers with shaking his head.

Matthew. But observe the *catastrophe*, now:

> "And I in duty will exceed all other,
> As you in beauty do excel love's mother."

55   *Edward.* [*To Wellbred.*] Well, I'll have him free of the Wit-Brokers, for he utters nothing but stol'n remnants.

Wellbred. Oh, forgive it him.

38–39 THIS . . . MOTTE *Edward accuses Wellbred of having provided Matthew with his Latin phrase to make him call himself a fool.*

39 MOTTE *motto, pithy quotation, often prefixed to a literary work; with pun on the meaning "quip, scoff, jest"; and further play on colloquialism for* mons veneris *(Cotgrave, F&H).*

40 BENCHERS *meaning uncertain; either* 1. *loafer in an ale house;* 2. *magistrate or senator;* 3. *senior member of the Inns of Court.* PAUCA VERBA *few words; a current catch phrase (see HS for examples). N.*

41–44, 47–48, 53–54 *slightly misquoted from Christopher Marlowe's extremely popular* Hero and Leander *(I.199–204), posthumously published in 1598.*

52 CATASTROPHE *denouement.*

55 HAVE . . . OF *have him given the freedom of—i.e. admitted to the City Company of.*

Edward. A filching rogue? Hang him! —And from the dead? It's worse than sacrilege.

Wellbred. [*To Bridget.*] Sister, what ha' you here? Verses? Pray 60 you, let's see. Who made these verses? They are excellent good!

Matthew. O, Master Wellbred, 'tis your disposition to say so, sir. They were good i' the morning, I made 'em *extempore* this morning.

Wellbred. How? *Extempore*?

Matthew. Aye, would I might be hanged else; ask Captain 65 Bobadill. He saw me write them, at The— pox on it— The Star, yonder.

Brainworm. [*To Edward.*] Can he find in his heart to curse the stars so?

Edward. Faith, his are even with him: they ha' cursed him enough 70 already.

Stephen. [*Aside to Edward.*] Cousin, how do you like this gentleman's verses?

Edward. Oh, admirable! The best that ever I heard, cos!

Stephen. [*Aloud, to the company.*]
Body o' Caesar! They are admirable! 75
The best that ever I heard, as I am a soldier.

(*Enter Downright.*)

Downright. I am vexed, I can hold ne'er a bone of me still! Heart, I think they mean to build and breed here!

Wellbred. Sister, you have a simple servant, here, that crowns your beauty with such *encomions* and devices; you may see what 80 it is to be the mistress of a wit! —that can make your perfections so transparent that every blear eye may look through them, and see him drowned over head and ears in the deep well of desire. Sister Kitely, I marvel you get you not a servant that can rhyme and do tricks, too. 85

80 ENCOMIONS *encomiums; the Greek form.*

135

Downright. Oh, monster! Impudence itself! Tricks?

Dame Kitely. [*To Wellbred.*] Tricks, brother? What tricks?

Bridget. Nay, speak, I pray you, what tricks?

Dame Kitely. Aye, never spare anybody here: but say, what
90 tricks?

Bridget. Passion of my heart! Do tricks?

Wellbred. 'Slight, here's a trick vied and revied! Why, you
monkeys, you, what a caterwauling do you keep? Has he not given
you rhymes, and verses, and tricks?

95 *Downright.* Oh, the fiend!

Wellbred. Nay, you—lamp of virginity, that take it in snuff so!
Come, and cherish this tame poetical fury in your servant; you'll
be begged else, shortly, for a concealment: go to, reward his muse.
You cannot give him less than a shilling, in conscience, for the
100 book he had it out of cost him a teston at least. How now, gallants?
Mr. Matthew? Captain? What? All sons of silence? No spirit?

Downright. [*To Wellbred.*] Come, you might practice your ruffian
tricks somewhere else, and not here, I wuss; this is no tavern, nor
drinking-school, to vent your exploits in.

105 *Wellbred.* How now! Whose cow has calved?

---

86 TRICKS *The word, of course, lends itself to* double entendres; *besides, it had
become ambiguous through the widely used pun on "merry tricks" and* meretrix,
prostitute. N.

92 TRICK *pun on the meaning in a card game.* VIED AND REVIED *bid and rebid (i.e.
raised).*

96 LAMP OF VIRGINITY *partial title of book entered in the Stationers Register, 1581,
as* The Lamp of Virginity and Mirror for Matrons. *N.* TAKE . . . SNUFF *take
offense at it (perhaps alluding to the unpleasant smell of an extinguished wick or
"snuff"; perhaps simply equivalent to modern "sniff at"). Here a play on the
snuff of a lamp: the socket in which the wick burned.*

97 POETICAL FURY *the traditional* furor poeticus: *poetic frenzy, inspiration.*

98 CONCEALMENT. *N.*

100 TESTON *colloquial for sixpence.*

Downright. Marry, that has mine, sir. Nay, boy, never look askance at me for the matter; I'll tell you of it, I, sir, you and your companions; mend yourselves, when I ha' done!

Wellbred. My companions?

Downright. Yes, sir, your companions, so I say, I am not afraid 110 of you, nor them neither: your hang-bys here. You must have your poets, and your potlings, your *soldados*, and *foolados*, to follow you up and down the city, and here they must come to domineer and swagger. [*To Matthew and Bobadill.*] Sirrah, you, ballad-singer, and Slops, your fellow there, get you out; get you home; or (by 115 this steel) I'll cut off your ears, and that presently.

Wellbred. 'Slight, stay, let's see what he dare do; cut off his ears? Cut a whetstone. You are an ass, do you see? Touch any man here, and by this hand, I'll run my rapier to the hilts in you.

They all draw, and they of the house make out to part them.   *Downright.* Yea, that would I fain see, boy.   (*Enter Cash and some more of the house to part them; the women make a great cry.*) 120

Dame Kitely. O Jesu! Murder! Thomas, Gaspar!

Bridget. Help, help! Thomas!

Edward. Gentlemen, forbear, I pray you. 125

Bobadill. Well, sirrah, you, Holofernes: by my hand, I will pink your flesh full of holes with my rapier for this: I will, by this good heaven! Nay, let him come, let him come, gentlemen, *They offer to fight again, and are parted.* by the body of Saint George, I'll not kill him.

Cash. Hold, hold, good gentlemen. 130

Downright. You whoreson, bragging coistrel!

108 COMPANIONS *often used as a contemptuous term, like "fellows."*

112 POTLINGS *tipplers. Downright invents the word by a happy associative step from "poets."*

115 SLOPS *alluding to Bobadill's puffy breeches. Cf. II.2.21 and fn.*

126 HOLOFERNES *in the Bible, the general sent by Nebuchadnezzar to wreak terrible vengeance on those who had refused him support in war. The story of his murder by Judith was extremely popular on the stage. N.*

127 FULL OF HOLES *play on Holofernes.*

131 COISTREL *base scoundrel (originally servant connected with horses, groom).*

Act IV Scene 3

(*Enter Kitely.*) [*He goes*] *to them.*

Kitely. Why, how now? What's the matter? What's the stir here?
Whence springs the quarrel?—Thomas! Where is he?
—Put up your weapons, and put off this rage.
[*Aside.*]
My wife and sister, they are cause of this—
5   What, Thomas? Where is this knave?

Cash. Here, sir.

Wellbred. Come, let's go; this is one of my brother's ancient
humors, this.

Stephen. I am glad nobody was hurt by his ancient humor. (*Exit
Wellbred, Edward, Brainworm, Stephen, Bobadill, Matthew.*)

10   *Kitely.* Why, how now, brother, who enforced this brawl?

Downright. A sort of lewd rakehells, that care neither for God
nor the devil! And they must come here to read ballads, and
roguery, and trash! I'll mar the knot of 'em ere I sleep, perhaps:
especially Bob, there: he that's all manner of shapes! and Songs and
15   Sonnets, his fellow.

Bridget. Brother, indeed, you are too violent,
Too sudden, in your humor; and you know
My brother Wellbred's temper will not bear
Any reproof, chiefly in such a presence,

---

7 ANCIENT *long-accustomed, established, here equivalent to "good old."* N.

10 ENFORCED *brought on by rough and rude behavior.*

13 MAR *mangle, maim.*

14 HE . . . SHAPES *i.e. depending upon the configuration of his breeches.*

14–15 SONGS AND SONNETS *a popular title of the day for collections of lyrics.*

Where every slight disgrace he should receive   20
Might wound him in opinion and respect.

   Downright. Respect? What talk you of respect 'mong such
As ha' nor spark of manhood, nor good manners?
'Sdeynes, I am ashamed to hear you! Respect? (*Exit.*)

   Bridget. Yes, there was one a civil gentleman,   25
And very worthily demeaned himself!

   Kitely. Oh, that was some love of yours, sister!

   Bridget. A love of mine? I would it were no worse, brother!
You'd pay my portion sooner than you think for.

   Dame Kitely. Indeed, he seemed to be a gentleman of an exceed- 30
ing fair disposition, and of very excellent good parts! (*Exit Bridget,
Dame Kitely.*)

   Kitely. [*To himself.*] Her love, by heaven! My wife's minion!
Fair disposition? Excellent good parts?
Death, these phrases are intolerable!
Good parts? How should she know his parts?   35
His parts? Well, well, well, well, well, well!
It is too plain, too clear.—Thomas, come hither.
What, are they gone?

   Cash.   Aye, sir, they went in.
My mistress, and your sister.

   Kitely. Are any of the gallants within?   40

   Cash. No, sir, they are all gone.

   Kitely. Art thou sure of it?

   Cash. I can assure you, sir.

   Kitely. What gentleman was that they praised so, Thomas?

   Cash. One, they call him Master Knowell, a handsome young 45
gentleman, sir.

29 PORTION *dowry.*
31 PARTS *qualities.*
32 MINION *sweetheart. Trisyllabic.*

Kitely. Aye, I thought so: my mind gave me as much.
I'll die, but they have hid him i' the house,
Somewhere; I'll go and search, go with me, Thomas.
50   Be true to me, and thou shalt find me a master. (*Exeunt.*)

50 A MASTER *i.e. worthy of the name.*

Act IV Scene 4

[*Outside Cob's house.*]

(*Enter Cob.*)

Cob. [*Knocks at the door.*] What, Tib! Tib, I say!

Tib. [*Within.*] How now, what cuckold is that knocks so hard?
[*She opens the door.*] O, husband, is't you? What's the news?

Cob. Nay, you have stunned me, i' faith! You ha' giv'n me a
5   knock o' the forehead will stick by me! Cuckold? 'Slid, cuckold?

Tib. Away, you fool, did I know it was you that knocked?
Come, come, you may call me as bad, when you list.

Cob. May I? Tib, you are a whore.

Tib. You lie in your throat, husband.

10   *Cob.* How, the lie? And in my throat, too? Do you long to be
stabbed, ha?

Tib. Why, you are no soldier, I hope?

Cob. Oh, must you be stabbed by a soldier? Mass, that's true!
When was Bobadill here? Your Captain? That rogue, that foist,
15   that fencing Burgullian? I'll tickle i'faith.

7 LIST *like.*
10–12 *Cf. II.4.4 and fn.*
13 OH . . . SOLDIER *a double entendre.*
14 FOIST *slang for pickpocket.*
15 BURGULLIAN *alternate form of Burgonian: Burgundian. A topical reference.* N.

Tib. Why, what's the matter, trow?

Cob. Oh, he has basted me rarely, sumptiously! [*Takes out the warrant.*] But I have it here in black and white—for his black and blue—shall pay him. Oh, the Justice! The honestest old brave Trojan in London! I do honor the very flea of his dog. A plague 20 on him, though, he put me once in a villainous filthy fear; marry, it vanished away like the smoke of tobacco; but I was smoked soundly first. I thank the devil, and his good angel, my guest. Well, wife, or Tib (which you will), get you in, and lock the door, I charge you, let nobody in to you; wife—nobody in—to you: those are my 25 words. Not Captain Bob himself, nor the fiend in his likeness; you are a woman; you have flesh and blood enough in you to be tempted: therefore, keep the door—shut upon all comers.

Tib. I warrant you, there shall nobody enter here, without my consent. 30

Cob. Nor with your consent, sweet Tib, and so I leave you.

Tib. It's more than you know, whether you leave me so.

Cob. How?

Tib. Why, sweet.

Cob. Tut, sweet or sour, thou art a flower, 35
Keep close thy door, I ask no more.

(Exeunt.)
[Cob goes down the street; Tib into the house.]

---

16 TROW *here merely emphatic.*
17 BASTED *lambasted.* SUMPTIOUSLY *sumptuously; a current form.*
20 TROJAN *standard colloquial epithet of commendation—for conviviality, valor, hard work, or (as here) trustworthiness. N.*
22 SMOKED *given a hot time.*

Act IV Scene 5

[*A street.*]

(*Enter Edward, Wellbred, Stephen, Brainworm.*)

Edward. Well, Brainworm, perform this business happily,
And thou makest a purchase of my love forever.

Wellbred. I'faith, now let thy spirits use their best faculties. But,
at any hand, remember the message to my brother: for there's no
5   other means to start him.

Brainworm. I warrant you, sir, fear nothing: I have a nimble soul
has waked all forces of my fant'sy by this time, and put 'em in true
motion. What you have possessed me withal, I'll discharge it
amply, sir. Make it no question. (*Exit Brainworm.*)

10   *Wellbred.* Forth, and prosper, Brainworm.—Faith, Ned, how
dost thou approve of my abilities in this device?

Edward. Troth, well, howsoever; but it will come excellent, if it
take.

Wellbred. Take, man? Why, it cannot choose but take, if the
15   circumstances miscarry not—but, tell me, ingenuously, dost thou
affect my sister Bridget, as thou pretend'st?

Edward. Friend, am I worth belief?

[A STREET.] *The young men are not likely to have abandoned their* "hang-bys"
*wordlessly for tavern cheer; they have preceded them up the street, and the group is
reunited in IV.7 while Wellbred is fetching Bridget.*

1 HAPPILY *successfully.*

8 POSSESSED ME WITHAL *entrusted to me, instructed me in.*

12 HOWSOEVER *in any case.*

16 AFFECT *feel affection for, inclination toward.* SISTER *i.e. sister-in-law.* PRETEND'ST
profess, claim.

Wellbred. Come, do not protest. On faith, she is a maid of good ornament, and much modesty; and, except I conceived very worthily of her, thou shouldest not have her. 20

Edward. Nay, that I am afraid will be a question yet, whether I shall have her, or no.

Wellbred. 'Slid, thou shalt have her; by this light, thou shalt.

Edward. Nay, do not swear.

Wellbred. By this hand, thou shalt have her: I'll go fetch her 25 presently. 'Point but where to meet, and as I am an honest man, I'll bring her.

Edward. Hold, hold, be temperate.

Wellbred. Why, by— what shall I swear by? Thou shalt have her, as I am— 30

Edward. Pray thee, be at peace, I am satisfied, and do believe thou wilt omit no offered occasion to make my desires complete.

Wellbred. Thou shalt see, and know, I will not. (*Exeunt.*)

18–19 OF GOOD ORNAMENT *equipped with proper and desirable qualities* (*from Lat.* ORNAMENTUM: *equipment*).

Act IV Scene 6

[*The street near Justice Clement's house.*]

(*Enter Knowell, Formal, meeting Brainworm.*)

Formal. Was your man a soldier, sir?

Knowell. Aye, a knave; I took him begging o' the way, This morning, as I came over Moorfields!

[*Enter Brainworm.*]

Oh, here he is! Yo'have made fair speed, believe me! Where, i' the name of sloth, could you be thus—

Brainworm. Marry, peace be my comfort, where I thought I should have had little comfort of your Worship's service.

Knowell. How so?

Brainworm. O, sir! Your coming to the City, your entertainment
10 of me, and your sending me to watch—indeed, all the circumstances either of your charge, or my employment—are as open to your son as to yourself!

Knowell. How should that be! Unless that villain, Brainworm, Have told him of the letter, and discovered
15 All that I strictly charged him to conceal? 'Tis so!

Brainworm. I am partly o' the faith 'tis so, indeed.

Knowell. But how should he know thee to be my man?

Brainworm. Nay, sir, I cannot tell; unless it be By the black art! Is not your son a scholar, sir?
20 *Knowell.* Yes, but I hope his soul is not allied Unto such hellish practice: if it were, I had just cause to weep my part in him, And curse the time of his creation. But where didst thou find them, Fitzsword?
25 *Brainworm.* You should rather ask where they found me, sir, for I'll be sworn I was going along in the street, thinking nothing, when (of a sudden) a voice calls, "Mr. Knowell's man!" another cries, "Soldier!" and thus half a dozen of 'em, till they had called me within a house where I no sooner came, but they seemed men,
30 and out flew all their rapiers at my bosom, with some three- or fourscore oaths to accompany 'em, and all to tell me I was but a

29 they] F_2; thy F_1

---

9 ENTERTAINMENT *engagement.*

19 BLACK . . . SCHOLAR *The connection between learning (which entered upon subjects "forbidden" to ordinary men, especially philosophy and divinity), and the ability to conjure or perform black magic, was part of popular tradition.*

23 CREATION *four syllables.*

29 SEEMED MEN *made their manhood, or manly valor, appear.*

dead man, if I did not confess where you were, and how I was employed, and about what; which when they could not get out of me (as, I protest, they must ha' dissected and made an anatomy o' me first, and so I told 'em) they locked me up into a room i' the   35
top of a high house, whence, by great miracle (having a light heart) I slid down, by a bottom of packthread, into the street, and so 'scaped. But, sir, thus much I can assure you, for I heard it while I was locked up, there were a great many rich merchants' and brave citizens' wives with 'em at a feast, and your son, Mr. Edward,   40
withdrew with one of 'em, and has 'pointed to meet her anon, at one Cob's house, a water-bearer that dwells by the Wall. Now there your Worship shall be sure to take him, for there he preys, and fail he will not.

    Knowell. Nor will I fail to break his match, I doubt not.   45
Go thou along with Justice Clement's man,
And stay there for me. At one Cob's house, say'st thou?

    Brainworm. Aye, sir, there you shall have him. [*Exit Knowell.*]
                                 [*To himself.*] Yes—invisible!
Much wench, or much son! 'Slight, when he has stayed there three or four hours, travailing with the expectation of wonders,   50
and at length be delivered of air: oh, the sport that I should then take to look on him, if I durst! But, now, I mean to appear no more afore him in this shape. I have another trick to act yet. Oh that I were so happy as to light on a nupson, now, of this Justice's novice. [*To Formal.*] Sir, I make you stay somewhat long.   55

    Formal. Not a whit, sir. Pray you, what do you mean, sir?
    Brainworm. I was putting up some papers—
    Formal. You ha' been lately in the wars, sir, it seems.

---

34 ANATOMY *body cut up in a dissection.*
37 BOTTOM *ball or skein.*
47 THERE *at Justice Clement's.*
54 NUPSON *simpleton.* OF *in.*

Brainworm. Marry have I, sir; to my loss—and expense of all,
60 almost—

Formal. Troth, sir, I would be glad to bestow a pottle of wine o'
you, if it please you to accept it—

Brainworm. Oh, sir—

Formal. But to hear the manner of your services, and your devices
65 in the wars; they say they be very strange, and not like those a man
reads in the Roman histories, or sees at Mile-end.

Brainworm. No, I assure you, sir; why, at any time when it please
you, I shall be ready to discourse to you all I know— [*Aside.*] and
more too, somewhat.

70 *Formal.* No better time than now, sir; we'll go to The Windmill:
there we shall have a cup of neat grist, we call it. I pray you, sir,
let me request you to The Windmill.

Brainworm. I'll follow you, sir—[*Aside.*] and make grist o' you, if
I have good luck. (*Exeunt.*)

61 POTTLE *two-quart tankard.*
66 MILE-END *see fn. to II.5.136.*
71 GRIST *malt that has been ground for brewing. A modest joke alluding to the tavern's name.*
73 GRIST *i.e. a source of profit.*

Act IV Scene 7

[*A street.*]

(*Enter Bobadill, Edward, Matthew, Stephen.*)

Matthew. Sir, did your eyes ever taste the like clown of him,
where we were today, Mr. Wellbred's half-brother? I think the
whole earth cannot show his parallel, by this daylight.

s.d.] F₁ includes Downright in head list of characters, then erroneously prints *To them* as
s.d. beside Bobadill instead.

1 CLOWN *cloddish fellow, bumpkin.*

Edward. We were now speaking of him: Captain Bobadill tells
me he is fall'n foul o' you, too.   5

Matthew. Oh, aye, sir, he threatened me with the bastinado.

Bobadill. Aye, but I think I taught you prevention, this morning,
for that— You shall kill him, beyond question: if you be so generously minded.

Matthew. Indeed, it is a most excellent trick!   10

Bobadill. Oh, you do not give spirit enough to your   *He [Matthew]*
motion, you are too tardy, too heavy! Oh, it must be   *practices at a*
                                                        post.
done like lightning— [*He draws and lunges.*] *Hai*!

Matthew. Rare Captain!

Bobadill. Tut, 'tis nothing and't be not done in a— [*He lunges.*]   15
punto!

Edward. Captain, did you ever prove yourself upon any of our
masters of defense, here?

Matthew. O, good sir! Yes, I hope he has.

Bobadill. I will tell you, sir. Upon my first coming to the City,   20
after my long travail for knowledge (in that mystery only), there
came three or four of 'em to me, at a gentleman's house where it
was my chance to be resident at that time, to entreat my presence
at their schools, and withal so much importuned me, that (I protest
to you as I am a gentleman) I was ashamed of their rude demeanor,   25
out of all measure; well, I told 'em that to come to a public school,
they should pardon me, it was opposite (in diameter) to my humor;
but if so they would give their attendance at my lodging, I protested

8–9 GENEROUSLY *nobly (because gallantly).*

13 HAI! *Italian, a hit (literally, " you have it").*

16 PUNTO! *Italian, instant (point of time); with pun on the technical name for a
thrust with the point (cf. 71).*

17 PROVE *try out.*

18 MASTERS *teachers.*

20–27 *N.*

21 TRAVAIL *1. travel; 2. labor.*

30 to do them what right or favor I could, as I was a gentleman, and so forth.

    Edward. So, sir, then you tried their skill?

    Bobadill. Alas, soon tried! You shall hear, sir. Within two or three days after, they came; and, by honesty, fair sir, believe me, I graced them exceedingly, showed them some two or three tricks
35 of prevention have purchased 'em, since, a credit to admiration! They cannot deny this; and yet now they hate me, and why? Because I am excellent, and for no other vile reason on the earth.

    Edward. This is strange and barbarous, as ever I heard!

    Bobadill. Nay, for a more instance of their preposterous natures,
40 but note, sir. They have assaulted me some three, four, five, six of them together, as I have walked alone, in divers skirts i' the town, as Turnbull, Whitechapel, Shoreditch, which were then my quarters; and since upon the Exchange, at my lodging, and at my ordinary: where I have driven them afore me the whole length of a
45 street, in the open view of all our gallants, pitying to hurt them, believe me. Yet all this lenity will not o'ercome their spleen: they will be doing with the pismire, raising a hill a man may spurn abroad with his foot at pleasure. By myself, I could have slain them all, but I delight not in murder. I am loth to bear any other
50 than this bastinado for 'em: yet I hold it good polity not to go disarmed, for though I be skillful, I may be oppressed with multitudes.

    Edward. Aye, believe me, may you, sir; and (in my conceit) our whole nation should sustain the loss by it, if it were so.

---

35 A . . . ADMIRATION *an amazing credit or reputation.*

40–41 THREE . . . THEM. *N.*

41 SKIRTS *outskirts, suburbs.*

42 TURNBULL . . . SHOREDITCH *thoroughly disreputable neighborhoods. N.*

43–44 AND SINCE . . . ME. *N.*

47 PISMIRE *ant.*

Bobadill. Alas, no: what's a peculiar man, to a nation? Not seen.   55

Edward. Oh, but your skill, sir!

Bobadill. Indeed, that might be some loss; but who respects it? I will tell you, sir, by the way of private, and under seal: I am a gentleman, and live here obscure, and to myself; but were I known to her Majesty and the Lords—observe me—I would undertake   60 (upon this poor head and life) for the public benefit of the state not only to spare the entire lives of her subjects in general, but to save the one half, nay, three parts of her yearly charge in holding war, and against what enemy soever. And how would I do it, think you?   65

Edward. Nay, I know not, nor can I conceive.

Bobadill. Why, thus, sir. I would select nineteen more to myself, throughout the land; gentlemen they should be of good spirit, strong and able constitution; I would choose them by an instinct, a character, that I have: and I would teach these nineteen the special   70 rules, as your *punto*, your *reverso*, your *stoccata*, your *imbroccata*, your *passada*, your *montanto*: till they could all play very near, or altogether, as well as myself. This done, say the enemy were forty thousand strong, we twenty would come into the field, the tenth of March, or thereabouts; and we would challenge twenty of the   75 enemy; they could not, in their honor, refuse us—well, we would kill them; challenge twenty more, kill them; twenty more, kill them; twenty more, kill them too; and thus would we kill, every man, his twenty a day, that's twenty score; twenty score, that's two hundred; two hundred a day, five days a thousand; forty thousand   80

---

55 PECULIAR *individual*.

57 RESPECTS *pays attention to, is aware of*.

71–72 PUNTO . . . MONTANTO *technical Italian terms for various cuts and thrusts:* punto, *evidently, with the point;* reverso, *a cross blow;* stoccata, *apparently a straightforward thrust;* imbroccata, *apparently a thrust with the wrist turned;* passada, *a pass with foot advanced;* montanto, *? an upward (Cotgrave: "upright") thrust. N.*

—forty times five, five times forty—two hundred days kills them all up, by computation. And this will I venture my poor gentleman-like carcass to perform (provided there be no treason practiced upon us) by fair and discreet manhood—that is, civilly by the sword.

85   *Edward.* Why, are you so sure of your hand, Captain, at all times?

   Bobadill. Tut, never miss thrust, upon my reputation with you.

   Edward. I would not stand in Downright's state, then, an' you meet him, for the wealth of any one street in London.

90   *Bobadill.* Why, sir, you mistake me! If he were here now, by this welkin, I would not draw my weapon on him! Let this gentleman do his mind; but I will bastinado him (by the bright sun) wherever I meet him.

   Matthew. Faith, and I'll have a fling at him, at my distance.

95   *Edward.* Godso, look where he is: yonder he goes.   *Downright walks over the*

   Downright. [*To himself.*] What peevish luck have I, I *stage.* cannot meet with these bragging rascals?

   Bobadill. It's not he, is it?

   Edward. Yes, faith, it is he. [*Exit Downright.*]

100   *Matthew.* I'll be hanged, then, if that were he.

   Edward. Sir, keep your hanging good for some greater matter, for I assure you that was he.

   Stephen. Upon my reputation, it was he.

   Bobadill. Had I thought it had been he, he must not have gone so;

105 but I can hardly be induced to believe it was he, yet.

   Edward. That I think, sir. But see, he is come again!

   Downright. O, Pharaoh's Foot, have I found you? *[Re-enter Downright.]*

99 he.] Q; he? Ff.

---

91 WELKIN *sky, heaven.* THIS GENTLEMAN *Matthew.*

Come, draw, to your tools: draw, gipsy, or I'll thresh you.

Bobadill. Gentleman of valor, I do believe in thee; hear me—

Downright. Draw your weapon, then.   110

Bobadill. Tall man, I never thought on it till now (body of me):
I had a warrant of the peace served on me, even now, as I came
along, by a water-bearer; this gentleman saw it, Mr. Matthew.

Downright. 'Sdeath, you will not draw, then?

Bobadill. Hold, hold! Under thy favor, forbear!   *He beats him,*   115
Downright. Prate again, as you like this, you whore-   *and disarms him:*
son foist, you! You'll control the point, you?—Your   *Matthew runs*
away.
consort is gone? Had he stayed, he had shared with you, sir. (*Exit
Downright.*)

Bobadill. Well, gentlemen, bear witness, I was bound to the
peace, by this good day.   120

Edward. No, faith, it's an ill day, Captain, never reckon it other;
but, say you were bound to the peace, the law allows you to defend
yourself: that'll prove but a poor excuse.

Bobadill. I cannot tell, sir. I desire good construction, in fair sort.
I never sustained the like disgrace, by Heaven—sure I was strook   125
with a planet thence, for I had no power to touch my weapon.

Edward. Aye, like enough, I have heard of many that have been
beaten under a planet; go, get you to a surgeon. [*Exit Bobadill.*]
'Slid, an' these be your tricks, your *passadas* and your *montantos,*

108ff. *N.*

108 TOOLS *dagger and rapier.* GIPSY *used contemptuously to mean a shiftless rascal
who lives by cunning; with pun on the sense "Egyptian," since Bobadill is always
swearing by the foot of Pharaoh (Sale).*

111 TALL *goodly, valiant.*

125–26 STROOK WITH *struck by. N.*

126 THENCE *from Heaven.*

128 PLANET *pun on the name for a priest's chasuble or outer mantle; the joke alludes
to the current widespread anti-Catholicism.*

130 I'll none of them. Oh, manners! That this age should   [*Stephen picks*
   bring forth such creatures! That Nature should be at   *up Downright's*
   leisure to make 'em! Come, cos.   *fallen cloak.*]

   Stephen. Mass, I'll ha' this cloak.

   Edward. God's will, 'tis Downright's.

135   *Stephen.* Nay, it's mine now; another might have ta'en it up,
   as well as I. I'll wear it, so I will.

   Edward. How an' he see it? He'll challenge it, assure yourself.

   Stephen. Aye, but he shall not ha'it; I'll say I bought it.

   Edward. Take heed you buy it not too dear, cos. (*Exeunt.*)

135 ta'en it up] tane it up Q; tane up F₁; tane 't up F₂.

Act IV Scene 8

[*A room in Kitely's house.*]

Kitely, Wellbred, Dame Kitely, Bridget.

   Kitely. Now, trust me, brother, you were much to blame,
T'incense his anger, and disturb the peace
Of my poor house, where there are sentinels
That every minute watch to give alarms
5 Of civil war, without adjection
Of your assistance, or occasion.

   Wellbred. No harm done, brother, I warrant you; since there is
no harm done. Anger costs a man nothing; and a tall man is never
his own man till he be angry. To keep his valure in obscurity is to

5 ADJECTION *adding on; four syllables.*
6 OCCASION *grammatically parallel with* "*adjection*"; *four syllables.*
9 HIS OWN MAN *truly himself.* VALURE 1. *valor;* 2. *value.*

keep himself, as it were, in a cloak-bag. What's a musician, unless   10
he play? What's a tall man, unless he fight? For, indeed, all this
my wise brother stands upon absolutely; and that made me fall
in with him so resolutely.

Dame Kitely. Aye, but what harm might have come of it, brother!

Wellbred. Might, sister? So might the good warm clothes your   15
husband wears be poisoned, for anything he knows; or the wholesome wine he drunk, even now at the table—

Kitely. [Aside.] Now, God forbid: O me! Now I remember,
My wife drunk to me last—and changed the cup—
And bade me wear this cursèd suit today.   20
See if Heav'n suffer murder undiscovered!
[*To Bridget.*] I feel me ill; give me some mithridate,
Some mithridate and oil, good sister, fetch me;
Oh, I am sick at heart! I burn, I burn.
If you will save my life, go, fetch it me.   25

Wellbred. [Aside.] Oh, strange humor! My very breath has poisoned him.

Bridget. Good brother, be content, what do you mean?
The strength of these extreme conceits will kill you.

---

10 CLOAK-BAG *suitcase.*

12–13 FALL IN *join.*

15–17 N.

21 SUFFER *permit.*

22 MITHRIDATE *general antidote against poison or infection, named for Mithridates,
King of Pontus, who was supposed to have invented it. (Elyot, Preface, Aii v).
This belief derives from the legend of Mithridates' immunity to poison, which he
created gradually by taking progressively larger doses of deadly drugs.*

24 SICK AT HEART *1. afflicted with palpitations, nausea, pain in the chest; 2. ?
mortally ill (English Dialect Dictionary); with pun on 3. the psychological
meaning.*

28 CONCEITS *fancies, delusions.*

Act IV Scene 8

    Dame Kitely. Beshrew your heart-blood, brother Wellbred, now,
30 For putting such a toy into his head.
    Wellbred. Is a fit simile a toy? Will he be poisoned with a simile?
Brother Kitely, what a strange and idle imagination is this? For
shame, be wiser. O' my soul, there's no such matter.
    Kitely. Am I not sick? How am I, then, not poisoned?
35 Am I not poisoned? How am I, then, so sick?
    Dame Kitely. If you be sick, your own thoughts make you sick.
    Wellbred. His jealousy is the poison he has taken.
             (Enter Brainworm.)
    Brainworm. Mr. Kitely, my master, Justice Clement, *He comes dis-*
salutes you; and desires to speak with you, with all *guised like*
40 possible speed. *Justice Clement's*
    man.
    Kitely. No time but now? When I think I am sick? very sick!
Well, I will wait upon his Worship. [*Calls.*] Thomas!
Cob! [*Aside.*] I must seek them out, and set 'em sentinels
Till I return. —Thomas! Cob! Thomas! (*Exit.*)
45   *Wellbred.* This is perfectly rare, Brainworm! But how got'st thou
this apparel of the Justice's man?
    Brainworm. Marry, sir, my proper fine penman would needs
bestow the grist o' me, at The Windmill, to hear some martial
discourse; where I so marshaled him that I made him drunk with
50 admiration! And because too much heat was the cause of his dis-
temper, I stripped him stark naked as he lay along asleep, and
borrowed his suit, to deliver this counterfeit message in, leaving
a rusty armor and an old brown bill to watch him till my return:

41–44] F₁ prints as prose.
49 I so] Q; so I F₁.

---

30 TOY *foolish notion.*
53 OLD . . . HIM *A bill was a kind of halberd or pike with a hooked point, used by
foot soldiers and watchmen; the brown bill was the particular emblem of the constable. N. "Brown" seems to have described the rusty head, which was not painted
black like that of a soldier's bill to preserve its appearance.*

154

which shall be when I ha' pawned his apparel, and spent the better
part o' the money, perhaps.   55

    Wellbred. Well, thou art a successful merry knave, Brainworm;
his absence will be a good subject for more mirth. I pray thee, return
to thy young master, and will him to meet me and my sister Bridget
at the Tower instantly; for here, tell him, the house is so stored
with jealousy there is no room for love to stand upright in. We   60
must get our fortunes committed to some larger prison, say; and,
than the Tower, I know no better air, nor where the liberty of the
house may do us more present service. Away! (*Exit [Brainworm].*)
            (*Enter Kitely, to him Cash.*)

    Kitely. Come hither, Thomas. Now my secret's ripe,
And thou shalt have it: lay to both thine ears.   65
Hark what I say to thee. I must go forth, Thomas.
Be careful of thy promise, keep good watch,
Note every gallant, and observe him well,
That enters in my absence, to thy mistress:
If she would show him rooms, the jest is stale;   70
Follow 'em, Thomas, or else hang on him
And let him not go after; mark their looks;
Note, if she offer but to see his band,
Or any other amorous toy about him;
But praise his leg; or foot; or if she say   75

59 TOWER " *They could be married at once within the precincts of the Tower, which
     was extra-parochial" (HS).*
60 LOVE . . . IN *a* double entendre.
61 COMMITTED *pun on 1. entrusted; 2. sent to jail.*
62–63 LIBERTY . . . HOUSE *degree of freedom sometimes allowed a prisoner in private
     custody. In this allusion to the Tower as prison, Wellbred puns on two other special
     senses of "liberty": 1. district within the limits of a county but exempt from the
     Sheriff's jurisdiction; 2. the precincts of a prison, outside the walls, over which its
     authority extended.*
70 STALE *play on the meaning "whore," and on the basic general sense which in-
     volves decoying, or else pretending one aim to achieve another.*

The day is hot, and bid him feel her hand,
How hot it is; oh, that's a monstrous thing!
Note me all this, good Thomas, mark their sighs,
And, if they do but whisper, break 'em off:
80   I'll bear thee out in it. Wilt thou do this?
Wilt thou be true, my Thomas?

    Cash. As truth's self, sir.

    Kitely. Why, I believe thee—Where is Cob, now? —Cob? (*Exit Kitely.*)

    Dame Kitely. He's ever calling for Cob! I wonder how he employs Cob so!

85   *Wellbred.* Indeed, sister, to ask how he employs Cob is a necessary question for you, that are his wife, and a thing not very easy for you to be satisfied in: but this I'll assure you, Cob's wife is an excellent bawd, sister, and oftentimes your husband haunts her house—marry, to what end I cannot altogether accuse him, imagine what

90   you think convenient. But I have known fair hides have foul hearts ere now, sister.

    Dame Kitely. Never said you truer than that, brother, so much I can tell you for your learning. Thomas, fetch your cloak and go with me, I'll after him presently: I would to fortune I could take

95   him there, i'faith. I'd return him his own, I warrant him. (*Exeunt Cash and Dame Kitely.*)

    Wellbred. So, let 'em go—[*Aside.*] This may make sport anon. —Now, my fair sister-in-law, that you knew but how happy a thing it were to be fair and beautiful!

    Bridget. That touches not me, brother.

100   *Wellbred.* That's true; that's even the fault of it: for, indeed, beauty stands a woman in no stead, unless it procure her touching. But, sister, whether it touch you or no, it touches your beauties;

---

80 BEAR . . . OUT *back . . . up.*

and I am sure they will abide the touch; an' they do not, a plague
of all ceruse, say I; and it touches me too in part, though not in the—
Well, there's a dear and respected friend of mine, sister, stands very 105
strongly and worthily affected toward you, and hath vowed to
inflame whole bone-fires of zeal at his heart, in honor of your
perfections. I have already engaged my promise to bring you
where you shall hear him confirm much more. Ned Knowell is the
man, sister. There's no exception against the party. You are ripe 110
for a husband; and a minute's loss to such an occasion is a great
trespass in a wise beauty. What say you, sister? On my soul he
loves you. Will you give him the meeting?

Bridget. Faith, I had very little confidence in mine own constancy,
brother, if I durst not meet a man; but this motion of yours savors 115
of an old knight-adventurer's servant a little too much, methinks.

Wellbred. What's that, sister?

Bridget. Marry, of the squire.

Wellbred. No matter if it did; I would be such an one for my
friend—[*Enter Kitely.*] But see! Who is returned to hinder us? 120

Kitely. What villainy is this? Called out on a false message?
This was some plot! I was not sent for. Bridget,
Where's your sister?

Bridget.   I think she be gone forth, sir.

Kitely. How! Is my wife gone forth? Whether, for God's sake?

Bridget. She's gone abroad with Thomas. 125

---

103 TOUCH *pun on "test for quality or genuineness" (applied to gold and silver by
rubbing them upon a touchstone).*

104 CERUSE *cosmetic preparation of refined white lead, much used.*

107 BONE-FIRES *original form of bonfires; but there may be a pun on bone-fire as the
bone-ache, venereal disease.* N.

110 PARTY *match.*

118 SQUIRE *pun on the meaning "pander."*

124 WHETHER *whither. In view of l. 128, perhaps a misprint; but cf. "thether"
IV.10.73.*

Kitely. Abroad with Thomas? Oh, that villain dors me.
He hath discovered all unto my wife!
Beast that I was to trust him! Whither, I pray you,
Went she?
   Bridget. I know not, sir.
   Wellbred.   I'll tell you, brother,
Whither I suspect she's gone.
130   *Kitely.*   Whither, good brother?
   Wellbred. To Cob's house, I believe; but keep my counsel.
   Kitely. I will, I will— To Cob's house? Doth she haunt Cob's?
She's gone a'purpose, now, to cuckold me
With that lewd rascal, who, to win her favor,
Hath told her all. (*Exit.*)
135   *Wellbred*   Come, he's once more gone.
Sister, let's lose no time; th'affair is worth it. (*Exeunt.*)

126 DORS *dupes, makes a fool of.*

Act IV Scene 9

[*A street.*]

(*Enter Matthew and Bobadill.*)

Matthew. I wonder, Captain, what they will say of my going
away? Ha?

Bobadill. Why, what should they say, but as of a discreet gentleman?—quick, wary, respectful of nature's fair lineaments: and
5 that's all.

Matthew. Why, so! But what can they say of your beating?

Bobadill. A rude part, a touch with soft wood, a kind of gross
battery used, laid on strongly, borne most patiently: and that's all.

Matthew. Aye, but would any man have offered it in Venice— as you say?   10

Bobadill. Tut, I assure you, no: you shall have there your *nobilis*, your *gentilezza*, come in bravely upon your reverse, stand you close, stand you firm, stand you fair, save your *retricato* with his left leg, come to the *assalto* with the right, thrust with brave steel, defy your base wood! But wherefore do I awake this remembrance? 15 I was fascinated, by Jupiter—fascinated; but I will be unwitched, and revenged by law.

Matthew. Do you hear? Is't not best to get a warrant, and have him arrested and brought before Justice Clement?

Bobadill. It were not amiss; would we had it.   20

(*Enter Brainworm.*)

Matthew. Why, here comes his man; let's speak to him.

Bobadill. Agreed, do you speak.

Matthew. [*To Brainworm.*] Save you, sir.

Brainworm. With all my heart, sir!

Matthew. Sir, there is one Downright hath abused this gentleman 25 and myself, and we determine to make our amends by law; now, if you would do us the favor to procure a warrant to bring him afore your master, you shall be well considered, I assure you, sir.

11 NOBILIS *Bobadill (or the printer) has inadvertently added an English ending to the already plural Italian* nobili, *gentlemen.*

12 GENTILEZZA *nobility.* REVERSE *perhaps a pun on the meaning "adverse change of fortune, defeat."*

13 RETRICATO *Bobadill has entered the realm of pure fantasy; there is no such word.* Rintricato, *entangled, is perhaps just suggestive enough to incite his imagination. As in "reverse," he seems to be thinking of both a fencing stroke and the desperate position (entanglement) from which one is always saved in Venice.*

14 ASSALTO *attack. N.*

15 BASE WOOD *probably a pun on baste-wood, bastinado. N.*

16 FASCINATED *bewitched.*

Brainworm. Sir, you know my service is my living; such favors
30 as these, gotten of my master, is his only preferment; and therefore
you must consider me as I may make benefit of my place.

Matthew. How is that, sir?

Brainworm. Faith, sir, the thing is extraordinary, and the gentleman may be of great accompt; yet, be what he will, if you will lay
35 me down a brace of angels in my hand, you shall have it; otherwise
not.

Matthew. How shall we do, Captain? He asks a brace of angels;
you have no money?

Bobadill. Not a cross, by fortune.

40 *Matthew.* Nor I, as I am a gentleman, but twopence left of my two
shillings in the morning for wine and radish; let's find him some
pawn.

Bobadill. Pawn? We have none to the value of his demand.

Matthew. Oh, yes. I'll pawn this jewel in my ear, and you may
45 pawn your silk stockings, and pull up your boots—they will ne'er
be missed. It must be done, now.

Bobadill. Well, an' there be no remedy— I'll step aside, and pull
'em off.

Matthew. [*To Brainworm.*] Do you hear, sir? We have no store of
50 money at this time, but you shall have good pawns: look you,

29–30 MY SERVICE . . . PREFERMENT *The sense is: my living is made out of being in
the service of a justice; instead of advancement, he gives me warrants and similar
favors when I ask, and I get what I can for them.*

34 ACCOMPT *account.*

35 A . . . ANGELS *The lawful fee seems to have been ten groats; the "clerk" is making
a 500 per cent profit. N.*

39 CROSS, BY FORTUNE *a play on being forced by Fortune to "bear a cross." The pun
on cross as money (a cross was imprinted on the penny and halfpenny) and as
misfortune was common.*

44 JEWEL . . . EAR *Matthew follows the fashion current among courtiers and dashing
gentlemen of wearing one jeweled earring.*

sir, this jewel, and that gentleman's silk stockings; because we would have it dispatched ere we went to our chambers.

Brainworm. I am content, sir; I will get you the warrant presently. What's his name, say you? Downright?

Matthew. Aye, aye, George Downright.   55

Brainworm. What manner of man is he?

Matthew. A tall big man, sir; he goes in a cloak, most commonly, of silk russet laid about with russet lace.

Brainworm. 'Tis very good, sir.

Matthew. Here, sir, here's my jewel.   60

Bobadill. And, here—are stockings.

Brainworm. Well, gentlemen, I'll procure you this warrant presently; but who will you have to serve it?

Matthew. That's true, Captain: that must be considered.

Bobadill. Body o' me, I know not! 'Tis service of danger!   65

Brainworm. Why, you were best to get one o' the varlets o' the City, a sergeant. I'll appoint you one, if you please.

Matthew. Will you, sir? Why, we can wish no better.

Bobadill. We'll leave it to you, sir. (*Exeunt Bobadill and Matthew.*)

Brainworm. This is rare! Now will I go pawn this cloak of the   70
Justice's man's at the broker's, for a varlet's suit, and be the varlet myself; and get either more pawns or more money of Downright, for the arrest. (*Exit.*)

60 jewel.] iewell? Q, Ff.

---

58 SILK . . . LACE. *N.*

66 VARLETS *sergeants-at-mace of the City Counters; minor police officers who made arrests or summoned before the court.*

Act IV Scene 10

[*Outside Cob's house.*]

(*Enter Knowell.*)

Knowell. Oh, here it is; I am glad: I have found it now.
[*He knocks.*] Ho? Who is within, here?
   Tib. [*Within.*] I am within, sir, what's your pleasure?
   Knowell. To know who is within besides yourself.
5   *Tib.* Why, sir, you are no constable, I hope?
   Knowell. Oh! Fear you the constable? Then, I doubt not,
You have some guests within deserve that fear—
I'll fetch him straight.
   Tib. [*Opens the door.*] O' God's name, sir!
   Knowell.   Go to.
Come, tell me, is not young Knowell here?
   Tib.   Young Knowell?
10 I know none such, sir, o' mine honesty!
   Knowell. Your honesty? Dame, it flies too lightly from you;
There is no way but fetch the constable.
   Tib. The constable? The man is mad, I think. (*Claps to the door.*)
          [*Knowell starts to go out.*]
         (*Enter Cash and Dame Kitely.*)
   Cash. [*Knocks.*] Ho, who keeps house here?

6 not,] Q; not. Ff.

---

13 *s.d.* CLAPS . . . KITELY *Tib's door is center stage; Knowell proceeds towards a side
exit, while Cash and Dame Kitely enter from the other side without seeing him.
Until Kitely discovers him at l. 42, Knowell's comments are all to himself.*

Knowell. Oh, this is the female copesmate of my son!   15
Now I shall meet him straight.
    Dame Kitely.   Knock, Thomas, hard.
    Cash. [*Knocking.*] Ho, good wife?
    Tib. [*Opens.*]   Why, what's the matter with you?
    Dame Kitely. Why, woman, grieves it you to ope your door?
Belike you get something to keep it shut.
    Tib. What mean these questions, pray ye?   20
    Dame Kitely. So strange you make it? Is not my husband here?
    Knowell. Her husband!
    Dame Kitely.   My tried husband, Master Kitely.
    Tib. I hope he needs not to be tried here.
    Dame Kitely. No, dame: he does it not for need, but pleasure.
    Tib. Neither for need nor pleasure is he here.   25
    Knowell. This is but a device, to balk me withal.
                  [*Enter Kitely.*]
Soft, who is this? 'Tis not my son, disguised?
    Dame Kitely. O, sir, have I forestalled your honest   *She spies her*
      market?   *husband come*
                                             and runs to him.
Found your close walks? You stand amazed, now,
    do you?
I'faith, I am glad I have smoked you yet at last!   30
What is your jewel, trow? In: come, let's see her;

---

15 COPESMATE *confederate; with a sexual sense derived from the inviting generality
of "cope," encounter. (Cf. Iago's "Where, how, how oft, how long ago, and
when | He hath, and is againe to cope your wife."—O, IV.1.99–100.)*

22 TRIED *choice, select. The word seems to be used for the sake of the pun which
follows.*

23 TRIED *pun on "accosted sexually, solicited." N.*

30 SMOKED *smoked you out: forced you to reveal your haunts.*

31 TROW *here equivalent to "may I ask?"*

Act IV Scene 10

[*To Tib.*] Fetch forth your huswife, dame—
                    [*To Kitely.*] if she be fairer,
In any honest judgment, than myself,
I'll be content with it; but she is change,
35 She feeds you fat, she soothes your appetite,
And you are well! Your wife, an honest woman,
Is meat twice sod to you, sir? O, you treacher!
    Knowell. She cannot counterfeit thus palpably.
    Kitely. Out on thy more than strumpet's impudence!
40 Steal'st thou thus to thy haunts? And have I taken
Thy bawd, and thee, and thy companion,
This hoary-headed lecher, this old goat,   *Pointing to old*
Close at your villainy, and would'st thou 'scuse it   *Knowell.*
With this stale harlot's jest, accusing me?
45 O, old incontinent, dost not thou shame,   *To him.*
When all thy powers' inchastity is spent,
To have a mind so hot? And to entice
And feed th'enticements of a lustful woman?
    Dame Kitely. Out, I defy thee, I, dissembling wretch!
50 *Kitely.* Defy me, strumpet? Ask thy pander, here,   *By Thomas.*
Can he deny it? Or that wicked elder?
    Knowell. Why, hear you, sir.
    Kitely.   Tut, tut, tut: never speak.

46 powers' inchastity] powers inchastitie Q; powers in chastitie F₁. N.

---

32 HUSWIFE *hussy.*
37 SOD *boiled (sod= sodden, past participle of seethe).*
41 BAWD *i.e. Thomas.* COMPANION *four syllables.*
42 N.
43 CLOSE *both "secretly" and "close together." Since Knowell would be half the*
   length of the stage away, Kitely's choice of word contributes to the general madness.
45–47 N.
46 POWERS' INCHASTITY. N.
50 s.d. BY THOMAS [*He says this*] *about, in reference to, Thomas.*

164

Thy guilty conscience will discover thee.

Knowell. What lunacy is this, that haunts this man?

Kitely. Well, goodwife Ba'd, Cob's wife; and you,   55
(Enter Cob.)
That make your husband such a hoddy-doddy;

And you, young apple-squire; and the old cuckold-maker;

I'll ha' you every one before a justice:

Nay, you shall answer it; I charge you, go.

Knowell. Marry, with all my heart, sir: I go willingly.   60

[*Aside.*] Though I do taste this as a trick, put on me

To punish my impertinent search—and justly;

And half forgive my son for the device.

Kitely. [*To Dame Kitely.*] Come, will you go?

Dame Kitely.   Go? To thy shame, believe it.

Cob. Why, what's the matter here? What's here to do?   65

Kitely. O, Cob, art thou come? I have been abused,

And i' thy house. Never was man so wronged!

Cob. 'Slid, in my house? My master Kitely? Who wrongs you

in my house?

Kitely. Marry, young lust in old, and old in young, here: 70

Thy wife's their bawd, here have I taken 'em.

Cob. How? Bawd? Is my house come to that? Am I   He falls upon his

preferred thether? Did I charge you to keep your   wife and beats

her.

doors shut, Is'bel? And do you let 'em lie open for all comers?

Knowell. Friend, know some cause, before thou beat'st thy wife;   75

55 GOODWIFE BA'D *pun on good, bad, and bawd.*

56 HODDY-DODDY *negligible and ridiculous figure (literally, small shell-snail); esp. a cuckold (alluding to the snail's horns).*

57 APPLE-SQUIRE *man kept by the earnings of a prostitute and soliciting customers for her.*

61 TASTE *perceive tentatively, "get the flavor of."*

73 PREFERRED *promoted.* THETHER *thither.*

74 IS'BEL *probably a play on "Jezebel" (Sale), proverbial for treacherous woman.*
     LET . . . COMERS *a double entendre.*

165

This's madness in thee.

    Cob.   Why, is there no cause?

    Kitely. Yes, I'll show cause before the justice, Cob;
Come, let her go with me.

    Cob.   Nay, she shall go.

    Tib. Nay, I will go. I'll see an' you may be allowed to make a
80 bundle o' hemp o' your right and lawful wife thus, at every
cuckoldly knave's pleasure. Why do you not go?

    Kitely. A bitter quean. Come, we'll ha' you tamed. (*Exeunt.*)

80 HEMP *The cut stems of the hemp plant were beaten to detach the fiber, used in rope.*
82 QUEAN *harlot; disyllabic.*

Act IV Scene 11

[*A street.*]

(*Enter Brainworm alone* [*disguised as a sergeant*].)

Brainworm. Well, of all my disguises yet, now am I most like
myself, being in this sergeant's gown. A man of my present profession never counterfeits, till he lays hold upon a debtor and says he
'rests him, for then he brings him to all manner of unrest. A kind of
5 little kings we are, bearing the diminutive of a mace, made like a
young artichoke, that always carries pepper and salt in itself. Well,

5 MACE *a City sergeant's staff of office; heavy club with a metal head.*
6 ARTICHOKE *The mace's metal head was composed of decorative vertical leaves
radiating from the central staff.* PEPPER AND SALT *a play on the "mace" always
carried by the sergeant as being spice.*

I know not what danger I undergo by this exploit; pray Heaven I come well off.

(*Enter Bobadill and Matthew.*)

Matthew. See, I think yonder is the varlet, by his gown.

Bobadill. Let's go in quest of him.   10

Matthew. Save you, friend, are not you here by appointment of Justice Clement's man?

Brainworm. Yes, an't please you, sir: he told me two gentlemen had willed him to procure a warrant from his master (which I have about me) to be served on one Downright.   15

Matthew. It is honestly done of you both; and see where the party comes you must arrest: serve it upon him, quickly, afore he be aware—

(*Enter Stephen [in Downright's cloak].*)

Bobadill. Bear back, Master Matthew.

Brainworm. Master Downright, I arrest you i' the Queen's name,   20
and must carry you afore a justice, by virtue of this warrant.

Stephen. Me, friend? I am no Downright, I. I am Master Stephen; you do not well to arrest me, I tell you, truly: I am in nobody's bonds nor books, I would you should know it. A plague on you heartily, for making me thus afraid afore my time.   25

Brainworm. Why, now, are you deceived, gentlemen?

Bobadill. He wears such a cloak, and that deceived us. But see, here a comes, indeed! This is he, officer.

(*Enter Downright.*)

Downright. [*To Stephen.*] Why, how now, Signior Gull! Are you turned filcher of late? Come, deliver my cloak.   30

Stephen. Your cloak, sir? I bought it even now, in open market.

Brainworm. Master Downright, I have a warrant I must serve upon you, procured by these two gentlemen.

Downright. These gentlemen? These rascals?

12 man?] man. F₁.
24 books, I would] Q; books, I, would F₁.

35   *Brainworm.* Keep the peace, I charge you in her Majesty's name.

Downright. I obey thee. What must I do, officer?

Brainworm. Go before Master Justice Clement, to answer what they can object against you, sir. I will use you kindly, sir.

Matthew. Come, let's before, and make the justice, Captain—

40   *Bobadill.* The varlet's a tall man! Afore heaven! (*Exeunt Bobadill and Matthew.*)

Downright. [*To Stephen.*] Gull, you'll gi' me my cloak?

Stephen. Sir, I bought it, and I'll keep it.

Downright. You will.

Stephen. Aye, that I will.

45   *Downright.* [*Gives Brainworm money.*] Officer, there's thy fee, arrest him.

Brainworm. Master Stephen, I must arrest you.

Stephen. Arrest me! I scorn it. There, take your cloak, I'll none on't.

50   *Downright.* Nay, that shall not serve your turn now, sir. Officer, I'll go with thee to the justice's; bring him along.

Stephen. Why, is not here your cloak? What would you have?

Downright. I'll ha' you answer it, sir.

Brainworm. [*To Downright.*] Sir, I'll take your word, and this

55   gentleman's too, for his appearance.

Downright. I'll ha' no words taken. Bring him along.

Brainworm. Sir, I may choose to do that: I may take bail.

Downright. 'Tis true, you may take bail, and choose—at another time: but you shall not now, varlet. Bring him along, or I'll swinge

60   you.

Brainworm. Sir, I pity the gentleman's case. Here's your money again.

40 s.d. before 40 in Q.

---

39 MAKE *win over.*

53 ANSWER *give satisfaction for.*

Downright. 'Sdeynes, tell not me of my money, bring him away,
I say.

Brainworm. I warrant you he will go with you of himself, sir.   65

Downright. Yet more ado?

Brainworm. [*Aside.*] I have made a fair mash on't.

Stephen. Must I go?

Brainworm. I know no remedy, Master Stephen.

Downright. [*To Stephen.*] Come along, afore me, here. I do not   70
love your hanging look behind.

Stephen. Why, sir. I hope you cannot hang me for it.—Can he,
fellow?

Brainworm. I think not, sir. It is but a whipping matter, sure!

Stephen. Why, then, let him do his worst, I am resolute. [*Exeunt.*]   75

Act V Scene 1

[*A room in Justice Clement's house.*]

Clement, Knowell, Kitely, Dame Kitely, Tib, Cash, Cob, Servants.

Clement. Nay, but stay, stay, give me leave: [*To servant.*] my chair, sirrah. You, Master Knowell, say you went thither to meet your son.

Knowell. Aye, sir.

5   *Clement.* But who directed you thither?

Knowell. That did mine own man, sir.

Clement. Where is he?

Knowell. Nay, I know not, now; I left him with your clerk, and appointed him to stay here for me.

10   *Clement.* My clerk! About what time was this?

Knowell. Marry, between one and two, as I take it.

Clement. And what time came my man with the false message to you, Master Kitely?

4 sir.] sir ? Q, F₁.

---

1 CHAIR *an uncommon article of furniture at this time; only men of great dignity or wealth appear to have had them for personal use. Clement evidently uses his as judgment seat. It would probably be an oak box surmounted by arms and a high back, a massive object from which a man might well have to be "helped off" (see 3.32 below).*

Kitely. After two, sir.

Clement. Very good; but, Mistress Kitely, how that you were at   15
Cob's? Ha?

Dame Kitely. An' please you, sir, I'll tell you: my brother Wellbred
told me that Cob's house was a suspected place—

Clement. So it appears, methinks: but, on.

Dame Kitely. And that my husband used thither, daily.   20

Clement. No matter, so he used himself well, mistress.

Dame Kitely. True, sir, but you know what grows by such haunts,
oftentimes.

Clement. I see, rank fruits of a jealous brain, Mistress Kitely;
but did you find your husband there, in that case, as you suspected?   25

Kitely. I found her there, sir.

Clement. Did you so? That alters the case. Who gave you knowledge of your wife's being there?

Kitely. Marry, that did my brother Wellbred.

Clement. How? Wellbred first tell her? Then tell you, after?   30
Where is Wellbred?

Kitely. Gone with my sister, sir, I know not whither.

Clement. Why, this is a mere trick, a device; you are gulled in this
most grossly, all! Alas, poor wench, wert thou beaten for this?

Tib. Yes, most pitifully, an't please you.   35

Cob. And worthily, I hope: if it shall prove so.

Clement. Aye, that's like, and a piece of a sentence. [*Enter First
Servant.*] How now, sir, what's the matter?

First Servant. Sir, there's a gentleman i' the court without desires
to speak with your Worship.   40

Clement. A gentleman? What's he?

First Servant. A soldier, sir, he says.

Clement. A soldier? Take down my armor, my   [*He takes off his
sword, quickly: a soldier speak with me! [*To servants.*]   Justice's cap.*]
                                                          *He arms him-
                                                          self.*

37 PIECE . . . SENTENCE *bit of a wise utterance: a scrap of wisdom.*
43–V.2.5. N.

171

45 Why, when, knaves? Come on, come on, hold my cap there, so;
give me my gorget, my sword— [*To the company.*] Stand by, I will
end your matters anon—[*To First Servant.*] Let the soldier enter:
now, sir, what ha' you to say to me?

(*Enter Bobadill and Matthew.*) [*Exit First Servant.*]

46 GORGET *piece of armor to protect the throat.*

Act V Scene 2

Bobadill. By your Worship's favor—
Clement. [*To Matthew.*] Nay, keep out, sir, I know not your pretense; [*To Bobadill.*] you send me word, sir, you are a soldier: why,
sir, you shall be answered here, here be them have been amongst
5 soldiers. Sir, your pleasure.
Bobadill. Faith, sir, so it is, this gentleman and myself have been
most uncivilly wronged, and beaten, by one Downright, a coarse
fellow about the town, here; and for mine own part, I protest,
being a man in no sort given to this filthy humor of quarreling, he
10 hath assaulted me in the way of my peace; despoiled me of mine
honor; disarmed me of my weapons; and rudely laid me along
in the open streets: when I not so much as once offered to resist
him.
Clement. Oh, God's precious! Is this the soldier? [*To servants.*]
15 Here, take my armor off quickly, 'twill make him swoon, I fear;
he is not fit to look on 't that will put up a blow.
Matthew. [*From the doorway.*] An't please your Worship, he was
bound to the peace.

2–3 PRETENSE *claim to attention.*

Clement. Why, and he were, his hands were not bound, were
they? 20

[*Enter First Servant.*]

First Servant. There's one of the varlets of the City, sir, has brought
two gentlemen here, one upon your Worship's warrant.

Clement. My warrant?

First Servant. Yes, sir. The officer says, procured by these two.

Clement. Bid him come in. [*To servants.*] Set by this [*Exit First
Servant.*] (*Enter* 25
picture. What, Mr. Downright! Are you brought at *Brainworm*
Mr. Freshwater's suit, here? *with Downright
and Stephen.*)

26 PICTURE *Bobadill, who is a soldier only in appearance.*
27 MR. FRESHWATER'S *i.e. Bobadill's. A freshwater soldier was one who had seen no
action (by analogy with freshwater sailor, one who has never been on the sea);
the title's implication is stated plainly by Florio (1598): "a goodly, great milk-
sop" (Cited F &H).*

Act V Scene 3

Downright. I'faith, sir. [*Indicates Stephen.*] And here's another
brought at my suit.

Clement. [*To Stephen.*] What are you, sir?

Stephen. A gentleman, sir. [*He sees Knowell.*] Oh, uncle!

Clement. Uncle? Who? Master Knowell? 5

Knowell. Aye, sir! This is a wise kinsman of mine.

Stephen. God's my witness, uncle, I am wronged here mon-
strously, he charges me with stealing of his cloak, and would I
might never stir if I did not find it in the street by chance.

Downright. Oh, did you find it, now? You said you bought it, 10
erewhile.

Stephen. And you said I stole it; nay, now my uncle is here, I'll
do well enough with you.

Clement. Well, let this breathe a while; [*To Bobadill and Matthew.*]
15 you, that have cause to complain, there, stand forth: had you my
warrant for this gentleman's apprehension?

Bobadill. Aye, an't please your Worship.

Clement. Nay, do not speak in passion so; where had you it?

Bobadill. Of your clerk, sir.

20 *Clement.* That's well! An' my clerk can make warrants, and my
hand not at 'em! Where is the warrant? [*To Brainworm.*] Officer,
have you it?

Brainworm. No, sir, your Worship's man, Master Formal, bid me
do it for these gentlemen, and he would be my discharge.

25 *Clement.* Why, Master Downright, are you such a novice, to be
served, and never see the warrant?

Downright. Sir. He did not serve it on me.

Clement. No? How then?

Downright. Marry, sir, he came to me, and said he must serve it,
30 and he would use me kindly, and so—

Clement. Oh, God's pity, was it so, sir? He must serve it? [*To
servants.*] Give me my long-sword there, and help me off; so. Come
on, sir varlet, I must cut off your legs, sirrah: [*Brain-*   He flourishes
worm falls on his knees.] nay, stand up, I'll use you   over him with his
long-sword.
35 kindly; I must cut off your legs, I say.

Brainworm. O, good sir, I beseech you; nay, good Master Justice.

Clement. I must do it; there is no remedy. I must cut off your
legs, sirrah, I must cut off your ears, you rascal, I must do it; I
must cut off your nose, I must cut off your head.

40 *Brainworm.* O, good your Worship!

19 sir.] Q, F₂; sir ? F₁.

---

14 BREATHE *have a rest.*
18 NAY . . . SO *perhaps meaning "do not speak so pathetically"; more likely, a piece
of sarcasm directed at Bobadill's milk-and-water reply.*
24 BE MY DISCHARGE *take the responsibility.*

Clement. Well, rise; how dost thou do, now? Dost thou feel thyself well? Hast thou no harm?

Brainworm. No, I thank your good Worship, sir.

Clement. Why, so! I said I must cut off thy legs, and I must cut off thy arms, and I must cut off thy head; but I did not do it: so you said you must serve this gentleman with my warrant, but you did not serve him. You knave, you slave, you rogue, do you say you must? [*To servant.*] Sirrah, away with him, to the jail. [*To Brainworm.*] I'll teach you a trick for your *must*, sir.

Brainworm. Good sir, I beseech you, be good to me.

Clement. Tell him he shall to the jail—away with him, I say.

Brainworm. Nay, sir, if you will commit me, it shall be for committing more than this: I will not lose by my travail any grain of my fame, certain. [*He throws off his disguise.*]

Clement. How is this!

Knowell. My man, Brainworm!

Stephen. Oh, yes, uncle. Brainworm has been with my cousin Edward and I all this day.

Clement. I told you all there was some device!

Brainworm. Nay, excellent Justice, since I have laid myself thus open to you, now stand strong for me: both with your sword, and your balance.

Clement. Body o' me, a merry knave! [*To servants.*] Give me a

---

53 LOSE . . . TRAVAIL *either "lose by my own act (work)" or "lose by omitting any effort of mine."*

57–58 WITH . . . I *an acceptable construction in Jonson's time.*

60 JUSTICE *pun on judge's title and name of goddess; the latter meaning becomes evident in ll. 61–62.*

60–61 LAID . . . OPEN *1. revealed myself; 2. made myself vulnerable.*

61–62 SWORD . . . BALANCE *the traditional symbols of the goddess Justice, which she holds in her hands. The joke has additional point because Clement has just threatened Brainworm with his sword.*

bowl of sack!—If he belong to you, Master Knowell, I bespeak your
65 patience.

Brainworm. That is it I have most need of. [To Knowell.] Sir, if
you'll pardon me only, I'll glory in all the rest of my exploits.

Knowell. Sir, you know I love not to have my favors come hard
from me. You have your pardon: though I suspect you shrewdly
70 for being of counsel with my son against me.

Brainworm. Yes, faith, I have, sir; though you retained me doubly
this morning for yourself: first, as Brainworm; after, as Fitzsword.
I was your reformed soldier, sir. 'Twas I sent you to Cob's, upon the
errand without end.

75 Knowell. Is it possible! Or that thou should'st disguise thy
language so, as I should not know thee?

Brainworm. O, sir, this has been the day of my metamorphosis!
It is not that shape alone that I have run through, today. I brought
this gentleman, Master Kitely, a message too, in the form of Master
80 Justice's man, here, to draw him out o' the way, as well as your
Worship—while Master Wellbred might make a conveyance of
Mistress Bridget to my young master.

Kitely. How! My sister stol'n away?

Knowell. My son is not married, I hope!

85 Brainworm. Faith, sir, they are both as sure as love, a priest, and
three thousand pound (which is her portion) can make 'em: and
by this time are ready to bespeak their wedding supper at The
Windmill, except some friend here prevent 'em, and invite 'em
home.

64 BOWL shallow cup.
71 RETAINED Brainworm plays on the legal meaning of "counsel" (l. 70).
73 REFORMED discharged (see fn. to III.5.14).
80 HERE refers to Master Justice.
81 MAKE A CONVEYANCE legal term for transferring property in due form; Brainworm continues the wordplay from l. 71.
85 SURE securely joined.
88 PREVENT forestall.

Clement. Marry, that will I—I thank thee for putting me in mind 90
on't. [*To Second Servant.*] Sirrah, go you and fetch 'em hither, upon
my warrant. [*Exit Second Servant.*] Neither's friends have cause to be
sorry, if I know the young couple aright. [*To Brainworm.*] Here, I
drink to thee, for thy good news. But, I pray thee, what hast thou
done with my man Formal? 95

Brainworm. Faith, sir, after some ceremony past—as making him
drunk, first with story, and then with wine (but all in kindness),
and stripping him to his shirt—I left him in that cool vein, departed,
sold your Worship's warrant to these two, pawned his livery for
that varlet's gown to serve it in; and thus have brought myself, 100
by my activity, to your Worship's consideration.

Clement. And I will consider thee in another cup of sack. Here's
to thee!—Which having drunk off, this is my sentence: Pledge me.
Thou hast done or assisted to nothing, in my judgment, but deserves
to be pardoned for the wit of the offense. If thy master, or any man 105
here, be angry with thee, I shall suspect his ingine while I know him
for't. [*A tumult without.*] How now? What noise is that?

(*Enter [First] Servant, then Formal [in a suit of armor].*)

First Servant. Sir, it is Roger come home.

Clement. Bring him in, bring him in. —What! drunk in arms
against me? Your reason, your reason for this? 110

95 Formal ?] Formal Ff.

---

106 INGINE *native wit (cf. ingenuity).*
106–07 I . . . FOR'T *probably "I shall suspect . . . for the rest of our acquaintance-*
ship, because he is angry with you"; but perhaps "I shall suspect . . . as long as I
know him to be angry."
109 *in arms. N.*

Act V Scene 4

Formal. I beseech your Worship to pardon me: I *To them.* happened into ill company by chance, that cast me into a sleep, and stripped me of all my clothes—

Clement. Well, tell him I am Justice Clement, and do pardon him;

5 but what is this to your armor? What may that signify?

Formal. And't please you, sir, it hung up i' the room where I was stripped; and I borrowed it of one o' the drawers, to come home in, because I was loth to do penance through the street i' my shirt.

(Enter Edward, Wellbred, Bridget.)

Clement. Well, stand by a while. Who be these? Oh, the young

10 company, welcome, welcome. Gi' you joy. Nay, Mistress Bridget, blush not; you are not so fresh a bride but the news of it is come hither afore you. Master Bridegroom, I ha' made your peace, give me your hand; so will I for all the rest, ere you forsake my roof.

7 DRAWERS *liquor-drawers: tapsters or waiters.*
13 SO WILL I *i.e. make your peace.*

Act V Scene 5

[Edward, Well-bred, Bridget go] to them.

Edward. We are the more bound to your humanity, sir.

Clement. [*Indicates Bobadill and Matthew.*] Only these two have so little of man in 'em, they are not part of my care.

Wellbred. Yes, sir, let me pray you for this gentleman; he belongs

5 to my sister, the bride.

4 GENTLEMAN *Matthew.*

Clement. In what place, sir?

Wellbred. Of her delight, sir, below the stairs, and in public: her poet, sir.

Clement. A poet? I will challenge him myself, presently, at *extempore.*   10

> "Mount up thy Phlegon Muse, and testify
> How Saturn, sitting in an ebon cloud,
> Disrobed his podex white as ivory,
> And through the welkin thundered all aloud."

Wellbred. He is not for *extempore,* sir. He is all for the pocket-   15
muse; please you command a sight of it.

Clement. Yes, yes, search him for a taste of his vein.

[*The servants search Matthew, who resists.*]

Wellbred. [*To Matthew.*] You must not deny the Queen's justice, sir, under a writ of rebellion.

[*They produce Matthew's papers.*]

Clement. What! All this verse? Body o' me, he carries a whole   20

---

6 PLACE *position, capacity; Wellbred puns on the meaning "location."*

7 BELOW THE STAIRS *in the servants' hall: i.e. as a servant; but like the place "of her delight," suggestive of a* double entendre.

11 MOUNT UP *either 1. "mount upon" or 2. "cause to mount upward."* PHLEGON *either the Greek adjective "burning" (in conjunction with meaning 2. of "mount up"), or one of the horses of the Sun—perhaps a likely steed for a Muse because of the connection with Apollo. N.*

12–14 N.

13 PODEX *rump.* Saturni podex *was proverbial for anything or anyone decrepit, worn out, or senseless (Erasmus, III.3.58; cited HS).*

17 SEARCH . . . VEIN *a medical pun: to "search" was to probe or examine; to "taste the vein," to feel the pulse.*

19 UNDER *under penalty of.* WRIT OF REBELLION *issued for the arrest, as a rebel, of one who had failed to present himself in court even though summoned by proclamation.*

realm, a commonwealth of paper, in's hose! [*A servant brings him the papers.*] Let's see some of his subjects! [*He reads.*]

> "Unto the boundless ocean of thy face,
>> Runs this poor river, charged with streams of eyes."

25 How? This is stol'n!

Edward. A parody! A parody! With a kind of miraculous gift to make it absurder than it was.

Clement. Is all the rest of this batch? Bring me a torch; lay it together, and give fire. Cleanse the air. [*The papers are set on fire.*]
30 Here was enough to have infected the whole city, if it had not been taken in time! See, see, how our poet's glory shines! Brighter and brighter! Still it increases! Oh, now it's at the highest; and now it declines as fast. You may see. *Sic transit gloria mundi.*

Knowell. There's an emblem for you, son, and your studies!

35 *Clement.* Nay, no speech or act of mine be drawn against such as profess it worthily. They are not born every year, as an alderman. There goes more to the making of a good poet, than a sheriff, Mr. Kitely. You look upon me! Though I live i' the city here amongst

---

21 REALM *ream. Since the spelling "ream" was a common variant of "realm" (short vowel), the word "ream (of paper)" (long vowel) developed by analogy the occasional variant spelling "realm" (as here). The ream/realm pun was popular. "Subjects" in l. 22 continues the pun.*

23–24 *a burlesque on the opening lines of Samuel Daniel's sonnet sequence, "To Delia" (1592): "Unto the boundless ocean of thy beauty, / Runs this poor river, charged with streams of zeal."*

28 OF THIS BATCH *of this same quality. For the metaphor, see fn. to I.2.77.*

29–31 *Clement pretends to be protecting the city against the plague by the oft-used and highly regarded technique of burning unhealthy rubbish and "disinfecting the air."*

33 AS FAST *as fast as may be: immediately.* SIC . . . MUNDI *So passes the glory of the world.*

35 DRAWN *1. brought forward, adduced; 2. construed.*

36 THEY . . . ALDERMAN *a favorite saying of Jonson's, adapted from a Latin couplet.* N.

you, I will do more reverence to him, when I meet him, than I will
to the Mayor, out of his year. But these paper-peddlers! These ink-   40
dabblers! They cannot expect reprehension, or reproach. They have
it with the fact.

Edward. Sir, you have saved me the labor of a defense.

Clement. It shall be discourse for supper, between your father and
me, if he dare undertake me. But, to dispatch away these: [*To Boba-*   45
dill and Matthew.] you sign o' the Soldier, and picture o' the Poet
(but both so false, I will not ha' you hanged out at my door till
midnight), while we are at supper, you two shall penitently fast it
out in my court, without; and, if you will, you may pray there that
we may be so merry within as to forgive or forget you, when we   50
come out. [*Indicates Formal.*] Here's a third, because we tender your
safety, shall watch you; he is provided for the purpose. [*To Formal.*]
Look to your charge, sir.

Stephen. And what shall I do?

Clement. Oh! I had lost a sheep, an' he had not bleated! Why,   55
sir, you shall give Mr. Downright his cloak: and I will entreat him
to take it. A trencher and a napkin you shall have, i' the buttery,
and keep Cob and his wife company, here; whom I will entreat

---

40 OUT . . . YEAR *the Mayor's term of office is one year.*

41 EXPECT *?wait for; this would seem to be sarcasm. Just possibly it is a misprint for
except: object to, protest against. The context seems to demand some such word as
"escape," which is in fact the sense of the Latin passage Jonson has in mind (see
N. to l. 42).*

42 WITH THE FACT *in the deed itself. N.*

46 SIGN, PICTURE *Clement likens the two to badly executed shop or tavern signs.*

48 MIDNIGHT *when it is too dark for you to be seen.*

51 TENDER *value, cherish.*

52 PROVIDED *furnished as a watchman, with his brown bill.*

57 BUTTERY *provision room; a kind of large-scale pantry, where servants ate and
drank.*

58 HERE *refers to "Cob . . . wife."*

first to be reconciled, and you to endeavor with your wit to keep
60 'em so.

    Stephen. I'll do my best.

    Cob. Why, now I see thou art honest, Tib, I receive thee as my
dear and mortal wife again.

    Tib. And I you, as my loving and obedient husband.

65   *Clement.* Good complement! It will be their bridal night, too.
They are married anew. Come, I conjure the rest to put off all discontent. You, Mr. Downright, your anger; you, Master Knowell,
your cares; Master Kitely and his wife, their jealousy.
For, I must tell you both, while that is fed,
70 Horns i' the mind are worse than o' the head.

    Kitely. Sir, thus they go from me— [*He embraces his wife.*]
                                Kiss me, sweetheart.

        See, what a drive of horns fly in the air,
        Winged with my cleansèd and my credulous breath!
        Watch 'em, suspicious eyes, watch where they fall.
75   See, see! On heads that think th'have none at all!
        Oh, what a plentous world of this will come!
        When air rains horns, all may be sure of some.
I ha' learned so much verse out of a jealous man's part in a play.

    Clement. 'Tis well, 'tis well! This night we'll dedicate
80 To friendship, love, and laughter. Master Bridegroom,
Take your bride, and lead; every one, a fellow.

---

77 some] Q, F$_2$; fame F$_1$.

---

63 MORTAL *malapropism for moral; perhaps with pun on "*mort,*" slang for harlot,
ordinarily used for the mistress of a beggar or thief.*

65 COMPLEMENT *either* 1. *consummation, completion; or* 2. *ceremony, formal polite-
ness; probably both.*

81 EVERY . . . FELLOW *parallel with the first clause;* "*take*" *is understood.* FELLOW
partner.

Here is my mistress—Brainworm! to whom all my addresses of courtship shall have their reference. Whose adventures this day, when our grandchildren shall hear to be made a fable, I doubt not but it shall find both spectators, and applause.

85 APPLAUSE *Clement's last sentence is an invitation to the audience to applaud, as at the end of* EO, V, *et al. The entire cast is on stage, and remains there to take its bows.*

THE END.

Notes

CAMDEN *William Camden (1551–1623), noted English antiquary and historian, author of two important and highly regarded works of the time:* Britannia *(1586), a description of customs and antiquities of the British Isles, and* Annales rerum . . . regnante Elizabetha *(London, 1615 and 1627), a history of the reign of Queen Elizabeth. Jonson was a student of his at the Westminster School, of which Camden later became headmaster; indeed, Camden is said to have financed Jonson's studies there. Jonson conceived of his teacher as having determined his own dedication to the intellectual life, and wrote of him in the* Epigrams *as "Camden! . . . to whom I owe / All that I am in arts, all that I know" (Epigram XIV). Camden became the model, for Jonson, of the truly learned man—Jonson's own ideal.*

CLARENTIAUX *The title of the second highest officer of the Heralds' College, who has authority over all matters of heraldry south of the River Trent (from Latin "Clarentia", the dukedom of Clarence, named from Clare in Suffolk). Camden had been appointed to this office, which obviously demanded a minute knowledge of regional history, in 1597.*

3 *Plays were at this time considered entertainment rather than "works", and Jonson incurred much ridicule for publishing the collection in which the revised EI appeared. He may well have this low current opinion of stage plays at heart in his rather defensive opening, though his own firm conviction that the playwright is a poet leads him to speak of poetry in general. With what must have been a certain amount of belligerence, he dignified every one of the plays in the Folio with a separate dedication; it is very possible that he established the practice of dedicating plays (D. Nichol Smith, Shakespeare's England, II.211; cited HS).*

PROLOGUE

4 ILL CUSTOMS *The romantic plays of the time, wide-ranging and melodramatic, were the very opposite of the classical drama which Jonson felt should be the playwright's model. The Prologue has been seen as an attack on Shakespeare, chief exponent of the romantic drama; he is certainly implicated, and his huge success may have given stimulus to Jonson's one-man crusade for reform, but Jonson's estimate of Shakespeare's worth as playwright and man was ultimately as high as that of present-day criticism (see his " To the Memory of . . . Mr. William Shakespeare . . . ,"* 1623, *and his comments in the* Discoveries, 647*ff.). Jonson's attacks on the stage's "ill customs" echoed the opinions of classically oriented critics at home and abroad; the "abuses" he cites were general in contemporary English and European drama.*

7–9 *The reference may or may not be pointed at Shakespeare's* Winter's Tale *(1611) or* Pericles *(?1608); literary criticism had been complaining for years about Elizabethan dramatists' cavalier treatment of the unity of time. Of course Jonson knew Sidney's famous take-off on the typical romantic plot some twenty years before* (Defence of Poesie, 1595): *" ordinary it is, that two young Princes fall in love, after many traverses she is got with child, delivered of a fair boy: he is lost, groweth a man, falleth in love, and is ready to get another child, and all this in two hours space . . ." Even this was only a reworking of a version seventeen years earlier by George Whetstone (Epistle printed with* Promos and Cassandra, 1578): *" in three hours runs he through the world: marries, gets children, makes children men, men to conquer kingdoms . . ."*
    It is likely that Jonson based his lines directly on the most recent statement of this kind in English, Shelton's translation of Don Quixote *(1612): " What greater absurdity can [there] be . . . than to see a child come out in the first scene of the first act in his swaddling clouts, and issue in the second already grown a man, yea, a bearded man ?" (Pt. i, Bk. iv, ch. 21; cited Carter, but not in this translation, so the verbal parallel is not very evident.)*

9 WITH . . . SWORDS *Cf. Sidney: " two armies fly in, represented with four swords and bucklers . . . ," and Shakespeare's* Henry V: *" And so our scene must to the battle fly; | Where, O for pity! we shall much disgrace | With four or five most vile and ragged foils, | . . . | The name of Agincourt." (IV, Prol. by Chorus, ll. 48–52).*

11 JARS *This allusion to the* Wars of the Roses *is almost certainly a hit at Shakespeare's cycle of plays on the subject:* Henry VI, Richard III, Richard II, *and* Henry IV *were all acted between 1592 and 1600.*

14 *For Jonson's aims, and the appreciation accorded his achievement, cf. Francis Beaumont's tribute (prefixed to* Volpone, *1607):*

> *I would have shown*
> *To all the world, the art, which thou alone*
> *Hast taught our tongue, the rules of time, of place,*
> *And other rites, delivered with the grace*
> *Of comic style, which only, is far more*
> *Than any English stage hath known before.*

15–16 CHORUS . . . DOWN *The Chorus was a single actor, one of whose functions was to advise the audience of major changes in locale.* Henry V *(1598–99) employs such a speaker to "waft" the audience from England to France, and has often been thought the target of Jonson's sarcasm; but this was actually a very modest trip compared to that in, say, Heywood's* The Four Prentises of London *(?ca. 1600) to France, Italy, and Ireland, "With the Conquest of Jerusalem" at the end; or in* The Travels of the Three English Brothers, *"the action of which ranges widely over the inhabited world" (Chambers, III.117–18), in which Fame hopefully nourishes the audience's impressions of the stage: "Think this England, this Spain, this Persia." Cf. Cervantes: "I myself have seen comedies whose first act began in Europe, the second in Asia, and the third ended in Africa . . ." (loc. cit.).*

CREAKING THRONE *Prophets, goddesses, and their ilk were apt to appear or vanish in thrones let down from above the stage by a system of ropes and pulleys. One descended to music to herald the vision of heaven in* Dr. Faustus *(Chambers, III.77, n.3); when in Act IV of* The Tempest *"Juno descends," she very likely uses this conveyance.*

17 SQUIB *Squibs were useful for lightning, and for that reason are mentioned in close conjunction with the storm sound effects; but they were also prominent in supernatural events, and so follow easily upon the mention of the throne (e.g. in Heywood's* The Silver Age, *1612, IV: "Thunder, lightnings, Jupiter descends in his majesty . . ." "As he toucheth the bed it fires, and all flies up"; quoted Chambers, III.110, n.1).*

21-24 *Jonson's definition of Comedy alternates Cicero (ll. 21, 23) and Aristotle (ll. 22, 24). According to Cicero, "Comedy is an imitation of life, a mirror of custom ..."; in Aristotle's terms, "Comedy ... is a representaton of inferior people, not indeed in the full sense of the word bad, but the laughable is a species of the base or ugly. It consists in some blunder or ugliness that does not cause pain or disaster ..." (Poetics V. 1-2). Cicero's definition also occurs in the section of* Don Quixote *cited before: "the comedy, as Tully affirms, ought to be a mirror of man's life, a pattern of manners, and an image of truth ..."*

PERSONS

JUSTICE CLEMENT *With his character as a "mad, merry old fellow" (III.5.44), cf. Justice Shallow (2 H IV, III.2.16-17): "I was once of Clement's Inn; where (I think) they will talk of mad Shallow yet."*

WATER-BEARER *Before all London houses had their own water, a system of pipes brought it from the Thames or suburban streams to conduits (large stone cisterns with spigots), erected by charitable citizens and by the city in strategic locations. Hired water-bearers then carried it from the conduits to individual houses in their tankards—wooden containers tapering toward the top, which held about three gallons.*

PAUL'S MAN *"The aisles [of St. Paul's] ... were the recognized haunts of loiterers, needy adventurers, and broken-down gallants" (Kingsford, II.349). They were used regularly as a place to transact business, both legitimate and illegal: "The south alley for Popery and usury, the north for simony, and the horse fair in the midst for all kinds of ... brawlings, murders, conspiracies ..." (Pilkington, 1561; quoted Kingsford, II.316). The middle aisle, being the busiest, was best for chance meetings, the latest news, and possible invitations to dinner.*

Act I, Scene 1

15-19 *An imitation of a passage in Thomas Kyd's popular melodrama,* The Spanish Tragedy *(V.1.67-70):*
> *When I was young I gave my mind*
> *And 'plied myself to fruitless poetry:*
> *Which though it profit the professor naught,*
> *Yet is it passing pleasing to the world.*

Since The Spanish Tragedy *provided a never-ending stimulus to ridicule for authors of the day, perhaps Knowell's easily recognized speech raised a laugh and so undercut the dignity of his objections. Jonson himself had some years before acted the leading role of Hieronimo (who speaks these lines) in the* Tragedy; *this must have increased the joke for those in the know.*

27–28 HOW DO *Stephen would seem not to merit in this case the indulgent contempt of HS, who call this form a "vulgarism"; cf. its use by at least two distinctly non-vulgar writers, John Philpot* (Examinations and Writings, 1553: *"He ... do confess"—p. 333, 1842 ed.) and William Cuningham* (The Cosmographical Glass, 1559: *"Geography do delineate ..."—p. 6). Pepys still takes it for granted in 1610: "Sir Arthur Haselrigge do not yet appear in the House"* (Diary, 1875 ed., I.62).

32 BOOK ... HUNTING *Such books enjoyed tremendous popularity at the time; at least 12 appeared between 1575 and 1620, some reprinted two and three times. They were practical manuals setting forth the equipment and techniques necessary for these exceedingly fashionable and exceedingly expensive sports.* The Gentleman's Academy *(a 1595 reissue of* The Book of St. Albans, 1486*) offers 39 different remedies for as many diseases of hawks, besides instruction on the best type of cage, the correct manner of taming, proper care during moulting, training for the hunt, appropriate rewards, suitable time and amount of feeding, and all other complicated details incident to what was indeed a "science."*

40–41 HAWKING ... LANGUAGES *Each action, attribute, and physical part of the hawk, for example, had its technical appellation.* The Gentleman's Academy *contains a nine-and-one-half-page section entitled "The kindly terms that belong to hawks" which includes seven paragraphs on the names of the feathers, besides a shorter section on "The manner to speak of hawks from an egg to they be able to be taken."*

Stephen's hoped-for accomplishments in "languages" and "the sciences" parody the two great traditional divisions of learning which together subsumed the seven liberal arts: readings in classical language (the "trivium": logic, rhetoric, grammar) and practical sciences (the "quadrivium": arithmetic, music—regarded as a branch of mathematics—geometry, astronomy). In the sixteenth and seventeenth centuries the liberal arts became the nucleus of an expanded concept of a broad liberal education in science and humanities. This ideal of education, in which Jonson himself was much interested, is travestied

by Stephen's ideals as Jonson believed it was by the aspirations of most contemporary youths. Cf. NI, where the typical young man's education for life
is seen as a corrupt inversion of real learning (I.3.81–85):

> These are the arts,
> Or seven liberal deadly sciences
> Of Pagery, or rather Paganism,
> As the tides run. To which, if he apply him,
> He may, perhaps, take a degree at Tyburn . . .

83–86 The sentiment is Seneca's (Epistle xliv) by way of Juvenal (Satire VIII,
"On Gentility"): "What avail your pedigrees? . . . so that we may admire
you, not yours, provide something of your own which I may inscribe among
your titles" (ll. 1, 68–69). Characteristically, Jonson also transposes into
l. 85 an image on the same subject but from a quite different context: "In a
flying chariot, fat Lateranus is swept past the dust and bones of his ancestors"
(Juvenal, 146–47).

Act I, Scene 2

115–27 This speech owes much to the opening soliloquy of the foster father in
Terence's Adelphoi: "I overlook things—I do not hold it necessary to manage
everything by my authority, . . . things that other sons do secretly from their
fathers, that youth does . . . I believe that to restrain children by modesty and
kindness is more effective than to do it by fear. . . . This is the difference
between a father and a slave-owner. . . . He who does his duty compelled by
punishment trembles just so long as he believes a thing will be found out;
if he expects to be undetected, he goes back to his own bent. He whom you
link to you by kindness acts from the heart, is eager to repay you equally, and
will be the same present and absent" (ll. 51–53, 57–58, 76, 69–73).

Act I, Scene 3

22 SCANDER-BAG A translation of the life of "Scanderbeg" had been published in
1596; a dramatic version was acted not long before 1601 (HS).

27 WISP . . . HARD Cf. TT: "What? wispes o' your wedding day . . . ? . . . I
would ha' had bootes o' this day . . ." "I did it to save charges . . . I got on my
best straw-colour'd stockins, | And swaddeld 'hem over to zave charges; I"
(I.4.2–9).

53 GELT *Edward alludes to the* castrati, *Italian male sopranos and contraltos whose boyhood voices were preserved by this means for amplification by adult tone and breath. The witticism was particularly appropriate to the original Italian setting; but it lost little in the transposition, for in 1595 the Court had been edified by scandalous rumors that the music master Mr. Champernoun was using the Italian technique on his choirboys* (SALISBURY PAPERS, *Vol. V, 155, 436; quoted Harrison II, p. 18).*

Act I, Scene 4

58 "MO FOOLS YET" *Used, e.g., as epigraph for the anonymous* Ulysses upon Ajax *(1596) and as title for a book of epigrams by Roger Sharpe (1610).*

63 INVINCIBLY *This was a recognized blunder of the time; see* Wits, Fits, and Fancies *(1595), in the chapter entitled "Of Improper Speech": "One telling a plain fellow, that divers were in such a place talking evil of him, he said: O that I had now but an invincible cloak . . . [to] stand amongst them . . ." (quoted Shaaber, III.2.313n.).*

81 ACTION *Either Bobadill pretends he is going to be employed in the next campaign, or he gets money for war news which he intercepts or invents (HS), or he borrows on the strength of his character as supposed participant in the action; or he has told Cob that he has a lawsuit pending which will bring him money.*

Act I, Scene 5

101 CHARTEL *Bobadill's foreign terms are very à la mode. The fine Continental art of dueling, by strictly defined rules, with rapier and dagger, was a subject of current controversy. It had become as popular among gentlemen as hawking, and its foreign terminology was even more indispensable to their education (at least seven treatises on the subject appeared between 1590 and 1623). Teachers began to import themselves to London about 1570, and after the arrival of the "great" Vincentio Saviolo in 1590–91, the new techniques rapidly replaced in favor the old English contest with sword and buckler. For Bobadill and Saviolo, see N. to IV.7.20–27.*

105 MYSTERY *"Brantôme [ca. 1540–1614] . . . informs us that the Italian masters of the science of defence made a great mystery of their art and mode of instruction, that they never suffered any person to be present except the scholar who*

was to be taught, and even examined beds, closets, and other places of probable concealment." (Wheatley, p. xlvi).

110–13 *Of course Bobadill's disclaimer is feigned modesty, but it may also reflect a certain opprobium which attached to expert knowledge of this deadly science:* "according to Montaigne [of whose Essays two copies, one in French and one in English, were in Jonson's library], 'gentlemen avoided the reputation of good fencers as injurious to them, and learn'd with all imaginable privacy to fence as a trade of subtilty' (Essay 84)." (Wheatley, p. xlvi). *Cf. also the sinister aura surrounding the figures of Tybalt and Osric, both experts.*

Act II, Scene 2

18 RANKEST COW *Cf.* "they be as chaste as a cow I have, that goeth to bull every moon, with what bull she careth not." (Harman, s.v. "Autem-Mort")

21 *A tumbril was a cart with a body constructed to tilt back for emptying. Downright's metaphor refers not only to the clumsiness of the lumbering cart, but also to its use for carrying loads—especially dung. The breeches, like the tumbril,* "were stuffed out with rags, wool, tow, or hair, and sometimes, indeed, with articles of a more cumbrous nature . . ." (Strutt, Dress and Habits, etc. I.259, quoted Carter). *Cf.* SW IV.5.117–19: "If he could but victual himself for half a year, in his breeches, he is sufficiently armed to overrun a country."

22 GARAGANTUA *Jonson himself knew Rabelais from the time of CA (1597–98), and drew upon him often and in detail; but at the time of EI* "Garagantua" *would have meant Rabelais' character mainly to literary men—his work was known, for example, to Gabriel Harvey, John Eliot, Sir John Harington, Joseph Hall. The general public of the 1590s would have had its knowledge of Gargantua from popular chronicles; one circulating as early as 1572 was perhaps identical with an English version of Girault's* Chroniques admirables *(containing, probably unknown to its readers, three chapters by Rabelais) current by 1592, which in turn may have been a version of* "the history of Gargantua" *entered in the Stationers Register in 1594.* "Gargantua his prophecy" *(entered 1592) may be the Prophecy of Rabelais' Pantagruel, with the prophet's name altered to that currently familiar in England (Brown, pp. 31–94).*

Act II, Scene 3

Variant TO THEM. *This, taken with F₁'s "Dow" at 55, might conceivably mean that Downright does not exit at the end of II.2; but F₁'s head list of characters for II.3 is "Kitely, Cob, Dame Kitely." In Q there is no change of scene; the s.d.'s are as in the present text.*

28 IMPOSITIONS *Kitely is exhibiting a medically recognizable condition of melancholic jealousy, which is expanded in detail in 58ff. below. Here he demonstrates how "the brain dispossessed of right discerning faineth unto the heart . . . and the heart answering his passion . . . causeth the senses ["eyes and ears," l. 27] . . . preposterously to conceive, as the heart vainly feareth." (Bright, pp. 104, 108).*

46 NEW DISEASE *Dame Kitely's diagnosis is medically and symbolically accurate. In a book on this fever in 1659, H. Whitmore declared that the part chiefly affected was the heart; besides headache, another important symptom was "a sudden faintness of spirits and weakness without any manifest cause." (p. 72, quoted Carter).*

58–73 *Throughout this speech, Kitely is medically very exact in both his description of the brain's anatomy and his understanding of the cause, progress, and effects of his disease. Jealousy was considered in current medical theory to be a form of melancholy, caused by an excess of choler; often, as in Kitely's case, such "humor superfluous is . . . gathered in to the brain" (Elyot, Bk. III, Cap. 2, p. 53n.), where it encounters "an innate burning untemperateness, turning . . . choler into melancholy" (Burton, I.II.5.3)—the "vapor" of l. 65 (cf. footnote to II.1.95). This is the disease Burton classifies as nonnatural head-melancholy, caused by "choler adust" (burnt)—the very worst kind of melancholy, often leading to madness. (See also Bright, Ch. XVIII.)*

59–64 *"That melancholic humor . . . passing up to the brain, counterfeiteth terrible objects to the fantasy, and . . . causeth it . . . to forge monstrous fictions, . . . which the judgment taking as they are presented by the disordered instrument, . . . the instrument of discretion is depraved by these melancholic spirits, and a darkness and clouds of melancholy vapors [cf. l. 72] . . . obscure the clearness . . . Neither only is common sense and fantasy thus overtaken with delusion, but memory also receiveth a wound therewith . . . The memory being thus fraight with perils past . . . causeth the fantasy . . . to forge new matters of sadness and fear . . ." (Bright, pp. 102 [erroneously printed 82], 104, 105).*

Act II, Scene 4

11–12 WEAR ... END "*Servants were, by way of punishment for notorious faults, stripped of their liveries and compelled to appear in a parti-coloured coat, the common habiliment of domestic fools*" (Gifford). *But if this is true (and I have not been able to trace it), Brainworm's joke "and ... know" (l: 12) is redundant and therefore pointless, since resemblance to a fool is the stated object of the punishment. On the other hand, "motley" also meant a coarse cloth; perhaps "wear motley" is equivalent to "be dismissed and reduced to suits of coarse, plain cloth (instead of our blue livery)"—which would make the second "motley" a pun on the fool's garb, a joke with some point.*

18 LANCE-KNIGHTS *The feigned ex-soldier was a familiar denizen of the Elizabethan underworld, known in the trade as a Ruffler:* "*A ruffler goeth with a weapon to seek service, saying he hath been a servitor in the wars, and beggeth for his relief. But his chiefest trade is to rob poor wayfaring men ...*" *(Awdeley, p. 53). Numbers of these vagabonds, however, really were former soldiers, discharged with a few shillings' severance pay after a foreign campaign, with no trade and no resources. Their situation was a problem which legislation of the time repeatedly attempted to solve, without success.*

The outskirts of London, such as Moorfields, were infested with Rufflers and others on the fringes of society. Cf. EH I.1.137–41: "*Methinks I see thee already walking in Moorfields without a cloak, with half a hat, ... borrowing and begging threepence.*"

37–38 THE ... SWEETER *Cf. Barry's* Ram-Alley, *I.1.298–305:* "*you hold us widows | But as a pie ... | That hath had many fingers in't before, | ... | Yet says the proverb, the deeper is the sweeter.*"

46–51 *Brainworm here slides up the recognized scale of vagabondage to the character of* "*A Courtesy-man," who will "walk side by side, and talk on this fashion:*
'*Oh, sir, you seem to be a man, and one that favoureth men, and therefore I am the more bolder to break my mind unto your good mastership. Thus it is, sir, there is a certain of us ... which have come lately from the wars ... And further, whereas we have been wealthily brought up, and we also have been in good estimation, we are ashamed now to declare our misery ... Which if we had to suffice our want and necessity, we should never seek thus shamefastly to crave on such good pitiful men as you seem to be, ... and also such a one as pitieth the miserable case of handsome men ...*' " *(Awdeley, p. 56).*

49–50 DIE . . . SHAME *Paraphrase of Lyly's* Euphues and his England *(1580), treasurehouse of elevated sentiments and elegant style: " Hard is the choice . . . when one is compelled either by silence to die with grief, or by writing to live with shame . . ." (p. 123; Jonson used the passage again in EO V.10.34–36).*

54–62 *Brainworm adopts the typical " maund" (begging speech) of the counterfeit soldiers: " bestow your reward upon poor soldiers, that are utterly maimed and spoiled in her Majesty's late wars, as well for God's cause as her Majesty's and yours." (?Dekker,* O per se O, *p. 373). In the geographical and temporal spread of the battles, Jonson satirizes the extravagant claims typical of such beggars.*

The joke was awkward in its original Italian context, for Italian mercenaries or " lance-knights" were much in demand for European wars, and by the same token did not constitute a social problem. In the revision Jonson improved the joke further by going out of his way to keep the campaigns as unlikely as possible for an English soldier; he deleted the location of the galleys in America (where Drake and Hawkins had indeed fought) and substituted the battles named in ll. 57–58 (to which it does not appear that England sent more than encouragement). The audience must have appreciated Jonson's ostentatious neglect of England's own important wars with Scotland, France, and Spain under both Henry VIII and Elizabeth, especially when Brainworm weeps at the memory of service " in his prince's cause" (II.5.84).

58 ADRIATIC GULF *Since the dates of all Brainworm's imaginary campaigns lie between ca. 1515 and the 1530s, this could be an allusion to the summer of 1537, when the Turks occupied Valona on the Adriatic, and from that base launched an attack on Corfu just beyond the straits. More likely, however, the famous battle of Lepanto is meant, in which the Spanish, Venetian, and Papal forces overwhelmed the Turks (1571). This would extend Brainworm's fourteen years to fifty-five and make the joke much clearer.*

82 HIGGINBOTTOM *In 1579 the Earl of Shrewsbury had a dispute with his tenants, in which one of them, Otwell Higgenbotham, was so active in stirring up resistance that he was several times called before the Privy Council for examination. (Gifford) His name may have survived as shorthand for " a belligerent lower-class fellow." (There is a semi-comic Higginbottom in " A Tale of Drury Lane" [*Rejected Addresses, *1812] who might be descended from Higgenbotham: a valiant fire chief, he urges his subordinates into action, and we hear of " The cane he had, his men to bang." Carter calls attention to him.)*

Act II, Scene 5

5–9 *Juvenal's "Depravity was something rare and astonishing in those days"
(Satire XIII.53) provides the generality out of which Jonson, characteristically, makes the concrete and specific l. 5. Juvenal, too, proceeds to discuss respect for age (ll. 54–58), but Jonson's immediate model in ll. 6–9 is Ovid
(Fasti, ll. 57–58, 69–70): "Great was the reverence, of old, for a gray head
. . . Who would have dared to speak words worthy of a blush in the presence
of an old man? Advanced old age conferred the right to censure." Again the
abstractions (in the last sentence) are transformed into a concrete situation which
shadows forth a dramatic scene (ll. 7–8).*

12–36 *Knowell's speech is a mosaic of adaptation, a fascinating study in Jonson's
way of using classical sources. Here the passages which provide a matrix for
Jonson's invention are primarily from Juvenal (Satire XIV), with a good admixture of Quintilian (Institutio Oratoria, I.1 and 2) and a return to
Horace when Juvenal's reworking of him proves less suggestive than the original (Epistle I.1):*

> 12–13 *Cf. Juvenal (Satire XIV.56–58): "Whence should you get the
> countenance and forthright speech of a parent, since you, an old man,
> do worse things yourself?"*

> 14–17 *A synthesis of Juvenal's opening, "There are many things . . . deserving
> evil fame . . . which parents themselves point out and hand on to their
> children," the same poet's "Nor is there any better hope for a youth . . .
> who has learned from his ne'er-do-well father . . ." (ll. 6, 9), and Quin-
> tilian's "Would that we did not ruin our children's character ourselves.
> We immediately begin soothing their infancy with delights . . ." (2.6);
> but the imagery of ll. 16–17 is an inversion of Quintilian's account of the
> sources of eloquence: "studies too have their infancy, and, as the education
> of bodies soon to be most strong takes its beginning from nursing and the
> cradle, so the man of future great eloquence . . ." (1.21). Jonson prefers
> Quintilian's more emphatic rhetoric, evidently ("Would that we did
> not . . ."); but Juvenal is more striking on the "parents themselves,"
> and his "hope for a youth" has more emotional interest (especially when
> Jonson adds "destroy") than "ruin . . . character." The principle is
> clear: Jonson adapts what is most vivid; if a generality ("soothing . . .
> infancy") reminds him of an effective image "nursing and the cradle"),*

*he simply plucks the image out of its own context and uses it in his.
(Juvenal's interesting ne'er-do-well father is saved for ll. 32ff.)*

18–19 *Juvenal gives the basic statement:* " *When his seventh year has passed
over the lad, before all his teeth have come in again . . . he will wish to
dine with sumptuous preparation" (ll. 10–13)—but Juvenal's child is
too old for Jonson; Quintilian can provide a younger, as well as the
forceful antithesis which particularizes "wish . . . preparation":* "He
cannot yet utter his first words, but already he is a connoisseur of luxury
[literally, of scarlet] . . . We train their palates before their lips . . ."
(2.7).*

19–24 *Whatever is specific in Quintilian, Jonson retains; what is vague or
roundabout, he dramatizes in specific detail:* " *We rejoice if they say
something particularly licentious: with laughter and a kiss we eagerly
catch up words which no one would tolerate even in an Alexandrian
favorite slave. No wonder: we teach them, they learn by listening to
us. . . . Every dinner party resounds with bawdy songs . . ." (2.7–8).*

25–31 *A dramatic expansion of Quintilian's abstract conclusion:* " *These
things breed habit first, then nature" (2.8); Jonson takes the lasting
stain (ll. 30–31) from Juvenal's opening ("There are many things . . .
which affix a lasting stain to bright actions, which parents . . . hand on
to their children"), but the deep dye comes from a different section of
Quintilian:* " *we are by nature most tenacious of those impressions which
we receive with unformed minds; just as . . . the dyes of the wool, by
which its pristine whiteness is altered, cannot be washed out" (1.5).*

32–36 *Based on Quintilian:* " *They see our mistresses, our minions, . . .
behold things which cannot be spoken for shame . . ." (2.8). Jonson
converts "see" and "behold" into a systematic list of sensual appeals
to four of the five senses.*

42–43 *A rearrangement of Juvenal: "The footprints of their fathers, which they
ought to flee from, lead the rest [sc. the majority of sons]—and the beaten
path of old crime, pointed out to them for so long already" (Satire XIV.36–37).*

47–51 *The picture of father instructing son in money-getting comes from Juvenal
(Satire XIII.189–91, 200–09), whose turn of phrase provides "the grammar*

197

of cheating" (Juvenal's Vitiorum elementa, l. 123), but the words of the lesson are closer to Horace: "make money, money— | If you can, honestly; if not, by whatever means, money!" (Epistles 1.1.65–66).

52–56 This portion of the speech is selected from Juvenal, with a reminiscent dash of Quintilian added.

> 52–55 "To peel truffles, to pickle the best kind of mushrooms and drown becaficos swimming in their own juice—this [the youth] has learned from his ne'er-do-well father, from the hoary gluttony which provided a demonstration . . ." (Juvenal, Satire XIV.7–10).

> 55–56 Basically Juvenal: "he will wish . . . not to degenerate from his grande cuisine" (Satire XIV.13–14); but Jonson's antithesis also reflects the Quintilian he has used in 18–19.

57–64 Gradually, Jonson (or Knowell) detaches himself from Juvenal. He begins by offering an approving reply (ll. 57–60) to Juvenal's strictures: "Let no foul speech or sight cross that threshold within which there is a father"; "most swiftly and rapidly do domestic examples of vices corrupt us" (Satire XIV. 44–45, 31–32). But then (ll. 61–64), still using Juvenal's imagery, Jonson suggests that his predecessor's solution is too simple: "When a guest is coming, none of your servants will slack off. 'Sweep the pavement! Polish the pillars! Let that whole dusty spiderweb come down! . . .' . . . And so you tremble, poor wretch, lest forecourts soiled by dog-filth displease the eyes of your friend . . . you take no trouble . . . that your son may behold a pure home . . ." (Satire XIV.59–69).

65–66 Knowell's speech comes full circle to Quintilian I.2.4: "nor is conversation safer among . . . the free-born who are none too modest" (than it is with slaves at home who offer a bad example).

Act III, Scene 1

107 STRIGONIUM There really were English volunteers serving against the Turks in the Holy Roman Empire at this time. Strigonium would have been a battle especially familiar in England because of the heroism there of Thomas Arundell, made a count by the Emperor and imprisoned by Elizabeth for accepting this foreign title.

Act III, Scene 3

36 CAPS *Win in* BF *has one (I.1.19–23), and Kate in* Taming of the Shrew *almost gets one—" a baby's cap," according to her husband (IV.1.63–85).*

61 *The image is taken from Terence's* Eunuchus, *l. 105; Q has the original* rimarum plenus.

66ff. *Parts of the ensuing scene bear strong similarities to King John's conversation with Hubert (*King John *III.3.22–62), as Gifford first pointed out. As usual, Jonson's technique is to expand here, contract there, and make his own pattern out of the elements of the original. Compare:*

EI

103   K. John. *Come hither* Hubert. *O my gentle* Hubert,
                We owe thee much: . . .

. . . .

93–95, 105   *And my good friend, thy voluntary oath*
                Lives in this bosome, deerely cherished.

70–72, 110–11   *Give me thy hand, I had a thing to say,*
                But I will fit it with some better tune [possibly time*].*

75–76   *By heaven* Hubert, *I am almost asham'd*
                To say what good respect I have of thee.

. . . .

126–29   *I had a thing to say, but let it goe:*

. . . .

137   *. . . If the mid-night bell*
                Did with his yron tongue, and brazen mouth
                Sound on into the drowzie race of night:
                If this same were a Church-yard where we stand,

. . . .

71–73   *Or if that thou couldst see me without eyes,*
                Heare me without thine eares, and make reply
                Without a tongue, using conceit alone,

103–04   *Without eyes, eares, and harmefull sound of words:*
                Then, in despight of brooded watchfull day,
                I would into thy bosome poure my thoughts:

66–67   *But (ah) I will not, yet I love thee well,*
                And by my troth I thinke thou lov'st me well.

Notes, Act III, Scene 4

67–69, 98–100   Hub. *So well, that what you bid me undertake,*
                      Though that my death were adjunct to my Act,
                      By heaven I would doe it.
101–02   K. John.   *Doe not I know thou wouldst?*

90 FAILS AND TICK-TACK *Gifford gives a description of Fails; for Tick-tack, see Cotton, p. 77.*

Act III, Scene 4

4 EMBER WEEKS *The name "Ember" is derived from OE "ymbryne," a cycle or revolution of time.*

48 HANNIBAL *Pistol in 2 Henry IV (cited HS) is similarly confused (II.4.166).*

51 COPHETUA *Q reads "Golias," i.e. Goliath, which sounds more like "Midas" but makes a cruder joke. In F, Cob mixes up not consonants but kings.*

55–57 FISHMONGER'S SON . . . SHOULD DO *Probably a political joke at the expense of William Cecil, Lord Burghley, Elizabeth's principal minister, responsible for the bill cited in fn. to l. 1 above, which included Wednesday as a fish-day. This clause was at last repealed, after 22 years, in 1585 (27 El. c. 11); by that time the whole unpopular measure was known as "Cecil's Fast" (Neale, I, 114–17).*

Cecil's rise from plain William Cecil to a title, to the Order of the Garter, and to the highest offices in the kingdom called attention to the unclarity of his origins, about which he was himself concerned. Much "research" done on his behalf produced at last a lengthy, distinguished, improbable official pedigree. His enemies did their "research" too, and in 1592 a Jesuit pamphlet appeared, issued in Latin in the Low Countries with an English digest in the form of a letter to Cecil's secretary, which asserted that Cecil himself had been a bell-ringer in Cambridge and that his grandfather "kept the best inn in Stamford." Francis Bacon (Cecil's nephew) wrote a reply which circulated widely in manuscript even before its eventual printing, giving the issue yet greater publicity. Although Cecil's grandfather, his first absolutely ascertainable fore-bear, was respectable and propertied, so persistently did slurs on Cecil's ancestry recur to the public memory that in 1662 Fuller (History of the Worthies of England) still found it necessary to repudiate them.

Cecil's Fast, too, continued to be a live issue. As soon as Cecil became Baron Burghley and moved off to the House of Lords, the Commons passed a bill which the Clerk entitled simply but eloquently "against Wednesdays." Cecil scotched this after one reading by the Upper House. When the original act expired in 1585, the bill to take its place passed in and out of committee, losing and acquiring Wednesdays as it went, one such addition the result of intervention by the Queen herself. Nevertheless, though Cecil drafted and urged a compromise bill, meatless Wednesdays were abolished; and although at the next parliament a general measure continued this abolition among other acts of 1584–85, feeling was so strong that a special clause was inserted to re-affirm the death of the Wednesday fish-day. Jonson could therefore count on his audience to know what son of a fishmonger was to be blamed for the extra-ordinary frequency of fish-days.

Act III, Scene 5

7 SEVEN WISE MASTERS *Not, in all probability, a learned allusion to the Seven Sages of ancient Greece, but a timely one to the familiar and popular Seven Wise Masters of Rome. These seven Roman philosophers, appointed tutors to the son of the widowed Diocletian, saved their pupil from execution when his new stepmother accused him of trying to ravish her. By each telling a tale to the Emperor, they succeeded in getting the execution put off from morning to morning in exchange for each day's story, despite the Empress's counter-attack each night with a tale of her own, allegorically importing the need to dispatch her stepson. The end of the week ended the spell she had cast over the youth, which assured that if he spoke within that time he would die; he was then able to tell a tale on his own behalf and exculpate himself. This originally oriental tale passed through Latin and Middle English into the sixteenth century with undiminished popularity. There were at least three prose versions (1548–61, 1558, 1565/6), and a Scottish metrical version went through four editions in the last quarter of the century. (Ellis) A dramatic version by Dekker, Chettle, and Haughton was produced by Henslowe in March 1599/1600. (Greg, Henslowe's Diary, I.118–19). The reference to the Masters, interestingly, is not in Q, which was acted before Henslowe's production appeared.*

65–80 *Jonson enlists Bobadill in the great tobacco controversy inaugurated in 1577 by John Frampton, who sang the praises of tobacco in his* Joyful news out of the new found world . . . *Explorers of the New World sincerely believed*

201

in the medicinal properties of tobacco, which the Indians used; Nicot (see fn. to l. 75) sent a specimen to Catherine de Medici with an account of its miraculous healing powers, and in 1571 a Spanish physician claimed to have cured 36 distinct maladies with it. Subsequently the story of its virtues, accompanying the substance itself, came to England; as the popularity of tobacco swiftly increased, pamphlets and poetry appeared claiming for it the most divine medical efficacy—and, very soon, the most deleterious physical effects. The controversy, heated and fanatical on both sides, grew until the productions for and against tobacco began to constitute a small independent branch of literature. In 1604 James I took a hand himself and published A Counterblast to Tobacco, buttressing its persuasive strength a few days later by raising the duty on tobacco from twopence the pound to six shillings tenpence, an increase of four thousand per cent. Both tobacco and the controversy throve.

Bobadill's claims and language closely follow the current literature; see following notes:

65–69 *Compare Frampton (translating Liébault, 1570):* "*Moreover the inhabitants* of Florida *do nourish themselves certain times, with the smoke of this herb . . .*" *(Arber, Tob., p. 84),* "*which smoke satisfieth their hunger, and therewith they live four or five days without meat or drink . . .*" *(Hakluyt, account of Hawkins's second voyage; cited HS).*

70, 73–74 *Compare Frampton (translating Liébault):* "*but for a truth this only simple herb, taken and applied as aforesaid, is of greater efficacy, notwithstanding one may make thereof an ointment, which is singular, to cleanse, incarnate, and knit together all manner of wounds . . .*" *(Arber, Tob., p. 84). Cf. also l. 69.*

75–78 *Compare Thomas Hariot's* Brief and true report of the new found land of Virginia . . . *(1588):* "*they [the colonists] use to take the fume . . . into their stomach and head; from whence it purgeth superfluous phlegm and other gross humors, openeth all the pores and passages of the body: by which means the use thereof not only preserveth the body from obstructions; but also if any be, . . . in short time breaketh them . . .*" *(Arber, Tob., p. 85).*

78–80 *Compare Frampton (translating Liébault):* "Nicotian . . . among all other medicinable herbs . . . deserveth to stand in the first rank, by reason of his singular virtues, and as it were almost to be had in admira-

tion ... Some have called this Herb the Queen's Herb, because it was first sent unto her ... Others have named it the great Prior's herb, ... for the great reverence that he bare to this herb, for the Divine effects therein contained ..." (Arber, Tob., pp. 82–83); Nicot himself "thought good to communicate the same into France, and did send it to King Francis the second, and to the Queen Mother, and to many other Lords of the Court, with the manner of ministering the same ..." (Frampton; Arber, Tob., p. 84)

90–98 Cob is as close to the standard arguments against tobacco as Bobadill is to those for it. Compare:

> ... this same poison, steepèd India weed,
> In head, heart, lungs, doth soot & cobwebs breed;
> With that he gasp'd, and breath'd out such a smoke
> That all the standers by were like to choke.
>
> (Samuel Rowlands, "Letting of Humours blood in the Head Vein," 1602, quoted Atkins, ix)

—and the famous warning of King James: "it makes a kitchen ... oftentimes in the inward parts of men, soiling and infecting them, with an unctuous and oily kind of soot, as hath been found in some great tobacco takers, that after their death were opened." (Arber, Tob., p. 111; cited HS).

97–98 incorporate one current pseudo-medical opinion; cf. Work for chimny-sweepers, or A warning for Tobacconists (1601): "it is the more dangerous for that it hath in it the effects of contrary and repug[n]ant poisons: ... it [hath] a stupefying and benumbing effect, not much unlike to Opium or Henbane: ... And albeit it be apt to suffocate or strangle like to gypsum or plaster of Paris, yet doth it purge & scour as violently as Precipitate or Quicksilver sublimed" (E 4v).

147 DRAWN OUT OED does not give this meaning, but Q makes it clear. There Wellbred's comment, "your cousin's discourse is simply suited, all in oaths" (a pun on the homonym "oats"—see Kökeritz, pp. 320–21—meaning coarse cloth) receives the reply, "Aye, he lacks nothing but a little light stuff [pun on "cloth" and "matter"] to draw them out withal, and he were rarely fitted to the time." Adulteration of foodstuffs was a constant contemporary abuse, repeatedly mentioned in legislation. ("Oatmeal" as a coarse fabric is not recorded in OED until the late nineteenth century, but the meaning is evident in Wellbred's pun.)

Act III, Scene 6

47–48 *With the detail of the smock, compare the testimony of the dying Robert Greene's landlady that "he was fain, poor soul, to borrow her husband's shirt whiles his own was a-washing." (Q reads "his owne shirt ha beene at washing"; F "one" may be a misprint. F₂ makes precisely this misprint for F "owne" in II.1.14.) Indeed, Bobadill's pathetic financial condition, his low-class lodging, and his drain on his host's resources through friendship with his hostess are all strikingly reminiscent of the circumstances surrounding the death of the poet Greene—circumstances turned into popular gossip in 1592 through their publication by his enemy Gabriel Harvey, who visited the dead author's landlady in order to ferret them out. With Cob's complaints about the selling of his platters, and his wistful hope that he will be paid the "forty shillings . . . besides his lodging" (I.4.79–80) that Bobadill owes him, compare Harvey's account: "his hostess Isam with tears in her eyes . . . told me . . . beside the charges of his winding sheet, which was four shillings; and the charges of his burial, . . . which was six shillings and fourpence; how deeply he was indebted to her poor husband: as appeared by his own bond of ten pounds . . ." (pp. 21–22).*

Act III, Scene 7

29–30 AN' . . . ME *This statute of limitations was apparently well known; cf. Shirley's* The Witty Fair One, *III.2.24–26, cited Gifford.*

58 SWEET OLIVER *None of this explains the joke, which seems to have been hilarious, judging by its contemporary vogue. Shakespeare, ca. 1598, in* As You Like It *(III.3.90–92), refers specifically to the ballad: "Farewel good Mr. Oliver [Sir Oliver Martext]: Not O sweet Oliver, O brave Oliver leave me not behind thee: But winde away, bee gone I say, I wil not to wedding with thee." ("O sweet Oliver, leave me not behind thee" was entered in the Stationers Register Aug. 6, 1584, and "The answer of O sweet Oliver" on Aug. 20—I take the latter to be the source of "wind away . . ." etc.) Besides this ballad reference, the principal young men in the play are, of course, Oliver and Orlando.*

The legendary Oliver may owe his epithet of "sweet" to the ballad Oliver, whose activities could also have produced the meaning "carouser" (attested to by Nashe's equation in LS, 1599, of "boni socii and Sweet Olivers"—p. 225; a bonus socius was a high liver: see Dekker's Honest Whore, *ca. 1608,*

Notes, Act IV, Scene 2

Pt. II, II.1.220–23). Or the two characters may have been identical from the first; the Peer Oliver is described in the popular romance Sir Ferumbras *as excessively handsome (ll. 1222–23), and he offers to prove himself a first-class wencher in "Charlemagne's Journey to Jerusalem . . . ," a chanson de geste popular in six languages (Child, Vol. I, pp. 274ff.). The ballad and answer might even have been based on Oliver's part in this story.*

Finally, in view of Nashe's synonyms, it is curious that in the medieval English romances Oliver is constantly called, as a kind of identifying tag, "his [sc. Roland's] fellow" or "his good fellow" (see e.g. Otuel and Roland, *ll. 2489–91, and* Sir Ferumbras, *passim). Perhaps the colloquial meaning of "good fellow" affected Oliver's reputation?*

Act IV, Scene 2

19–22 CAN . . . BAGPIPE *Perhaps a topical joke. There was a gentleman of the time who, it was known, "could not endure the playing on a bag-pipe" without reacting as Edward describes, according to a marginal note (1605) to the story of one who found himself incontinent at the sound of a phorminx (in a translation of de Loier's* A Treatise of Spectres). *Cf. Shakespeare,* MV *IV.1.51ff.: "Some men there are love not a gaping Pigge: | . . . | And others, when the bag-pipe sings i' th' nose, | Cannot containe their Urine for affection." But either or both of the playwrights may have had the original story in mind rather than their afflicted contemporary; the anecdote, according to Warburton, comes from Scaliger's* Exotericarum exercitationum *(344 Exer., Sec. 6), a book "then much in vogue." (See Furness's note to MV IV.1.53.)*

40 PAUCA VERBA *Proverbial phrases beginning thus were common ("few words are best," "few words and many deeds," "few words suffice for the wise"), but the specific application here is unknown: an exhortation to drink (HS)? a benchers' exclamation at formal legal disputations (NH)?*

86 TRICKS *HS cite examples; cf. Lodowick Barry's title* Ram-Alley: Or, Merry Tricks *for a play (1611) concerned with a set of sexual escapades in which a main character is a prostitute.*

96 LAMP OF VIRGINITY *The Bible makes frequent mention of seven lamps as symbolic or religious objects. Allusive uses of "lamp" grew out of these, especially allusions to "lamps" of spiritual qualities (from Rev. 4.5, where*

*the seven lamps are "the seven Spirits of God"). Nashe had used the phrase
"lamp of virginity" recently as a dedicatory appellation in* The Terrors of
the Night *(1594). (HS)*

98 CONCEALMENT *A topical reference. Queen Elizabeth had granted numerous
commissions to private persons for the searching out of "concealments,"
privately held lands formerly belonging to monasteries, which ought to have
passed into the Crown's possession when Henry VIII dissolved the monasteries. The finder of a concealment received a proportionate reward from the
Crown, often a part or even all of the land itself. Abuse of such commissions,
to claim land rightfully another's, was frequent, and had recently come to
public attention when* EI *was first acted: a claim against the Bishopric in
Norwich resulted in a special restraining statute in 1597–98.*

Wellbred's meaning is that Matthew has searched out the concealed Hero
and Leander; *now Bridget, who gave him his "commission" as her servant,
must forestall his claiming the whole book, by rewarding him proportionately—
apparently sixpence for labor and sixpence for expenses.*

126 HOLOFERNES *The Bible story provided matter for what was "probably a
traditional play" (Harbage); four versions of it appeared in English during
the sixteenth century, one possibly performed before Queen Mary when she
visited the Princess Elizabeth at Hatfield. In the seventeenth century the story
was produced as a droll at Bartholomew Fair, and revived toward the end of
the century on the legitimate stage. (Coleman, Harbage)*

Act IV, Scene 3

7 ANCIENT *Cf. Shakespeare,* C *IV.5.100–01: "present | My throat to thee, and
to thy Ancient Malice."*

Act IV, Scene 4

15 BURGULLIAN *In 1598 "John Barrose a Burgonian by nation, and a fencer by
profession, that lately was come over and had challenged all the fencers of
England [cf. Bobadill's plan in IV.7], was hanged . . . for killing of an officer
of the City, which had arrested him for debt . . ." (Stow,* Annales, *1631,
p. 787; cited HS). Marston, in* The Scourge of Villainy *XI (HS refer,
through a misprint, to IX), also 1598, presents a gallant "who ne'er dis-
courseth but of fencing feats" talking of "the Burgonian's ward [position of*

defense in dueling]" (ll. 53, 63). For Cob's possibly erroneous form of the word, see Marston's Jacke Drums Entertainment *(1601), in which a Frenchman says: "you see | Me kill a man, you see me hang like de Burgullian" (Act II, 87–88; quoted without title or act, line numbers by Davenport, p. 361, n.63).* OED *incorrectly defines the word as "bully" on the basis of Cob's speech.*

20 TROJAN *The Trojans may have acquired their Elizabethan reputation simply by being valiant in a hopeless situation, or more specifically by their opposition to the deceiving Greeks and the trickery which conquered Troy: the straightforward, "trusty" Trojans against the devious "merry Greeks." Certainly the Elizabethan view was influenced by the popular legend that the English were lineally Trojans, through Brut, the descendant of Aeneas who came to England. Cf. the play on "true Trojan" in* Fuimus Troes. The True Trojans *(printed 1633), "a story of the Britons' valor at the Romans' first invasion," which concludes with a league of amity between the two commanders, "Both come of Trojan race, both nobly bold" (V.6.50). In this play, as often, London was called Troynovant.*

Act IV, Scene 7

20–27 *The rivalry between the English masters of defense (teaching the management of the short sword) and Italian experts in the new art of rapier dueling was at its height in London in the 1590s. There were three notable Italian fencing experts in London between 1570 and 1600; Vincentio Saviolo, the best known, in 1595 published his* Practise, *a fashionably influential book combated in 1599 by George Silver's* Paradoxes of Defence, *which upheld the English methods. Bobadill seems intended in part as a take-off on Saviolo (see also next note), anecdotes about whom appear in Silver's book and were probably current in the late 1590s. With Bobadill's story of the English fencing masters' importunity, compare the following: "the [English] master of defence would not thus leave him [Vincentio], but prayed him again he would be pleased to take a quart of wine of him. Then said Vincentio, 'I have no need of thy wine.' Then said the master of defence: 'Sir, I have a school of defence in the town, will it please you to go thither.' 'Thy School?' said master Vincentio. 'What shall I do at thy school?' 'Play with me' (said the master) 'at the rapier and dagger, if it please you.' 'Play with thee?' said master Vincentio. . . . Then said the master of defence, . . . 'yet once again I heartily pray you, good sir, that you will go to my school, and play with me.'*

Notes, Act IV, Scene 7

'*Play with thee?*' *said master Vincentio (very scornfully)* ..." *(Silver, pp. 68–69).*

40–41 THREE ... THEM *Bobadill's trick of enumeration here seems to be an allusion to a recognizable peculiarity of Vincentio's speech. Cf.* "'*Play with thee?*' *said master Vincentio.* '*If I play with thee, I will hit thee 1.2.3.4. thrusts in the eye together.*' ... *Vincentio lustily start up,* ... *saying,* '*Very well: I will cause you to lie in the jail for this jeer, 1.2.3.4. years*'" *(Silver, p. 69).*

42 TURNBULL ... SHOREDITCH *Turnbull was a street well known for its prostitutes, Whitechapel a filthy maze of alleys inhabited by thieves, receivers of stolen goods, drunkards, prostitutes; Shoreditch, actually Sewer-Ditch, sufficiently characterized by its name. Bobadill's flight of imagination outsoars his prudence as he names his haunts. There is a characteristic, splendid disregard of mundane reality in his presentation of the main danger in these neighborhoods as a group of fencing teachers on the prowl.*

43–44 AND SINCE ... ME *With Bobadill's account of his victory against the whole group of fencing masters who set upon him at his ordinary, compare the following story:* "*the masters of defence of London* ... *[were] drinking of bottle ale hard by Vincentio's school, in a hall where the Italians must of necessity pass through* ...: *and as they were coming by, the masters of defence did pray them to drink with them, but the Italians being very cowardly, were afraid, and presently drew their rapiers: there was a pretty wench standing by, that loved the Italians; she ran with outcry into the street,* '*Help, help, the Italians are like to be slain!*' *The people with all speed came running into the house, and* ... *parted the fray* ... *The next morning after, all the Court was filled, that the Italian teachers of fence had beaten all the masters of defence in London, who set upon them in a house together*" *(Silver, p. 67).*

71–72 PUNTO ... MONTANTO *For the* reverso, *see Saviolo 15r, and,* "*with a sudden riversa cut the other's neck almost quite in sunder*" *(B—double floral design—2r); for some light on the* stoccata *and* imbroccata, *see the discussion of left-handed swordplay (M3v–M4r), where Saviolo recommends that a left-handed fencer use the one thrust wherever a right-handed fencer uses the other, and the comments that few left hands use* stoccatas, *but rather most depend upon* imbroccatas *(N2v). HS define these thrusts differently, evidently following Florio for the most part; but in view of his* "passata a passado, a word in fencing," *and* "stoccata a foyne, a thrust, a stoccado given in fence,"

I am inclined not to put much faith in his other definitions. His bibliography includes "Duello di messer Dário Attendolo," but not Saviolo's work; perhaps there were variant definitions afoot. In any case, Florio's definitely do not fit Saviolo's descriptions of the stoccata *and* imbroccata; *see 15r, K2r, M1v, which establish that either thrust may be given above or below the rapier.*

108ff. *Bobadill's behavior in this encounter runs true to the form reported with relish of the fencing masters, especially Vincentio. Cf. particularly:* "the master of defence was very much moved, and up with his great English fist, and struck master Vincentio such a box on the ear that he fell over and over, his legs just against a buttery hatch, whereon stood a great black jack [leathern tankard]; the master of defence fearing the worst, against Vincentio his rising, catcht the black jack into his hand, being more than half full of beer. . . . [Vincentio, instead of fighting, threatens the Englishman with jail—Bobadill's recourse—and he replies:] 'I drink to all the cowardly knaves in England, and I think thee to be the veriest coward of them all'—with that he cast all the beer upon him . . ." *which Vincentio bore, although he was armed with rapier and dagger and the Englishman only with the tankard (Silver, pp. 69–70).*

Of course Bobadill's beating is the time-honored come-uppance of the miles gloriosus; *but the Italian fencing masters seem to have been welcomed as contemporary examples of that type. The parallels between Vincentio's beating and Bobadill's are obvious; though Jonson need not have had this particular story in mind, similar anecdotes glorifying Vincentio's "downright" English opponents were evidently numerous and popular.*

125–26 STROOK WITH *Contemporary medicine and astrology agreed on the liability of planets to emit sudden, unpredictable malign influences (to strike). It was the practice for physicians to attribute seizures and sudden deaths beyond their diagnosis to planets; a common entry in the bills of mortality, giving the cause of death, was "Planet strucken," or "Planet and Blasted"—or, familiarly, "planet." (Wheatley)*

Act IV, Scene 8

15–17 *This passage shades over into verse, and should perhaps be read as three iambic lines, two of them irregular:* "So . . . wears, | be . . . knows, | or . . . table."

53 OLD . . . HIM *E.g.* Blurt, Master Constable, *1602:* "Which is the constable's house? | At the sign of the brown bill"; *quoted Wheatley.*

107 BONE–FIRES *"Bone" apparently had a short vowel in both words; see Nashe's pun in PP (p. 182): "'tis not their new bonnets will keep them from the old bone-ache [ʔbɒnətʃ]."*

Act IV, Scene 9

14 ASSALTO *The whole preceding speech is in true Saviolese. Compare: "He shall . . . remove with his right foot, which must be conveyed behind the left, and shall strike a rinversa at his scholar's head" (10 r, v); "the scholar shall let the middest of his left foot directly respect the heel of his right, and let him turn his body upon the right side, but let it rest and stay upon the left, and in the same time let him turn the rapier hand outward in the stoccata or thrust, . . . and take good heed that he come not forward in delivering the said stoccata, which is half an incartata" (10 r).*

15 BASE WOOD *Final "t" after "s" was dropped in a number of words—see Kökeritz, p. 302; specifically, "base" and "baste" coexisted as heraldic terms for the lowest part of a shield—see OED.*

35 A . . . ANGELS *Cf. Sir Thomas Overbury's A Wife, 1614, 5th ed., in the "Character" of a Tailor: "His actions are strong in Counters . . . A ten groats fee setteth them a foot . . ."; quoted HS.*

58 SILK . . . LACE *Russet was a coarse homespun woolen cloth, characteristic of country people's clothing. It may be that there was a more refined version of it called silk russet, and that Downright's lace was russet in color; but I strongly suspect that this description is a joke, signifying that although Downright makes the concession of wearing silk and lace, he is so belligerently countrified that he has russet silk and russet lace—rather like saying, "He wears a cloak of silk burlap, edged about with burlap lace."*

Act IV, Scene 10

23 TRIED *First cited 1713 OED, but cf. "tried virgin," harlot, cited 1694 F&H, and Shakespeare, PP, 1599: "She told the youngling how god Mars did trie her, | And as he fell to her, she fell to him." Sonnet 11, ll. 3–4.*

42 *Taken from a corrupt reading of Plautus' Mercator. Cf. Burton's translation: "Thou old goat, hoary lecher, naughty man" (III.III.4.2); he gives the*

Latin, which is not in the Mercator, *to which he ascribes it. If it were, it would immediately precede Act III, ll. 574–76, which Burton goes on to quote in their usual sixteenth-century form. The line perhaps came from one of the contemporary grammars or collections of sayings, which often contained misquotations; since "old goat" is in l. 575 of the Latin, yet both Burton and Jonson include it with the nonexistent first line, their source probably contained a translation of the passage.*

45–47 *Cf. Burton's description (III.III.4.2) of old men* "qui jam corpore impotenti, et a voluptatibus deserti, peccant animo" *(who, already impotent in body, and deserted by their lusts, sin with the mind); he ascribes this to Plutarch's* Contra Coleten. *The propinquity of the last two allusions in both Burton and Jonson suggests that both writers may be working from a treatise on love in old men (which quoted Plutarch in Latin).*

46 POWERS' INCHASTITY *HS justify the F reading, which all subsequent editors have followed, by means of other examples in which Jonson allows noun and verb to disagree. But all these contain singular nouns and plural verbs, and have the advantage of making sense; whereas l. 46 would demand the dubious substitution of "lawful sexual pleasure" for "chastity" in order to yield any meaning. The context, moreover, clearly demands a hit not at Knowell's marital state, about which Kitely neither knows nor cares, but at his disgraceful age. Kitely wishes to enforce the antithesis between "powers" and "mind" (l. 47).*

Act V, Scene 1

43–V.2.5 *Jonson took this piece of eccentricity from an anecdote published in 1595:* "A soldier coming about a suit to a merry Recorder of London, the Recorder seeing him out at the window, ran hastily into an inner room, & there put on a corslet and a head-piece, & then with a lance in his hand came down unto him, and said: How now Sirrah, are you the man that hath somewhat to say to me? Begin now when you dare, for behold (I trow) I am sufficiently provided for you" *(Antony Copley,* Wits, Fits, and Fancies; Or, A general and serious collection, of the . . . Behaviors, of all sorts of Estates . . .; *quoted HS).*

Act V, Scene 3

109 IN ARMS *The story of a man who, finding himself at an inn without clothes and without resources, puts on an old suit of armor to make his way through the*

town, was traditional. It appears in Merry Tales and Quick Answers *(ca. 1532),* Merry Tales of Skelton *(1567), and the* Merry Conceited Jests of George Peele *(1607; cited HS). See Horne, Ch. 5.*

Act V, Scene 5

11 PHLEGON *If Q* "Mount thee my Phlegonmuse" *is accurate, it suggests that Jonson intended the sense* "burning." *Cf. the opening lines of* Henry V: *"O, for a Muse of fire, that would ascend | The brightest heaven of invention."*

The horse Phlegon may also be meant as a primary or secondary allusion, serving here as the Muses' and poets' horse, the role more usually assigned to Pegasus. The latter acquired his poetic significance only in the Renaissance; in Hesiod's Theogony, *he lives in the halls of Zeus and brings him thunder and lightning. Later, however, two horses belonging to the Sun are identified as the horses of thunder and lightning (Hyginus, Fabula CLXXXIII). A general exchange or confusion of functions among heavenly horses seems possible. (See—with caution—Pauly, s. v. Musai, G, XVI.699.)*

Conceivably, Jonson in a learned mood might even intend a subsidiary allusion to Phlegon (second century A.D.), author of a book of marvels, since the Phlegonmuse is called upon to relate a divine occurrence.

12–14 *Saturn seems to have been given to this kind of activity toward the end of the sixteenth and beginning of the seventeenth century. In Tassoni's mock epic* The Rape of the Bucket *(La Secchia Rapita, 1615), Saturn attends a meeting of the gods just after taking a laxative; by way of beginning his speech,* "the old fellow smiled, and broke wind . . ." *(II.45). Saturn's scatological connections may have been accepted mock-mythology. He is the great-grandfather of Ajax (a jakes, a toilet) according to Harington, who calls him* "old Saturn. Alias dictus Stercutius" *with the note:* "Stercutius, the god of dung" *(Prologue, p. 71). This identification in itself is highly respectable, deriving from St. Augustine's pronouncement that the figure of Saturn was a mistaken deification of a farmer named Sterces or Stercutius who invented the technique of manuring fields (De Civitate Dei, XVIII.15). Perhaps Tassoni, Harington, and Jonson were all piously developing St. Augustine.*

36 THEY . . . ALDERMAN *Cf. D 2432–34.* "Every beggarly corporation affords the state a Mayor, or two Bailiffs, yearly: but, solus Rex, aut Poeta, non quotannis nascitur." *Jonson here gives the source as Petronius, but it is*

actually Florus (first and second centuries A.D.): "Consules fiunt quotannis et novi proconsules; / solus aut rex aut poeta non quotannis nascitur." *(*Anthologia Latina, *Vol. I, p. 73. Couplet quoted HS.)*

42 WITH THE FACT *The sentiment is modeled on Seneca:* "*You say, ' Shall he go without punishment?' Put the case that you wish it, nevertheless it will not be; for the greatest punishment of a misdeed done is to have done it . . ." (De Ira, III.26.2; cited HS).*

Appendix I
Text and Stage History

Every Man in His Humor exists in two versions, for each of which there is one authoritative text, apparently seen through the press by Jonson himself. For the first version, set in Italy, it is the Quarto of 1601; for the second, set in England, the 1616 Folio of Jonson's works. The present edition is based on the latter. I have incorporated into the text without comment all corrections made during the printing, even though some copies of the Folio were issued without them.

Surprisingly, quite a large number of misprints remained uncorrected. Some were altered in the 1640 Folio; some seem to be mistakes in setting type from the Quarto. I have noted at the foot of each page rejected Folio readings which in any way affect sense or vocal inflection, together with the Quarto and Second Folio variants which appear to correct them; I have omitted obvious misprints which have no bearing on meaning or connotation.

I should call attention to two passages in which I have broken with previous editorial tradition. One concerns the feast of which Brainworm claims to have overheard the proceedings. Originally, "there were a great many rich merchants, and brave citizens wives with 'hem at a feast" (IV.6.39–40); modernizing editors, triply misled by the Elizabethan lack of apostrophes, the punctilious comma between syntactically parallel nouns, and the apparent reference of the pronoun, have read "rich, merchants, and brave citizens' wives with 'em," thus undeservedly compromising the business community. I have removed the comma and added the missing apostrophe to restore the "rich merchants' and brave citizens' wives" ("with 'hem" refers back to the sinister "they" of the whole speech), a more pleasant and less irregular guest list. The other passage is Kitely's accusation of Knowell, which also hinges on an apostrophe. The compositor of the Folio unluckily left too much space in setting up the Quarto's "when all thy powers inchastitie is spent" and produced "when all thy powers in chastitie is spent" (IV.10.46). This was an easy error for Jonson to overlook, since it involved no change in words or punctuation; and Kitely has been exhausting his powers in chastity ever since. I have accepted the Quarto reading and supplied the needed apostrophe on "powers'." (See note to these lines for further discussion.)

All other deviations from the text of the First Folio, except for line arrangement, the modernized spelling and punctuation, and modification of the list of characters heading each scene, are also given at the foot of each page.

I have normalized the orthography to modern American spelling except where such a change seemed to affect pronunciation or implication. For the former reason I have retained Jonson's semi-elisions, such as "be'at" or "mother'herself"; for the latter, such forms as the Dedication's proudly Latinate "Clarentiaux" for "Clarencieux," "millaner's" (I.3.101) for "milliner's," "bone-fires" (IV.8.107) for "bonfires" (see footnotes).

Jonson's punctuation presents a much more complicated problem. His usage in the Folio is generally systematic, and wholly effective. In preparing his revision for publication, he greatly increased the amount of punctuation over what it had been in the Quarto, giving as much attention to its nuances as to the words themselves. He combined syntactic pointing with pointing to indicate tone, pace, and even inflection. To read the text with the original punctuation is to be as close as possible to the speaking voice of each character. Nevertheless, this punctuation is by no means always comprehensible to the untrained modern eye. Our marks for various kinds of syntactic differentiation are not the same as Jonson's, and our syntactic expectations when we see a particular mark get in the way of understanding a character's intonation.

In hopes of achieving for the text both accessibility and fidelity, I have made two kinds of change: when a non-modern punctuation mark was clearly syntactic, I substituted the modern punctuation if it did not violate the indicated tempo of the sentence; when such a mark was expressive, I tried to substitute an equivalent modern punctuation. So, for example, I have generally removed commas between two parallel nouns connected by "and," and before indirect discourse—but not always; I have preferred overpunctuation, where it is comprehensible, to removing a genuine indication of speech rhythm. On the other hand, in a line like the Folio's "And, here, are stockings" I have tried to translate the vital punctuation; in this case, into "And, here—are stockings" (IV.9.61). To remove that pause would be to rob the line of its immortality.

For the same reasons, I have retained almost all of Jonson's parentheses, which signal shifts to and from a different tone of voice. These semi-asides can create extremely funny interruptions of thought; their humor is vitiated if they are incorporated into the sentence. I have also dealt cautiously with question marks, which in Elizabethan punctuation often stood for exclamation points. Jonson uses them besides to indicate a questioning rise in the speaker's tone, as when Edward says to Stephen, "I told you thus much?" (III.1.155). When there is a reasonable possibility that such an indication is intended, I have let the question mark stand. Indeed, whenever there has been any doubt about the punctuation, I have tried to give the benefit to Jonson.

In preparing the play for the Folio, Jonson, following the example of Roman comedy, materially reduced the number of stage directions, even to the point of not marking entrances and exits. Since *Every Man in His Humor* is exceptionally dependent upon its stage business, the reduction is much to the disadvantage of the modern reader—or any reader. I have therefore restored the Quarto stage directions wherever their applicability has not been changed by Folio revision, and I have silently altered their Italian names to the English equivalents. All stage directions from the Quarto are enclosed in parentheses. Now and again, when a portion of such a direction was duplicated in the Folio or seemed inapplicable, I have taken the liberty of omitting it without comment. The addition of further clarifying stage directions provided a special problem. In principle I feel that an editor ought not to function as a director, or allow enjoyment of the text to become embroidery upon it. On the other hand, there are lengthy sections of *Every Man in His Humor* which are totally flat when the action is not visualized, but hilarious quasi-farce when it is—for example, those in which the gulls pass their sacred objects from hand to hand: the rapiers in III.1 and the tobacco in III.5. In others, the dialogue shifts among so many speakers so rapidly that it is easy to misunderstand what goes on. I have therefore added "Aside" or "To ——" before a speech wherever this seemed helpful; and I have indicated implied action which must occur at a certain point, and which is not perfectly plain from the dialogue. When an action or series of actions must be taking place in the course of a scene, but the details or timing are not fixed, I have indicated the action in the notes rather than in stage directions. All added material in the stage directions is enclosed in brackets.

Every Man in His Humor has been frequently revived on the stage, re-printed, and anthologized. Whether justly or not, it has proved itself among the most popular of Jonson's plays. Its appeal is reflected in its unusual stage history, which has had one high point in each century (let us allow 1598 to count as seventeenth-century).

There is a tradition that the play was accepted for production because of Shakespeare's recommendation; be that as it may, he acted in its initial per-formance. A list of the principal actors (at the end of the Folio text) gives his name first, which has been interpreted to mean that he played Knowell, whose name stands first in the list of characters. The famous comedians Will Slye and Will Kempe participated, too. This performance can hardly have been matched by any subsequent one; but in 1751 Garrick directed the play (with a text altered by him) in a production "perfectly 'cast'" (Fitzgerald, *Life of . . . Garrick*, quoted Carter, p. lxxi), in which he himself played Kitely. One of the spectators was "a little jealous for poor Shakespeare; for if Mr. Garrick often acts Kitely B. Jonson will eclipse his name" (*Correspondence of . . . Garrick*, I. 385, quoted Carter, p. lxxii). Sir Joshua Rey-nolds painted Garrick in his costume for the part.

A very different guiding spirit animated what is perhaps the play's most famous revival, that by Dickens in 1845. This private production met "with a success that out-ran the wildest expectation"; it had to be moved to a public theater, and in 1847 was taken on tour to the provinces (Carter, pp. lxxxii-iv; he quotes Forster, *Life of Dickens*, ed. 1874, 2.209ff.). Dickens played Bobadill, and even the roughest sketch of his performance makes the play's reception easily comprehensible: "at 'This a Toledo? Pish!' [III.1.151] he bent the sword into a curve; he leaned on his companion's

shoulder when puffing out his tobacco smoke as 'your right *Trinidado*';
and he rattled off his arithmetic in Act IV, Scene vii, making an invisible
sum of addition in the air and scoring it underneath with an invisible line"
(HS IX.184, summarizing Clarke, *Recollections of Writers*, pp. 310–11).

In 1937, at Stratford-upon-Avon, *Every Man in His Humor* received its
last major revival to date, with Donald Wolfit as Kitely, and Knowell made
up to look like Shakespeare. The production was a complete success; it
"made every incident lucid and . . . was a revelation of accomplished stage-
craft" (HS IX.185; for an exhaustive treatment of the play's stage history
see pp. 168–85; for a critical review of editions, pp. 13–157).

The most recent substantial editions of *Every Man In* are one by Arthur
Sale (1941, revised 1949), which I have consulted, and one by Martin
Seymour-Smith (London, Ernest Benn, 1966), which came out too late for
me to use. The standard editions, to all of which I owe greater or lesser
debts, are those by Peter Whalley (in *The Works . . .*), 1756; William Gifford
(in *The Works . . .*), 1816; H. B. Wheatley, 1876; P. Simpson, 1919 (with
critical material substantially reprinted in HS); H. H. Carter, 1921 (parallel
texts of Quarto and Folio); and the monumental edition of C. H. Herford
and E. and P. Simpson (in *Ben Jonson*, Vols. I, III, IX, with additional mentions in XI)—a mine, or rather labyrinth, of essential information.

Appendix II
The Dates of Composition

Every Man in His Humor was, in effect, composed twice; the dates of both versions have been the subject of prolonged argument. To settle the question for the first composition is relatively simple; for the revision, perhaps impossible. The question of dates is further complicated by the Prologue, which may or may not have been written at the same time as the new version of the play.

The Prologue, being complete in itself, should be dealt with independently. I believe it can be dated. It contains an undoubted verbal echo, besides further echoes in content, of Thomas Shelton's translation of *Don Quixote*. This was printed in 1611–12 by Stansby—who printed Jonson's own Folio around the same time. Here is Shelton's version of the village Canon pronouncing on modern comedies: "what greater absurdity can be in such a subject than to see a child come out in the first scene of the first act in his swaddling clouts, and issue in the second already grown a man, yea, a bearded man?" (Pt. IV, ch. xxi). Here is Jonson: "To make a child, now swaddled, to proceed / Man, and then shoot up, in one beard and weed, / Past threescore years ..." Cicero's definition of Comedy (Prol. 21, 23) immediately precedes, and the complaint about changes in locale (Prol. 15) is in the same paragraph, though Jonson was not seeing these for the first time. Compare also with the Prologue's six opening lines the Canon's explanation of why he did not finish his projected book of chivalry; his argument was "drawn from our modern Comedies, and thus made to myself: If those (as well the fictions, as historical ones) are all or the most part of them notorious fopperies, ... and yet are by the vulgar heard with such

---

Appendix II

1. *The Comedy of Humors*, a "new play," according to Henslowe, not in 1595–96 but in May 1597, was Chapman's *Humorous Day's Mirth*, which was "sundry times publicly acted ... by the Lord High Admiral his Servants" (title-page, quoted Chambers III.251) before its publication in 1599. The identification is rendered absolute by 1598 inventories of the Admiral's Men, which list as properties for *The Comedy* clothing for named characters in Chapman's play (Greg, *Henslowe's Diary*, II.184).

2. The Folio date is undoubtedly analogous to that given for *Sejanus*. This play, first acted in 1603, was revised in 1605 and provided with a preface for the specific purpose of pointing out that "this book ... is not the same with that which was acted on the public stage ..."; yet in 1616 the revision was printed in the Folio with title- and end-pages stating: "First acted in the year 1603." (See Carter, p. lxiii.)

3. Francis Meres' *Palladis Tamia: Wit's Treasury*, entered in the Stationers Register on September 7, 1598, gives a list of the English writers considered "the best for Comedy amongst us," which includes Chapman but not Jonson, who is mentioned as a writer of tragedy (on the basis of dramas referred to by Henslowe, but lost). Since Q made Jonson's reputation as a comic writer on the humors, the inference is that *EI* had not yet been acted.

4. On September 20, 1598, Toby Mathew wrote to Dudley Carleton that a gentleman had lost three hundred crowns at "a new play called Every Man's Humor." (See HS IX.168.)

5. Several topical allusions in Q, retained in F, refer to events in 1598 (see footnotes and notes for detailed explanations):

    a. Marlowe's "Hero and Leander" (IV.2.45) was published in 1598 with immense success; there were probably three editions during the year (Tucker Brooke, quoted Carter, p. 375).

    b. The problem of "concealments" unscrupulously claimed (IV.2.97–98) was brought to public attention by an act passed in the parliamentary session of 1597–98.

    c. In July, 1598, the "fencing Burgullian" (IV.4.15) was executed.

    d. On September 6 (Raikes, p. 16) or September 9 (Harrison, II.307), 1598, the office of Provost-Marshal for London and its outskirts (III.5.10–11) was instituted, as it occasionally was when rogues and vagabonds became unusually numerous and belligerent.

Internal and external evidence combine to produce a date for the first

delight . . . and . . . the authors that compose them . . . say, that they must be such as they be for to please the people's humors, . . . therefore it is better for them to gain good money and means by many, than bare opinion or applause by a few. The very same should be the end of my book . . . ; and I should remain only for a need . . . But because that Comedies are become a vendible merchandise, they affirm, and therein tell the plain truth, that the players would not buy them, if they were of any other than the accustomed kind, and therefore the Poet endeavors to accommodate himself to the humor of the player, who is to pay him for his labor . . . "

Shelton's was the first translation of this section of *Don Quixote* into any language. Jonson had heard of the novel by 1609 (see *SW* IV.1.57), and knew Beaumont and Fletcher's *The Coxcomb* (see *A* IV.7.39), based on a story narrated in *Don Quixote* which had been translated into French; but he seems to have had an erroneous idea of the novel's bias, for he couples it several times with *Amadis de Gaul* as, apparently, a genuine romance (*loci cit.*, *U* xliii.29), whereas *Amadis* is one of the books responsible for Don Quixote's madness, and narrowly escapes the general conflagration of his library. That Jonson had read Cervantes in the original seems improbable; the Spanish in *A* IV.3 leaves the definite impression that Jonson had no accurate working knowledge of that tongue (e.g. in l. 61 the use of *tan* is syntactically suspicious; in 62 *bien* should be *buena*; in 93 *tiengo* should be *tengo*). There is no record of any Spanish book in his library, though there are works in Italian and French; on the other hand, there is a translation from the Spanish. (See the two HS lists, in I and IX.) It seems reasonably certain that Shelton's translation provided Jonson's first opportunity for close verbal contact with *Don Quixote*. There is a slight possibility that he might have seen Shelton's manuscript before publication; it was written in 1607 or 1608 (Shelton's dedicatory epistle says "some five or six years ago"; his translation is based on the 1607 Brussels edition in Spanish). But if Shelton is to be trusted, he translated it especially for "a very dear friend," and "after I had given him once a view thereof, I cast it aside, where it lay long time neglected in a corner," until "at the entreaty of others my friends, I was content to let it come to light"—presumably ca. 1610, for it was entered in January 1611. There is no indication that Jonson was one of Shelton's friends; if Jonson was in touch with Stansby in 1611–12 about his own Folio, he might have seen Shelton's translation then, but probably no earlier.

This date accords with previous conjectures that the "tempestuous (Prol. 19) and "monsters" (30) refer to *The Tempest*, which Jonson attacked in the Induction to *BF* (using the words "monster" and " pests") and probably also in the address To the Reader prefixed to HS's discussion, X.51–52). The date would also fit in with the sugge offered by "foot-and-half-foot words" (Prol. 10), Jonson's own rend in his *Ars Poetica* of *sesquipedalia verba*, that Jonson had recently bee close touch with his Horace translation (originally done in 1604, but published until 1640). In 1611 Heinsius published a Latin edition of the *Poetica* with an entirely new line arrangement, which Jonson followed wh he published his own translation. As soon as he heard of the Heinsius must have wanted to see it; as soon as he saw it and read its systemat justification of the new ordering, he must have known that his labors ha entered a new stage. That he was looking attentively at his own version soo after 1611, and perhaps already rearranging and/or revising, is more than likely. The Prologue, at this late date, must definitely have been composed for the revised version of the play (hereafter called F) first published in the Folio, and not for the original Quarto (hereafter called Q); this confirms what is deducible from its insistence on "an image of the times," not very applicable to the Italian setting of Q.

Although the Italian version was entered in the Stationers Register in 1600 and published in 1601, its first performance is dated by the 1616 Folio. In this collection the revised play's title page describes it as "A Comedy. Acted in the year 1598," and the end page even more clearly states: "This Comedy was first acted in the year 1598." Both Q and F ascribe the play's performances to the Lord Chamberlain's Men. Gifford, editing the play in 1816, raised a great deal of critical dust by asserting that 1598 must have been the date when the revision was first acted. He argued that Q was presented in 1595 or 1596 by Henslowe's company, the Admiral's Men, and identified it with a play called *The Comedy of Humors*, which Henslowe mentioned in his diary on May 11, 1597. His arguments imply that Q was issued by Henslowe after F had been acted because Henslowe wanted to capitalize on, or get revenge for, the success of F in the hands of a rival company.

There are numerous weaknesses in Gifford's hypothesis, but it is unnecessary to analyze its probability, since various facts demolish this theory's strongest points and independently establish the date of 1598.

performance of *EI* between September 7, 1598 (when *Palladis Tamia* was entered), or even September 9 (if Harrison is right about the Provost-Marshal), and September 20, when Mathew mentions the play in his letter.

Unfortunately such factual clarity disappears in relation to the revision. The three twentieth-century scholars who have discussed the evidence most thoroughly have come to three different conclusions as to the date of F— a testimonial to the skill with which Jonson covered his tracks. There appears to be only one definite topical allusion added in F which would not have fitted the play's known and stated date of 1598, and that allusion, being Boba-dill's, is automatically suspect as to accuracy. All others would have been possible in 1598 and recognizable for a good while afterward.

Although theoretically F could have been composed at any time after 1598, in point of fact it could scarcely have been written before 1604. The recomposition was thorough, and Jonson was very busy (see Chronology). That four plays were his total output from 1598 to 1601 is corroborated by Dekker's jibe in *Satiromastix* (1601): "You and your itchy poetry break out like Christmas, but once a year" (V.2.218; quoted Chambers), and by Jonson's defiant response in the Apologetical Dialogue to *P*: "'Tis true. / I would they could not say that I did that." The Dialogue, a rejoinder to the storm of displeasure raised by *P*, ended by announcing Jonson's intention to "try / If Tragedy have a more kind aspect." One assumes that he would not have followed up this public advertisement of a change to the somber Muse with a revision of his first successful comedy.

By February 12, 1603 (HS II.3; not, as in HS I.30, February 2, 1602) Jonson had retired to the home of a patron of letters, where, a contemporary recorded in his diary, he "scorns the world" (Manningham, quoted HS). This accords with his plans in the Dialogue; presumably he was composing *S*. In view of his activity from 1602 through the first part of 1604 (see Chronology), the Court performance of *EI* in February 1605 seems the first plausible date for a production of F. If the Horace translation (see Chronology, 1605) extended, with its commentary, from 1602 to 1606, Jonson could conceivably have been sufficiently at leisure between May 1, 1604 and the last part of the year to revise *EI*, with still enough time after February 2, 1605 to collaborate on *EH* for presentation before summer cut off the playing season. He might then have gone to jail and been released, re-vised *S* for republication in the autumn (or performed these two feats in reverse), written his next masque, and with some crowding fitted in *V*, which "five weeks fully penned" (*V* Prol. 15), for performance in the first part of 1606.

The evidence in favor of a 1604 revision, then, is:

1. Jonson could hardly have done it before; perhaps he could have done it then; with the Court performance in prospect, perhaps he would have done it then.

2. He had just participated, for the first time, in composing a London comedy (*EH*). The possibilities of the setting might have struck him and suggested the change of scene for *EI*.

3. Bobadill's remark in F that the siege of Strigonium (1595; not 1596–97 as given HS I.332) had taken place some ten years before (III.1.105) would exactly fit the date of the Court performance.

4. Clement's burning of Matthew's poetry because "here was enough to have infected the whole city" (V.5.29–30) suggests that measures against the plague were currently very familiar. Author and spectators had, to an extent, the plague always with them; but from 1594 to 1603 there seems to have been no epidemic. 1603–04, however, was a plague year; the Coronation was curtailed, seasonal fairs suppressed, court terms deferred, and the theaters apparently closed from spring 1603 to spring 1604 (Chambers, IV. 349–50).

5. Mr. John Trundle, for whom Edward proposes to "troll ballads" (I.3.53–54), though admitted to the Company of Stationers in 1597, entered his first publication in the Register in 1603.

There are, on the other hand, several awkward considerations about this hypothesis:

1. Would the Court have picked out its entertainment for the following January in time for Jonson to revise *EI* and write a masque besides, when he was also working on his Horace? (Drummond dates the translation proper 1604; *CD* 86–88.)

2. If the Folio dates *V* according to the modern calendar, the play was presented toward the end of 1605; in that case its composition pushes back the presumable dates of other 1605 work so that *EH* falls almost necessarily in the last part of 1604, which makes the simultaneous revision of *EI* (with Horace not yet finished!) most unlikely.

3. Having recognized the comic potentialities of a London scene, would

Jonson have returned to Italy for his next—immediately following— comedy, and waited four years to use the English setting again ?

4. By February 1605, John Trundle had entered precisely one work in the S.R.; that was in 1603, and the piece was not a ballad. Though he may have been a bookseller at this time, the record suggests that early in 1605 "Trundle" was not a name to conjure with.

Bobadill's comment on Strigonium, too, is vague enough to fit a span of at least four or five years with sufficient accuracy. It would certainly be appropriate to the next likely opportunity for F's composition, the years 1606 to early 1609. The external evidence for a date within this period is better than that for 1604:

1. For all his experience and now highly developed skill in composing comedy, and despite the enthusiastic reception of *V*, Jonson wrote no new play for over three years. Of these, 1606 and 1608, at least, offered ample time for other projects (see Chronology).

2. The King of Denmark's state visit in the summer of 1606 would have been a logical occasion for a performance of F. Jonson, in high favor at Court, surely contributed something besides the recorded brief speeches of the Entertainment. (See Carter, p. lxv.)

3. If F falls between 1606 and 1609, it begins an unbroken series of comedies with English settings.

4. Certain topical allusions added in F would have been fresher at this time than later:

a. Bobadill's reference to Strigonium.

b. The mention of the Turkey Company's gifts to the Grand Signior (I.2.76–77). James I had reconstituted and rechartered the company in 1605; in July of that year, the merchants petitioned him to bear the cost of a present to the Sultan; in December, James granted them £5322 for the purpose—an enormous sum.

c. Edward's assurance to Stephen that he will not draw him "into any plot against the state" (I.3.80–81), which may glance at the Gunpowder Plot of November 1605.

d. Clement's remark on Matthew's poetry. The end of 1605 was again a time of plague; theaters were closed from October through the middle of December. The epidemic recurred in July 1606 (the month of the King of Denmark's visit) and continued until the end of the

Appendix II

year. In the second half of 1607 and the same part of 1608 there were repeated outbreaks.

5. By the end of 1609, John Trundle had published seventeen pieces entered in the S.R., nine of them in 1607, including a little burst of ballads (September–October). These pieces were almost exclusively ephemeral works on the latest sensational news, foreign and domestic; even if his productions were not mainly ballads, his reputation for publishing the stuff that ballads are made on would have been sufficiently established. In 1605 he entered six books, but in 1606 only two; and only one each in 1608 and 1609. Assuming that his work was being recorded with roughly the same degree of regularity throughout, his name would probably have been most easily recognizable in early 1606, or better late 1607 or early 1608.

6. To Kitely's assertion that Cash is no Puritan, F adds: "nor rigid Roman Catholic" (III.3.89). Simpson takes the addition of this phrase, its tone, and especially the word "Roman," as testimony that Jonson's own Catholic period (1598–1610) was over (Simpson, p. xxx). I agree that the phrase would hardly have been added by a sympathizer. There is, however, another possible explanation. In the first half of 1606, Parliament passed a mandatory Oath of Allegiance, denying the Pope's power over the King. From then on, and particularly in 1607 and 1608, Catholics carried on a raging controversy over the taking of the Oath. (See Harrison V, *passim*.) The Pope sent two letters declaring the Oath unacceptable by Catholics; the Archpriest of England, on the other hand, claimed that the Oath could be taken without violation of conscience, and took it himself in September 1607. English Catholics were split into two factions: those who, following the behests of Rome, steadfastly refused the Oath; and those who considered themselves Englishmen foremost, took the Oath if required, and decried the treasonous sentiments ascribed to the first group. Jonson was among the latter. Kitely, debating why Cash does not "lend an oath to all this protestation" (87), may be thinking not of Cash's soul, but of his loyalty; if a Catholic of the "rigid" and "Roman" type, he could not be brought to take Kitely's oath of allegiance. This interpretation favors the date of 1606–09, though without precluding a later date; in any case it lightens the weight of the phrase in establishing Jonson's return to Protestantism.

There are, inevitably, possible objections to this period as the date of F, which may be stated in ascending order of seriousness:

1. Bobadill is notoriously inaccurate, and he is obsessed with numbers. When these two tendencies coincide, they produce a joke (cf. "twenty score, that's two hundred"—IV.7.79–80). Is he not likelier to be wrong than right, then, in his remark about Strigonium?

2. The allusions in 4c and 4d are vague; they may not have been intended as topical references at all.

3. There are records of gifts to the Grand Turk by the company in the 1590s, so great as to "scandalize other nations" (State Papers, quoted Carter, q.v. on these gifts, pp. 285–86); they seem to have been a byword for opulence by 1603 at least, for in that year Dekker speaks of gifts "more worth then those that are given to the great ,Turk" (*The Wonderful Year*, Blr, quoted HS). The further munificence of 1605 may have made them proverbial for years thereafter.

4. There is a noticeable decrease in ballad entries in the S.R. between 1595 and 1620 (see Arber, *S.R.* III.26). Trundle may have published earlier or later ballads which were never entered.

5. In writing F, Jonson excised from Q a good many classical allusions and Latin quotations. Those left or added were easily recognizable: e.g. *sic transit gloria mundi* (V.5.33) and *veni, vidi, vici* (II.4.16). Those omitted were less commonplace: *quis contra divos?* (Q I.1.151), *rimarum plenus* (Q III.1.57), these lean *Pirgo*'s (alluding to Plautus' character Pyrgopolyneices; Q III.2.16), signior *Pythagoras*, he that's all manner of shapes (Q III.4.174–75), a Latin passage partly from Ovid's *Ars Amatoria* and partly unidentified or original (Q V.1.210–12), another from Seneca's *Medea* (Q V.1.236), the opening of the *Odyssey* as rendered in Horace's *De Arte Poetica* (Q V.1.263); and the last line of the play, the close of Vergil's third eclogue. (I disregard simpler allusions clearly deleted to improve characterization.) The total result was an impressive reduction in the smell of the lamp. But would Jonson have been moved to these changes when preparing his play to be heard by the most pedantic monarch ever to occupy the English throne, whose delight in the learning of others was exceeded only by his delight in his own? HS speak of "the scholastic fashions which his example encouraged; folios expanded, quotations multiplied, the phalanxes of authorities grew more serried" (I.35). Would Jonson have chosen a command performance before this King as the occasion on which to prune all but schoolboy allusions from his play?

6. By the same token, would he have deleted Edward's impassioned defence of "poesy . . . , / Blessed, eternal, and most true divine" (Q V.3.316–17ff.) for a performance before the author of *Essays of a Prentice in the Divine Art of Poesy*?

7. In May 1606 a statute was passed "for the preventing and avoiding of the great abuse of the holy Name of God in stage plays," directed against those who use "jestingly or profanely . . . the holy Name of God or of Christ Jesus or of the Trinity" (3 Jac. I, c. 21; in Chambers, IV.338–39). The oaths in Q are softened in F, which has been taken as evidence for a revision around this time. But this softening alone could just as well support the theory of a Court performance in 1605, by which time the King's feelings on the subject must have been known, or on the other hand a rewriting at any later date.

The curious fact is, however, that the oaths were not dealt with as scrupulously as one might expect. Utterances unusual enough to stand out as offensive disappear: e.g. *Rex regum* (Q II.1.17), *in saeculo saeculorum* (Q II.3.228), upon my salvation (Q III.2.123–24), by God's passion (Q III.3.113), I think they mean to build a tabernacle here (Q III.4.104), by God's bread (Q III.4.135), and a few others. Aside from these, the changes are inconsistent and by no means thorough. "God's my judge" (Q III.3.35) is eliminated, but "God's my comfort" (F II.5.70) remains. Stephen refrains from saying "By God's lid" (Q I.1.101), but exclaims "Oh, God's lid!" (F III.2.2). "Mass" (Q I.3.155) becomes "Troth" (F I.5.73), but both Cob and Matthew say "Mass" (F III.1.160, III.6.4). Stephen is restrained in Act I from saying "by God's will" (Q I.1.40), but by Act III it is permitted him (F III.2.12), after which Downright and Edward follow his example (F IV.1.12–13, IV.7.134). Would Jonson really have sent his play to Court, just before or just after James's decree, with characters who said "'Fore God" (III.5.6), "God's my life!" (IV.1.17), "by God's precious —" (III.7.64–65), and "O Jesu!" (IV.2.122)?

This carelessness about oaths speaks strongly against a revision for performance before James, and indeed against any performance ca. 1606. On the contrary, it suggests that in February 1605 Q would have been indulged as an old play from the previous licentious reign, while F would date from a time when nervousness of the new statute had died down (and Jonson's remembrance of his 1605 imprisonment had, too). Conceivably this might have happened as early as 1608, but a later time is likelier; clearly, by 1616 the restrictions admitted of generous interpretation, for the publication of F caused no trouble. The question then becomes, how late could Jonson have revised *EI*?

In 1615 Jonson had some leisure, but this is too late, for the plays had almost certainly been printed by then. On January 20, 1615, Stansby, publisher of the Folio, registered his rights to Jonson's unpublished masques (HS IX.13; not on June 20, given by HS IX.335). The masque section is the last item in the Folio, and the only one to contain pieces written after 1612—though it is quite inaccurate to say that the Folio "contains no work, and no allusions to events, of later date" (HS I.333), since there are four Court pieces dating from 1613 through 1616. But of the plays, the available *BF* is not included; neither are two 1614 poems which, according to HS (IX.15), would find a natural place in the *Epigrams*. That may be because Jonson considered the latter a finished unit after 1612 (indeed, they may have been published; Drummond claims to have read them in 1612–13; see HS IX.15); but the omission of *BF* strongly suggests that by late 1614 the printing had got beyond the dramas, into the *Epigrams* at least, so that Stansby would have had no room—and no inclination—to interpolate more plays (or poems). The 1616 masque could be added on easily at the end. It seems from the registration, too, that Stansby was ready or nearly ready to proceed with the masques. Jonson could hardly have been keeping *EI* out for special treatment, since the page signatures of the Folio follow one another without a break and F is the first work in the book.

That the first part of the Folio went to press as late as 1614 is also highly unlikely. Stansby was then completing Raleigh's *History of the World*, published in late 1614; this impressive folio had been in process since its licensing in April 1611 (HS IX.15) and must have cost him immense pains. Its completion evidently left him free to go on to the masques. It is hardly likely that in 1614, with the Raleigh three years in preparation and not finished yet, he would have taken on another major folio, printed roughly four-fifths of it while bringing out the Raleigh—and then used another year and a half for the remaining fifth.

More probably, Stansby undertook the Folio in 1613 or even 1612. If HS are correct, there are no allusions outside the masques to events after 1612; *SW* and the *Epigrams* had presumably reached their final form by then (see Chronology), *SW* having perhaps newly acquired its Second Prologue. On the other hand, Jonson seems to have been almost continuously occupied in 1611–12; he might have begun preparing the Folio, but probability favors late spring to fall of 1613 for most of the work.

All this, of course, demonstrates only that the Folio probably went to press ca. 1613; it contributes nothing except a terminal limit to the question of F's date. The main support for 1613 as the actual time of revision comes from whatever is improbable in the others; from the inherent likelihood of a revision for this formal publication of the Works; and from the demonstration, on the basis of Q peculiarities and errors reproduced in F, that F was printed from a corrected copy of Q (see HS III.294–95). The changes in format of acts and scenes, the reduction of stage directions and increase in punctuation, and the new way of listing characters for each scene must, in any case, all have been made for the forthcoming Folio, for none of them would have affected a performance. For neatness's sake if for no other, one prefers to imagine a copy of Q completely reworked into F, and not a copy interlined with textual alterations in 1606–09, then re-interlined in 1613 with changes of format and new punctuation; and a single recomposed Q is easier to deal with mentally than a partial recomposition copied into a second Q with further alterations. Nevertheless, both these possibilities exist.

There are other pieces of circumstantial evidence to support this date; none is very strong, but some are suggestive.

1. On November 13, 1613 Daborne, a playwright for the Lady Elizabeth's Men, wrote to Henslowe mentioning a forthcoming production of a play by Jonson. This may have been part of the 1613 revival of *EH*, which the Elizabeth's Men produced that autumn and then gave at court on January 25, 1614 (see Chambers, III.255). But if Greg's dating is right, *EH* went on the boards in August; November seems rather late for Daborne to worry that his own play may not be wanted because it cannot be ready "till Johnson's play be played" (*Henslowe Papers*, pp. 70–71, 78). Besides, would *EH*—the work of three men, and so little Jonson's own that he did not include any of it in the Folio—be spoken of as "Johnson's play"? It is tempting to conjecture that the new version of *EI*, just revised with the Folio in view, might have been the play to be performed, Prologue and all.

2. Mr. John Trundle, having dropped totally out of the S.R. during

1610 and 1611 and entered only one book in 1612, suddenly sprang back
into activity in January 1613 and registered four pieces of sensationalism
and one marriage triumph by mid-November.

3. The Royal Artillery Company, of which Stephen is a member in F
only (III.5.130–31), was more or less forcibly revived in 1610 by a lieutenant
of the company and some of its members. Its "military exercises . . . had
apparently been much neglected for some years past" (Raikes, I.39).
Though the general public might well have remained unaware of the internal reorganization, in 1612 the company "applied to the Privy Council for
permission to assemble, . . . and undertook, at their own private charge, to
have a weekly exercise after the modern and best fashion," for the better
fulfillment of which aim they erected "a handsome armoury" (ibid.). On
July 3 the Privy Council issued an Order confirming the company's right
to train, exercise, and have a membership up to 250, and in December the
members arranged with the Armorers for the use of their hall, kitchen, and
other facilities for feasts and general assemblies (Raikes, I.40). All this activity cannot have escaped attention—nor indeed amused attention, consider-
ing the lapse of exercises for some ten years past, during which the membership must have been well under the 250 set in 1612 as an ultimate goal. The
joke, to be sure, would have been appropriate while the company was
nearly defunct; but would it have been an easily recognizable reference then ?

4. Clement's allusion to preventive measures against the plague seems,
on the whole, unlikely to have raised a laugh while an epidemic was ravag-
ing London. It would come much better at a time when the danger was past,
but recent enough for the measures to be familiar. The recurrent epidemics
which had begun in late 1605 ceased at the end of 1610. From 1611 to 1616,
"plague was absent from London" (Chambers, IV.351); 1613 would be
early enough for memory of the five bad years to be vivid, but late enough
for allusions to them not to be painful. (Granting a little more callousness
to the Londoners' sensibilities, one might also consider early 1607 or the
first half of 1608, when plague deaths were under 30 a week, as appropriate
for Clement's jocularity.)

5. Jonson told Drummond that "the greatest sport he saw in France [i.e.
in 1612–13] was the picture of our Savior with the apostles eating the Pascal
Lamb that was all larded" (CD 462–63). In F (III.5.148–49) Edward makes
the following gratuitous joke about Stephen's interpolation of oaths into

his discourse: "'Tis larded with 'em. A kind of French dressing, if you love it." The possible objections are obvious; but the coincidence is peculiar, since this image evidently remained in the forefront of Jonson's mental picture of the French.

6. At the end of F, Clement declares that Brainworm's "adventures this day, when our grandchildren shall hear to be made a fable, I doubt not but it shall find both spectators and applause." Obviously Clement is not engrossed in inward calculation of the number of years this will take; "grandchildren" is an inexact projection into the future. Nevertheless, it is meant to apply to the audience of F, for it is a plea for their applause—or rather, an assurance of its certainty. Now, the revision was deliberately kept Elizabethan (see the references, not in Q, to the Queen—IV.7.60, II.20, II.35; V.5.18). In fact, it was kept consonant with the play's original date (except for the remark on Strigonium, which may show up Bobadill's exaggeration): Trundle became a Stationer in 1597; a huge gift for the Grand Turk was being prepared in 1598 (see Carter, p. 286); four years at most had then elapsed since public precautions against plague were considered by the City (Chambers, IV.349); in November 1598 a conspiracy to poison the Queen was discovered, providing a referent, if referent there must be, for Edward's "plot against the state"; the Artillery Company was in existence with a membership of 600, though few exercises (Raikes, I.36). Jonson's meticulousness is staggering. In view of such precision, might not "our grandchildren" sound somewhat odd to an audience only ten years younger than the events? In 1613, however, after a lapse of fifteen years, with perhaps no performance immediately in prospect, "our grandchildren" would come very suitably and naturally from a man a little older than Knowell, whose son is in 1598 just of marriageable age.

7. The Prologue was composed 1611–13—almost certainly 1612–13. But Jonson was perfectly capable of writing a prologue for an existing play (cf. SW's Second Prologue), especially with the motivation provided by a new performance or a first appearance in print.

The final consideration is the style of the revisions, which may be categorically said to belong to Jonson's period of most complete mastery of language. The best examples are the minutest alterations; with one stroke, he transforms stale, flat, and unprofitable jests into inspired comedy. The stroke may be one sentence; thus in Q, Knowell's agitated moral strictures on Wellbred's offensive letter culminate in a melodramatic assertion about staining "modest paper" (I.1.186–88), but in F, in a cry of pain from the heart: "Why should he think I tell my apricots?" (I.2.96). This brilliantly anticlimactic line exhibits the whole character of Knowell. Nor does Jonson need an entire sentence to turn dross into gold; in Bobadill's reply to the English fencing masters, that "to come to a public school, they should pardon me, it was opposite (in *diameter*) to my humor" (F IV.7.27), the parenthesis has been added; in his description of his kindness to them: "yet now they hate me, and why? Because I am excellent, and for no other vile reason on the earth" (F IV.7.37), the word "vile." Plainly, Jonson could accomplish comic wonders with one word; his command of nuance was total. Here is Matthew relating his seizures of melancholy, in Q: "then do I . . . write you your half score or your dozen of sonnets" (II.3.79–81); in F: "then do I . . . overflow you half a score, or a dozen of sonnets" (III.1.81–82). Matthew again, on Downright's intention to "give him the bastinado" (Q I.3.176–77): "I termed it so for the more grace"; in F: "I termed it so, for my more grace" (I.5.94–95). And finally, by a virtuoso change of a single syllable, Bobadill's self-judgment (F IV.7.51–52), "though I be skilful, I may be oppressed with multitudes," was created from "be suppressed" (Q IV.2.51).

It is tempting to put these alterations as close as possible to the composition of *A*, which offers similarly compact pleasures—consider the two-line characterization of Neighbor 6: "Some three weeks since, I heard a doleful cry / As I sat up, a-mending my wife's stockings" (V.1. 33-34), or the zestful bandying of one affected word, "Chiaus," in 1.2 (compare Bobadill's attempt to use "accommodate" in F 1.5). But 1612-13 is no closer to *A* than 1607-08; and the period of Jonson's surest touch extends from *V* throught *BF*.

In view of the finality with which HS declare the date of F to be ca. 1612, it is perhaps important to emphasize once more that there is no conclusive evidence for this date whatsoever—only compelling evidence that the Folio went to press at that time. In accepting a date of 1612 or 1613, the scholar has the convenience of envisioning only one set of alterations (including the Prologue), the satisfaction of knowing a reasonable motivation, and the pleasure of speculating on a 1613 production. Further, he realizes that John Trundle, the Artillery Company, Clement's joke about the plague, Kitely's uncomplimentary reference to Catholics, and the unregenerate oaths can all be advantageously accounted for. He will have to assume that the Grand Turk's gifts were familiar eight years after the fact; that Bobadill's allusion to Strigonium is an unfunny witticism which crept in, or that it had some secret way of being funny in 1613; that Jonson could have finished the *Epigrams*, prepared the remainder of the Folio for publication, composed a masque and an entertainment, and rewritten *EI* in the six or seven months available in 1612–13 (with some time perhaps used in 1611?); and that there is a satisfactory explanation for Jonson's strange inactivity for three years (1606–09) after his greatest comic success.

This inactivity offers the strongest support for a revision in 1606–09 and therefore the greatest objection to a total one in 1613. The scholar disposed to favor this period will find most to attract him in the last part of 1607 and the first part of 1608. Here Strigonium's tenth anniversary, the Grand Turk, and the Gunpowder Plot are comfortably near at hand; here Clement's remarks are in acceptable taste and a propos; here the controversy over the Oath of Allegiance is the latest news, the oaths of players very likely thrown into the shade by comparison; here and only here John Trundle is demonstrably connected with ballads. In the first part of 1608 the new revision could be performed; in the second half of that year and of 1607 it could not, for the theaters were closed on account of plague. The year 1606 is unpleasantly close to the act about stage oaths; late 1608, and 1609, too full of the plague and *The Silent Woman*. Such a scholar would have to assume that the oaths in F were for one reason or another not likely to cause trouble, that the Artillery Company was well known even in decay, and that Jonson's leisure from spring to October or November 1613 was sufficiently occupied with preparing his dramas for the press. (This period would scarcely be, even without the revision, a "lapse into sterility" at "the zenith of his career"; only a judicious omission of his absence in France makes this rhetoric plausible in HS IX.335–36.)

As for the hypothetical Court performance of 1606, I think it can safely be forgotten. With the act against oaths passed in May, even Jonson would hardly have had the face to offer his casual treatment of profanity to the King in July. Besides, since the King on this theory had heard and approved of Q in 1605, that would be the play he asked for in 1606—not a new version with all the Latin out.

The oaths, the removal of scholarly allusions, and the sheer quantity of work Jonson was engaged in during 1604 (two entertainments, a panegyric, a masque, a translation of Horace, and very possibly a collaboration on *EH*) make a revision of *EI* for the 1605 Court performance improbable. To add to this the presumable obscurity of John Trundle, and the unlikelihood of Jonson's following up two successful London comedies with a reversion to Italy, is to leave the date only a bare possibility.

It remains to add a sharp word of caution to all these intricate calculations. To argue from topical allusions in a work is the only procedure available when external evidence is lacking, but the method can be startlingly unreliable. Nature imitating art can create topical allusions in retrospect. Let me illustrate the unseen pitfalls with a brief demonstration:

1. In Q, Jonson is clearly poking fun at *Othello*; consider the following allusions:

> a. Kitely/Thorello (note the parodic name), who has just expressed his jealousy for the first time, is approached by his wife and asked to come to a waiting meal: "Sweetheart, will you come in to breakfast? ... I pray thee, good Muss, we stay for you." As her husband answers only by speaking aside, she asks, "What ail you, sweetheart, are you not well? Speak, good Muss." He replies, "Troth, my head aches extremely, on a sudden" (I.4.184–91).
>
> Othello, who has just expressed his jealousy for the first time, is approached by his wife and asked to come to a waiting meal:
> *Des.*   How now, my dear Othello!
> Your dinner, and the generous islanders
> By you invited, do attend your presence.
> *Oth.* I am to blame.
> *Des.*   Why do you speak so faintly?
> Are you not well?
> *Oth.* I have a pain upon my forehead here.
> (III.3.279–84)
>
> b. Kitely comes upon his associates, who have been brawling, while their swords are drawn, and exclaims, "Why, how now? What's the matter? What stir is here? Whence springs this quarrel? ... / Put up your weapons, and put off this rage" (III.4.160–62). This is an obvious

conflation of Othello's two reactions to the drawing of swords: "What is the matter here?... Why, how now, ho! From whence ariseth this?" (II.3.163, 169) and the famous "Keep up your bright swords, for the dew will rust them" (I.2.59). Kitely, like Othello, fails to get an answer to his questions; his subsequent "who enforced this brawl?" (170) is more than reminiscent of Othello's "put by this barbarous brawl:... Give me to know / How this foul rout began, who set it on" (II.3.172, 209–10).

c. Most impudent of all is Stephen's comment on Bobadill's beating by Downright: "would any man have offered it in Venice?" (IV.4.10) —a parody of Lodovico's comment on the blow Othello gives Desdemona: "this would not be believed in Venice" (IV.1.251).

2. Q has a clear allusion to King James's *A Counterblast against Tobacco*: Cob's statement that of two men on the point of death from tobacco, one has "voided a bushel of soot upwards and downwards" (III.2.102–03) is an echo of James's assertion that tobacco soils and infects the inner parts "with an unctuous and oily kind of soot, as hath been found in some great tobacco takers... after their death." The whole dispute between Cob and Bobadill obliquely lampoons a disputation at which James acted as moderator when he paid a royal visit to Oxford (Harrison IV.227): "An creber suffitus Nicotianae exoticae sit sanis salutaris?" (James had just raised the tax on tobacco several thousand percent.)

3. Cob's exclamation in Q, after he has been beaten by Bobadill, that he is "hammering revenge: oh, for three or four gallons of vinegar, to sharpen my wits: Revenge, vinegar revenge..." (III.3.44–45) seems merely pointless low comedy until one realizes that it is an allusion to the Gunpowder Plot, laid and carried out in Vinegar House, which adjoined the Houses of Parliament and had a basement through which the gunpowder was conveyed to its hiding place.

Othello was given at Court in November 1604; *A Counterblast* was published in October of that year, and the tobacco tax raised a few days later; the Oxford disputation took place at the end of August 1605; and the Gunpowder Plot, of course, at the beginning of November in that year. It seems clear beyond reasonable doubt that Q was composed in late 1605 at the earliest; probably in 1606, when the insinuation that the Gunpower Plot was caused by the King's opposition to tobacco would no longer be offensively jocose.

The publication of Q in 1601 can only be wondered at as a piece of Elizabethan duplicity.

We are left, then, with the almost certain knowledge that the Prologue was composed ca. 1612, and the belief that F was written between 1604 and 1614. The probabilities favor 1607–08 and 1612–13; but events do not always favor probabilities. And we have besides the disorderly but heartening certainty that there is nothing to stop a man of genius, who could write *Volpone* in five weeks, from sitting down and recomposing *Every Man In* at any time he chose.

Chronology Relevant to the Dates of *Every Man in His Humor*

(Unless otherwise specified, dates refer to first performance, not publication.)

May 1597	Chapman's *Humorous Day's Mirth*.
Sept. 1598	*Every Man In*.
Winter 1599	*Every Man Out*.
Christmas season 1600–01	*Cynthia's Revels*.
Late spring or early autumn 1601	*Poetaster*.
Late 1601	*Apologetical Dialogue* to *Poetaster*.
June 25, 1603	*Althorp Entertainment*.
Autumn or winter 1603	*Sejanus*.
March 15, 1604	*Coronation Entertainment* (Jonson wrote three sections of this).
March 19, 1604	Panegyric to the King on the opening of Parliament.
May 1, 1604	*Highgate Entertainment*.
Jan. 6, 1605	*Masque of Blackness*.
Feb. 2, 1605	*Every Man In* performed at Court.
Between end of 1604 and Sept. 1605	*Eastward Ho* (a collaboration with Chapman and Marston). *Westward Ho*, referred to and capitalized on by *EH*, appeared in the latter part of 1604; *EH* was published Sept. 1605.

Chronology

Between May 4 and Nov. 7, 1605	Jonson and Chapman in prison because of offensive passages in *EH*. On May 4 Lord Salisbury and the Earl of Montgomery received their titles, by which Jonson addresses them in letters from prison; on Nov. 7 he was asked to help investigate the Gunpowder Plot. In early Oct. he was at a Catholic supper party (see HS XI.578), but he could have spent the last weeks of that month in prison.
Latter part of 1605	Revision of *Sejanus* published. The play's rights were transferred to its new publisher on Aug. 6; prefatory verses allude to the release from prison.
Latter part of 1605	Translation of Horace's *Ars Poetica*, with commentary, finished or nearly finished (see preface to *S*).
Winter 1605–06	*Volpone.*
Jan. 5, 1606	*Hymenaei* (masque).
July 24, 1606	*Entertainment of the King of Denmark* (short speeches by three Hours, in English and Latin; some Latin inscriptions and epigrams).
May 22, 1607	*Theobalds Entertainment.*
July 16, 1607	Short speech for Merchant Tailors' banquet for the King. Lost (see Chambers, III.394).
Jan. 10, 1608	*Masque of Beauty.*
Feb. 9, 1608	*Hue and Cry after Cupid* (masque).
Feb. 2, 1609	*Masque of Queens.*
Winter 1609–10	*The Silent Woman.*
Jan. 6, 1610	*Prince Henry's Barriers.*
Spring 1610	*The Alchemist.* From July 12 to Nov. 29 the theaters would have been closed on account of plague; the play was entered to the publisher on Oct. 3.
Jan. 1, 1611	*Oberon* (masque).
Feb. 3, 1611	*Love Freed from Ignorance and Folly* (masque).
1611	*Catiline.*
Jan. 6, 1612	*Love Restored* (masque).
Early spring 1612	Jonson leaves for France as "governor" of Sir Walter Raleigh's son. The secretary of the English ambassador

in Paris writes on March 3, 1613 that the two have "spent some 12 months travel in this country." (See HS XI.581.)

Between early
April and June 29,
1613   Jonson returns to England. He was in Brussels ca. April 3, when some bills of exchange of his were sent to the acting English ambassador there (see HS XI.582). On March 11 he was about to leave or had just left Paris for Brussels (*ibid.*, p. 581); so he probably stayed well into April at least. On June 29 he was in London and witnessed the burning of the Globe (see "Execration upon Vulcan").

May 15, 1612   *Epigrams* registered.

Dec. 27, 1613   "A Challenge at Tilt" (introductory section of *Tilting*; see below).

Dec. 29, 1613   *The Irish Masque.*

Jan. 1, 1614   *Tilting* (entertainment). The verses to "Virtuous Somerset" also belong to this celebration of his marriage.

Oct. 31, 1614   *Bartholomew Fair.*

Jan. 6, 1615   Masque.★

Jan. 20, 1615   Masques registered.

Jan. 1, 1616   Masque.★

1616   *The Devil Is an Ass.*

1616   The First Folio published.

★The Masques of 1615 and 1616 were *Mercury Vindicated from the Alchemists* and *The Golden Age Restored*, but there is some question as to which was which.

Books Cited in Footnotes and Appendices

Note: All citations to individual Greek and Latin authors are to The Loeb Classical Library. In my notes, translations from the Greek are taken from these volumes; translations from the Latin are my own.

A. See Jonson.

Anthologia Latina. Franciscus Buecheler et A. Riese, eds., Fasciculus I, Lipsiae, 1894.

Arber, Edward, ed., Tob.: *English Reprints*, VIII (four works on tobacco), London, 1869.

—— S.R.: *A transcript of the registers of the company of stationers of London, 1554–1640.* London, 1875–77; Birmingham, 1894.

Atkins, S. H., ed., *Work for chimny-sweepers* (1601), Shakespeare Association Facsimiles No. 11, London, Oxford University Press, 1936.

Awdeley, John, *The Fraternity of Vagabonds* (1561), in *The Elizabethan Underworld*, ed. A. V. Judges, London, George Routledge & Sons, Ltd., 1930.

Barry, Lodowick, *Ram-Alley: or, Merry Tricks* (published 1611), in *A Select Collection of Old Plays*, ed. Isaac Reed *et al.*, Vol. V, London, 1825.

BF. See Jonson.

Bright, Timothy, *A Treatise of Melancholie* (1586), introduction by Hardin Craig, New York, Columbia University Press for The Facsimile Text Society, 1940.

Brown, Huntington, *Rabelais in English Literature*, Cambridge, Mass., Harvard University Press, 1933.

Books Cited

Burton, Robert, *The Anatomy of Melancholy*, ed. Shilleto, London, 1893.

CA. See Jonson.

Camden, William, *Remains Concerning Britain*, London, 1674.

Carter, H. H., ed., *Every Man in His Humor*, Yale Studies in English 52, New Haven, Yale University Press, 1921.

CD. See Jonson.

Chambers, Sir E. K., *The Elizabethan Stage*, Vols. III, IV, Oxford, Clarendon Press, 1923.

Child, Francis James, ed., *The English and Scottish Popular Ballads*, Vol. I, Boston, 1882.

Coleman, Edward D., *The Bible in English Drama*, New York, The New York Public Library, 1931.

Cotgrave, Randle, *A French and English Dictionary*, ed. Howell, London, 1673.

Cotton, Charles, *The Compleat Gamester* (1674), ed. Cyril Hartmann, London, George Routledge and Sons, Ltd. Reprinted in the English Library, 1930.

D. See Jonson.

Davenport. *See* Marston.

Dekker, Thomas, *The Honest Whore*, Pts. I & II, in *The Dramatic Works of Thomas Dekker*, ed. Fredson Bowers, Vol. II, Cambridge, Cambridge University Press, 1955.

———?*O per se O* (1612), in Judges (see Awdeley).

EH. See Jonson.

EI. See Jonson.

Ellis, George, *Specimens of Early English Metrical Romances*, Vol. III, London, 1805.

Elyot, Sir Thomas, *The Castel of Helth* (1541), introduction by Samuel A. Tannenbaum, New York, Scholars' Facsimiles and Reprints, 1937.

EO. See Jonson.

Erasmus, Desiderius, *Chiliades Adagiorum*, Coloniae, 1540.

F &H: Farmer, J. S. and W. E. Henley, *Slang and Its Analogues*, printed for subscribers only, n.p., 1890–1904.

Florio, John, *A World of Words*, London, 1598.

—— *Queen Anna's New World of Words*, London, 1611. The bibliography belongs to this edition, but not in all copies. I have seen it only in a presentation copy of Queen Anne's (Houghton Library).

Fuimus Troes. ? by Jasper Fisher, in Reed (*see* Barry), Vol. VII, 1825.

Gifford, William, ed., *The Works of Ben Jonson*, Vol. I, London, 1816.

Greg, W. W., ed., *Henslowe Papers*, London, A. H. Bullen, 1907.

—— *Henslowe's Diary*, 2 vols., London, A. H. Bullen, 1904, 1908.

Harbage, Alfred, *Annals of English Drama 975–1700*, rev. S. Schoenbaum, Philadelphia, University of Pennsylvania Press, 1964.

Harington, Sir John, *The Metamorphosis of Ajax* (1596), ed. E. S. Donno, London, Routledge and Kegan Paul, 1962.

Harman, Thomas, *A Caveat for Common Cursitors* (1566), in Judges (*see* Awdeley).

Harrison, G. B., [I.] *An Elizabethan Journal* (1591–94), New York, Cosmopolitan Book Corp., 1929.

—— [II.] *A Second Elizabethan Journal* (1595–98), New York, Richard R. Smith Inc., 1931.

—— [III.] *A Last Elizabethan Journal* (1599–1603), London, Constable & Co. Ltd., 1933.

—— [IV.] *A Jacobean Journal* (1603–06), New York, The Macmillan Co., 1941.

—— [V.] *A Second Jacobean Journal* (1607–10), Ann Arbor, University of Michigan Press, 1958.

Harvey, Gabriel, *Foure Letters and Certaine Sonnets . . .* (1592), in *The Works of Gabriel Harvey, D.C.L.*, ed. A. B. Grosart, Vol. I, London, 1884.

Horne, David H., ed., *The Life and Minor Works of George Peele*, Vol. I of *The Life and Works of George Peele*, gen. ed. Charles T. Prouty, New Haven, Yale University Press, 1952.

HS: Herford, C. H. and E. and P. Simpson, eds., *Ben Jonson*, Oxford, The Clarendon Press, 11 vols., 1925–52.

Books Cited

Jonson, Benjamin. (All citations are to the HS edition.)

A	*The Alchemist*
BF	*Bartholomew Fair*
CA	*The Case Is Altered*
CD	*Conversations with Drummond*
D	*Discoveries*
EH	*Eastward Ho*
EI	*Every Man in His Humor*
EO	*Every Man out of His Humor*
NI	*The New Inn*
P	*Poetaster*
S	*Sejanus*
SW	*The Silent Woman*
TT	*A Tale of a Tub*
U	*The Underwood*
V	*Volpone*

Kingsford. *See* Stow.

Kökeritz, Helge, *Shakespeare's Pronunciation*, New Haven, Yale University Press, 1953.

Lyly, John, *Euphues and his England*, in *The Complete Works*, Vol. II, ed. R. Warwick Bond, Oxford, The Clarendon Press, 1902.

Marston, John, *Poems*, ed. Arnold Davenport, Liverpool, Liverpool University Press, 1961.

Nashe, Thomas, *LS: Lenten Stuffe*, in *The Works of Thomas Nashe*, Vol. III, ed. R. B. McKerrow, London, Sidgwick & Jackson, Ltd., 1910. *PP: Pierce Penniless*, in McKerrow, Vol. I.

Neale, J. E., *Elizabeth I and Her Parliaments*, London, Jonathan Cape, Vol. I (1559–81), 1953, Vol. II (1584–1601), 1957.

NH: Nicholson, Brinsley and C. H. Herford, eds., *Every Man in his Humour*, in *Ben Jonson*, Vol. I, London, T. Fisher Unwin, n.d.

NI. *See* Jonson.

OED. *A New English Dictionary on Historical Principles*, ed. J. A. H. Murray, Oxford, The Clarendon Press, 1888–1933.

Otuel and Roland. Ed. M. I. O'Sullivan, Early English Text Society, Original Series, 198, London, Oxford University Press, 1935 (for 1934).

P. *See* Jonson.

Pauly, August Friedrich von, and Georg Wissowa, *Paulys real-encyclopädie der classischen altertumswissenschaft,* Stuttgart, J. B. Metzler, 1894–1965.

Raikes, George A., *The History of the Honourable Artillery Company,* Vol. I, London, 1878.

Ram-Alley. See Barry.

S. *See* Jonson.

Sale, Arthur, ed., *Every Man in his Humour,* London, University Tutorial Press, 1958 (first ed. 1941, rev. 1949).

Saviolo, Vincentio, *His Practise,* Bk. 1, London, 1595.

Shaaber. *See* Shakespeare, 2 *H IV.*

Shakespeare, William. (All citations are to the Variorum edition, Philadelphia, J. B. Lippincott Co.)

C	*Coriolanus,* ed. Furness, 1928.
2 H IV	*Henry IV,* Part II, ed. M. A. Shaaber, 1940.
	King John, ed. Furness, 1919.
MV	*The Merchant of Venice,* ed. Furness, 1888.
O	*Othello,* ed. Furness, 1886.
PP	*The Passionate Pilgrim,* in *The Poems,* ed. H. E. Rollins, 1938.

Shelton, Thomas, trans., *The History of the Valorous and Wittie Knight-Errant, Don-Quixote Of the "Mancha,"* London, 1612.

Sidney, Sir Philip, *Defense of Poesy,* ed. A. S. Cook, Boston, 1890.

Silver, George, *Paradoxes of Defence* (1599), Shakespeare Association Facsimiles No. 6, London, Humphrey Milford, 1933.

Simpson, Percy, ed., *Ben Jonson's Every Man In His Humour,* Oxford, The Clarendon Press, 1919.

Sir Ferumbras. Ed. S. J. Herrtage, Early English Text Society, Extra Series 34, London, 1879.

S.R., *Stationers Register. See* Arber.

Books Cited

Stow, John, *A Survey of London*, ed. C. L. Kingsford, 2 vols., Oxford, The Clarendon Press, 1908, 1927.

SW. See Jonson.
TT. See Jonson.
U. See Jonson.
V. See Jonson.

Whalley, Peter, ed., *Every Man in his Humour*, in *The Works of Ben Jonson*, London, 1756.

Wheatley, Henry B., ed., *Ben Jonson's Every Man in His Humour*, London, Longmans, Green, and Co., 1901.

Work for Chimney [sc. *chimny*]*-sweepers. See* Atkins.